D0916175

THE
Fightin' Phils

Other Books by Rich Westcott

The Phillies Encyclopedia (with Frank Bilovsky)

Diamond Greats

The New Phillies Encyclopedia (with Frank Bilovsky)

Phillies '93 — An Incredible Season

Masters of the Diamond

Mike Schmidt

Philadelphia's Old Ballparks

No-Hitters — The 225 Games, 1893-1999 (with Allen Lewis)

Splendor on the Diamond

Great Home Runs of the 20th Century

A Century of Philadelphia Sports

Winningest Pitchers — Baseball's 300-Game Winners

Tales from the Phillies Dugout, First and Second Editions

*Native Sons — Philadelphia-Area Baseball Players
Who Made the Major Leagues*

The Phillies Encyclopedia, Third Edition (with Frank Bilovsky)

Mickey Vernon — The Gentleman First Baseman

Veterans Stadium — Field of Memories

Phillies Essential

The Mogul — Eddie Gottlieb, A Philadelphia Sports Legend

Oddities, Insights, and Untold Stories

RICH WESTCOTT

Foreword by Harry Kalas

Camino Books, Inc.
Philadelphia

Copyright © 2008 by Rich Westcott

All Rights Reserved

No part of this book may be reproduced in any form or by any
electronic or mechanical means, including information storage and
retrieval systems, without permission in writing from the publisher,
except by a reviewer who may quote brief passages in a review.

Manufactured in the United States of America

1 2 3 4 5   11 10 09 08

Library of Congress Cataloging-in-Publication Data

Westcott, Rich.
    The Fightin' Phils : oddities, insights, and untold stories / Rich
Westcott ; foreword by Harry Kalas.
        p. cm.
    ISBN 978-1-933822-13-6 (alk. paper)
    1. Philadelphia Phillies (Baseball team)—History. 2. Philadelphia
Phillies (Baseball team)—Miscellanea. I. Title.

    GV875.P45W468 2008
    796.357'640974811—dc22   2008017488

Cover and interior design: Jerilyn Bockorick

This book is available at a special discount on bulk purchases for pro-
motional, business, and educational use. For information write to:

Camino Books, Inc.
P.O. Box 59026
Philadelphia, PA 19102

www.caminobooks.com

DEDICATION

To Fred Harzer, Wally Knief, and Jim Hamilton, wherever you three are, and to Ed Gebhart, Bob Armbruster, and Frank Bilovsky, each of whom at various points along the way played significant roles in the development of my career. I will always value the contributions all of you have made as mentors, friends, or both.

ACKNOWLEDGMENTS

For every book that is written, there are usually numerous people who chipped in to help. This book is no exception. Accordingly, I would like to thank all those who have provided assistance and without whom this project would not have been possible.

Thank you to Frank Bilovsky, Sam Carchidi, Skip Clayton, Clem Conley, Kit Crissey, Doc Daugherty, Jim Goings, Frank Vaccaro, and Bob Warrington. Also to Freddy Berowski and Tim Wiles of the Baseball Hall of Fame, Rob Holiday and Tina Urban of the Phillies, Jerry Emig at Ohio State University and Ben Adamson at Southwest Missouri State University.

A very special thanks to the scores of people who provided interviews and comments that appear in the pages of this book. Thanks also to Edward Jutkowitz of Camino Books and to Harry Kalas for his insightful Foreword.

Finally, my thanks, as always, to my wife Lois for her astute advice and suggestions as I put this book together, and for pitching in to help whenever necessary.

From a grateful author, thank you one and all.

CONTENTS

FOREWORD

Harry Kalas

s baseball fans, we are usually aware of our favorite team's players, their numbers, and their honors. But are we aware of the backgrounds of our favorite players and our favorite teams?

We know that Ryan Howard set the Phillies record for home runs in one season with 58. And we know that he was only the second player in major league history to win Rookie of the Year and Most Valuable Player awards in back-to-back seasons, joining Cal Ripken, who performed the feat in the 1982 and 1983 seasons with the Baltimore Orioles (Fred Lynn of the Boston Red Sox was both Rookie of the Year and MVP in 1975).

But what about Howard's youth? And what about his days on the high school and college playing fields? How did he perform in those years? What did his coaches and the scouts think about this young slugger? You're about to find out.

It was a tremendous honor to have watched Hall of Famer Steve Carlton take the mound over the years with the Phillies. In 1972, "Lefty" won 27 games for a last place team that won a total of only 59. What a feat for Carlton!

As we know, though, Carlton did not talk with the media during most of his playing days. But he did sit down with our esteemed author recently, and talked about that spectacular 1972 season.

The Phillies franchise is one of the oldest in major league baseball. Over the years, there have been many, many stories on things that took place with the club, both on the field and behind the scenes. For instance, the Phillies were the first major league team to hire a full-time woman scout. The Phillies once played a nine-inning game in 51 minutes. And the team had a lefthanded catcher who played with the Phils for 14 years.

These are just a few of the remarkable stories connected with Phillies teams. There are numerous others. Many of them appear amid the 33 chapters in this book. You'll be amazed at what you read.

Rich Westcott is a baseball writer and historian. Nobody does that job any better. Now, through tireless research and countless interviews, he has written a fascinating collection of stories of Phillies exploits, both past and present.

The Fightin' Phils — Oddities, Insights, and Untold Stories is as interesting a book as has ever been written about the team. It's different than most of them—many of which have been written by Rich. It's entertaining, and it tells wonderful stories. Many of these stories have never been told before, and even among those that have, there are details that most readers certainly never knew before.

I thoroughly enjoyed reading *The Fightin' Phils*. And I recommend it, not only to all Phillies fans, but to baseball fans everywhere and of all ages.

INTRODUCTION

s the fourth oldest franchise in major league baseball, the Phillies have proved to be not only durable but possessors of a rich history that is filled with interesting stories about players, events, and teams.

Some of the stories have happy endings. Some do not. With a franchise that's been around for 125 years, there is bound to be a vast mixture of stories that depict joy and satisfaction as well as ones that show pain and suffering.

It could be said that the latter far surpasses the former. But that's not the point here. The point is that through good times and bad, through sickness and in health, the Phillies are a team with a wealth of highly engaging stories. And this is a book that relates some of those stories.

It is common knowledge who leads the team in career home runs. Most people who follow the Phillies can also easily identify the team's only pitcher ever to hurl a perfect game. And it is hardly a secret how the Phils won the 1950 pennant, the name of the ballpark in which the team played its most games, or what player was the Phillies' last Rookie of the Year.

There are stories about these and other Phillies players and exploits that have been told before. Among avid Phillies followers, who are among the most knowledgeable in baseball, the stories are quite familiar. Indeed, very little over the years has escaped the attention of the legions of people who have an interest in Phillies history.

So what can be said about the Phillies that hasn't already been said? You're about to find out.

The Fightin' Phils — Oddities, Insights, and Untold Stories is a book composed of special (and unusual) stories about people, places, and events connected with the team. Most of these stories are not the usual big headline grabbers. In fact, quite a few have barely been covered or have never previously been told.

Who knows, for instance, that the Phillies were the first team to hire a full-time woman scout? Incredibly, that happened in 1946.

It is generally thought that John Kennedy was the first African American to wear the Phillies uniform. Not so. Chuck Randall was the Phils' first black player, and he appeared a full three years before Kennedy.

Who knew that the Phillies once could have fielded an outfield consisting of Hall of Famers Hank Aaron, Al Kaline, and Carl Yastrzemski? Or that a former Phils pitcher became a prominent member of the CIA? Or that the Phillies once had a left-handed catcher, that Mike Schmidt was originally a switch-hitting shortstop, or that basketball great Neil Johnston pitched in the Phillies' farm system?

Was Dickie Noles really throwing at George Brett in the 1980 World Series? Were the Phillies ever actually known as the Blue Jays, or is that a myth? Why did the Phillies trade Ryne Sandberg? And did you know that the Phils once played in a game that took 51 minutes? Or that nearly 100 players from the Philadelphia area have played with the Phillies?

Among recent developments, the postgame celebration following the team's remarkable 2007 division title clincher is described. There is also an in-depth account, somewhat glossed over by the media, of the Phillies' dramatic tarpaulin rescue in Denver. There's a look at the emergence of Ryan Howard as a power-hitter from his youth to the present. And if you ever wondered what the inside of the Phillies' clubhouse at Citizens Bank Park looks like, here's your chance to find out.

These stories and many more are included in the following pages. Numerous interviews were conducted in pursuit of this material. Steve Carlton talked about his 15-game winning streak. Delightful Edith Houghton, now a robust 96 years old, discussed her life as a woman scout. And Jimmy Rollins, Mike Schmidt, Ryne Sandberg, Dallas Green, Robin Roberts, Charlie Manuel, and many, many others were interviewed for chapters in this book.

To the best of my knowledge, no book of this kind has ever been written about any baseball team. It took not only interviews, but extensive research and considerable help from others to arrive at a finished product.

It was, though, a most enjoyable project. Now, it is your turn to enjoy it. I hope, like me, you will learn some things about the Phillies that you had no idea about before.

Rich Westcott

chapter 1

A REMARKABLE COMEBACK

Throughout their more than 125-year history, the Phillies have experienced many highs and many lows. The final weekend of September 2007 was one of the club's all-time highs.

It was a weekend in which the Phillies did what just a few weeks earlier seemed impossible, overcoming a seven-game deficit on September 12 to win the National League's East Division championship over the New York Mets. It was the first time in 14 years that the Phillies reached the postseason playoffs.

For the Mets, who had been in first place throughout the season but lost 12 of their last 17 games, it was the biggest collapse in baseball that late in the season. For the Phillies, who won 13 of their last 17 games and 23 of their final 34, it was their greatest comeback.

The Phillies entered the final weekend still trailing the Mets by one game, But a 6-0 Phillies win over the Washington Nationals on Friday night that was fueled by a 13-strikeout performance by the club's top pitcher, Cole Hamels, and a two-run homer by Ryan Howard, coupled with a 7-4 Mets loss to the Florida Marlins vaulted the Phillies into first place for the first time all season. The following day, however, the Phils fell back into a tie as they lost, 4-2, to the Nationals while the Mets were winning, 13-0.

That set the stage for the final day of the season. September 30. Mets against the Marlins at Shea Stadium. Phillies against the Nationals, who were coming off of a three-game sweep of the Mets in New York. Citizens Bank Park. Old left-hander Tom Glavine (41) pitching for the Mets. Older lefthander Jamie Moyer (44) hurling for the Phillies.

For the third straight game, the Phillies played before a sell-out crowd, the club's 24th sellout of the season. Before the game, streets surrounding the ballpark were jammed with traf-fic. The air was filled with the constant sound of policemen's whistles and the shouts of vendors selling their goods. And hardly a soul was without either a Phillies hat, a Phillies shirt, or both.

Meanwhile, deep in the bowels of the ballpark, far from the clatter outside, the Phillies' clubhouse rocked with the sound of music. Players chatted and joked and nibbled on pregame snacks. If there was pressure on the players, it wasn't notice-able. "We're just trying to have some fun, relax, and stay fo-cused," said Howard, the reigning National League Most Valu-able Player and home run champion.

As gametime approached, the noise in the stands became louder. The fans, in their red clothes with white rally towels—given out before each of the weekend games—ready to be waved, perched nervously on the edges of their seats. An elec-trifying atmosphere permeated the young, four-year-old ballpark like it had never previously experienced.

Finally, the Phillies took the field accompanied by thunder-ous cheers from the stands. The game was under way. History was in the making.

Before the first inning was even over, the scoreboard flashed with a message: Marlins 7, Mets 0 after one inning. Bedlam en-gulfed the stands.

Jimmy Rollins singled and scored in the first. Howard socked a two-run single in the third. Pinch-hitter Tadahito Iguchi's sac-rifice fly and a triple by Rollins each chased home runs in the sixth. And Howard's fourth home run in the last four games registered a final run in the seventh.

All the while, Moyer, a native son from nearby Souderton, a Philly guy through and through who had cut school as a kid to attend the Phillies' victory parade down Broad Street in 1980, pitching the biggest game of his life, was setting down the Nationals. When he finally departed with one out in the sixth, he had been touched for nothing more than one unearned run. It was a gritty, clutch performance if there ever was one.

With each Phillies hit, when each Phils pitcher got two strikes on a batter, with each new score in the Mets' game, the fans exploded with cheers. They stood and waved towels, so many that all you could see looking out over the stands was a sea of white. The noise got exceedingly loud whenever Chase Utley, Aaron Rowand, Howard, and Rollins—all key players in the Phils' amazing season—came to bat. With Rollins, chants of "MVP" pumped out of thousands of vocal chords.

Rollins had drawn a considerable amount of flack, especially in New York, when he had said before the season that the Phillies were the team to beat in the National League East. Hardened Philly fans loved the cocky pronouncement by the team's glittering shortstop. Now, with his statement holding up, Rollins had also played himself into a spot as the leading candidate for the league's MVP award. His final statistics while starting every one of the Phils' 162 games: an all-time major league record 706 at-bats, 212 hits, 30 home runs, 38 doubles, 20 triples, 94 RBI, 139 runs, 41 stolen bases, .296 batting average, which collectively rank among the finest in big league history—not to mention his brilliant fielding (just 11 errors all season) and spectacular base-running.

A few minutes before the end of the Phillies' game, the Mets' fate had been sealed. With Glavine suffering the worst first inning of his career, they were 8-1 losers. In Philadelphia, that alone was reason to celebrate.

At exactly 4:35 p.m., Brett Myers, who had thrown the first pitch of the season as opening day starter and who fired the last pitch of the season as ace closer, got Wily Mo Pena on a called third strike to end the game. The Phillies were 6-1 winners. As Myers heaved his glove high in the air and catcher Chris Coste dashed to the mound, the stadium's Liberty Bell began to ring and the celebration was officially under way.

Convening near the mound, the Phillies jumped, yelled, and pummeled each other with unbridled joy. Fireworks erupted. Policemen converged on the field. Up in the stands, the white towels and ear-splitting noise surfaced once again. And all over the Philadelphia area, people poured into the streets, car horns blared, and the celebration would go on throughout the night.

After starting the season with a 4-11 record, after using a club record 28 pitchers who registered the fourth-worst ERA (4.73) in the league, after players going on the disabled list 20 times, after losing the 10,000th game in franchise history and receiving scads of negative publicity because of it, after getting eliminated from the playoffs on the final day of the season in 2005 and the next-to-last day in 2006 and taking longer to re-enter the playoffs than all but three other teams, after one of the most improbable seasons imaginable—recording an 85-62 record (best in the majors since May) since their disastrous start—the Phillies had finally reached the postseason again for the first time since 1993.

They did it with a team that scored more runs (892) than any Phillies team since 1930, that ranked in the top three in the league in 12 offensive categories, that swept the Mets twice in September and three times during the season, that came from behind in 48 games, and that simply refused to give up even after a devastating 12-0 loss in mid-September to the Rockies and a game five days later in which they had an 11-0 lead and almost lost it to the Cardinals before winning, 13-11.

Afterward, in the Phils' clubhouse where lockers were covered with sheets of plastic and hats and T-shirts noting the just-won title were handed out to team members, players raucously sprayed beer and champagne on each other and anyone else—including the media. Empty bottles and ice cubes dumped from the tubs carrying the booze covered the floor. As the reserve players mostly stood around the perimeter watching the proceedings, the starters, surrounded in each case by a half-dozen or so media people, described their emotions at the moment and happily recapped the events of the day.

No word was used more frequently than "unbelievable." "It's just unbelievable," said Rowand, a hard-nosed team leader who became one of the Phillies' most popular players because of his feats as a hitter and center fielder with a willingness to crash into walls or dive to the turf to make spectacular catches. "Unbelievable," echoed Howard, the league's runnerup in home runs and RBI. "This is unbelievable," said a chorus of others.

Aaron Rowand (left) and Jimmy Rollins celebrated after the Phillies clinched the division title.

Players talked about the Phils' amazing comeback. "You never know what's going to happen in this game," said Rollins. Added Shane Victorino, a key player during the season (and with Rollins one of the reasons the team set an all-time success record by getting caught stealing only 19 times in 157 attempts), "We always stayed positive, always focused on the job all season long."

One of the topics most players modestly avoided was the overall character of the team and its extraordinary popularity with fans. The 2007 Phillies surely rank as one of the most likeable groups of athletes the club has ever assembled. For the most part, they are men with strong values, well-disciplined, agreeable, classy, in general a group of upstanding and stand-up individuals who, as manager Charlie Manuel said, were a team with "no quit in it." And because of this and, of course, because of its ability, this team is enormously popular, as evidenced by the fact that the Phils drew more than three million fans in 2007.

In the midst of the clubhouse celebration, players suddenly dashed back onto the field. Thousands of fans lingered in the stands, not wanting to leave the scene of such a heroic triumph. The players came back to give them a part in the celebration and to thank them for their support.

One by one, players ran to the edge of the stands to shake hands with the fans. Howard, Rollins, Rowand, Myers, J.C. Romero, who immediately following the game had rushed to the Washington dugout to extend good wishes to some of the Nationals who stayed to watch the celebration. Rollins grabbed public address announcer Dan Baker's microphone to thank the fans for their support. First Antonio Alfonseca, then Victorino grabbed a groundskeeper's hose and sprayed the fans in an attempt to make them a direct part of the celebration. And Myers picked up Rollins and carried him around in front of the dugout.

Manuel, unfairly maligned during the season and certainly a legitimate favorite to win the National League's Manager of the Year award (instead, Bob Melvin of the Arizona Diamondbacks, won it), stood quietly on the sidelines. Maybe he talked like a hillbilly, had an odd jiggle to his walk, and bobbed his head in a funny way. Maybe he even made a questionable strategic move here and there. But Charlie was the guy who held this team together when it was struggling. And he chased the tension out of the clubhouse, kept a positive attitude, talked to every player, and got the players to focus, relax and believe in themselves. For all of these, he was extremely popular in the clubhouse, and in no small measure it was his style that got this team to the playoffs.

More than one and one-half hours after the final out, some players remained on the field. Several thousand fans were still in the stands. Outside the ballpark, many more fans lingered while cars raced by, their horns blasting and their passengers cheering the Phillies.

Coming as it did on Sunday, September 30, it was only the second time a Phils team had won a title on the last day of the regular season. The only other time that was done was in 1950 when the Whiz Kids beat the Brooklyn Dodgers, 4-1, in 10 innings.

In that memorable game—made particularly so by Richie Ashburn's game-saving throw and Dick Sisler's game-winning home run—Robin Roberts, making his third start in five days, pitched all 10 innings in as marvelous a mound performance as the Phillies have ever received.

How ironic is it that September 30 is the birthday of none other than Robin Roberts? As the Phillies were winning their first title of any kind since 1993, their Hall of Fame pitcher was celebrating his 81st birthday. And before the game, he had even sent Manuel an e-mail wishing him good luck.

The Phillies' 2007 clincher in which they finished ahead of the Mets by one game, ending with an 89-73 record, was unlike any title the Phillies had won before. It was the first time a Phillies team had won a crown after never being in first place until the end. They were in first just one day all season, that being two days before the clincher.

In both 1978 and 1980, the club won division titles on the next-to-last days of the season (beating the Pittsburgh Pirates and Montreal Expos, respectively), but both had been in first place at various times during the season. Other division crowns were clinched at earlier dates and with far bigger leads.

In their other division races in the 1970s, the 1976 Phillies led by 10 games at the All-Star break and won the crown by nine games. The Phillies in 1977 were as much as eight and one-half games out of first early in the season before winning the East crown by five games.

The 1915 team won the National League pennant by six games after leading the race most of the time since the first day. The 1950 team led off and on early, went into first to stay in late July, opened a seven-game lead by the end of August, then collapsed in September before taking a one-game lead into the final game of the season.

In 1983, after the Phillies won 14 of their last 16 games, they captured the division title by six games. The 1993 club had as much as an 11 and one-half game lead in June, but a late-season slump knocked them down to a three-game lead at the end of the season.

The 2007 victory was different in other ways, too. While roosting in either second or third places since mid-May, the

Phils were seven games out of first on September 12. No Phillies team ever overcame a greater deficit that late in the season. In fact, no major league team ever overcame such a large disadvantage with so little time remaining.

The crash of the Mets out of their season-long perch in first place was, of course, the latest in the season that a team had ever blown a title when leading by that many games. The Pittsburgh Pirates led by seven on September 1, 1938 before losing the pennant to the Chicago Cubs, and the New York Giants had a seven-game cushion on September 6, 1934 before yielding to the St. Louis Cardinals.

Naturally, the question repeatedly arose: Did the Phillies' comeback and the Mets' fold erase the stigma of the infamous Phillies collapse in 1964 when the team blew a six and one-half game lead with 12 games left in the season? Can all those bad memories now be forgotten?

Of course they can't. The '64 team cannot be vindicated by the achievements of the 2007 club. Nor does the fact that the Mets' collapse outdid the 10 straight losses and the ultimate destruction of the '64 Phils. One happened in Philadelphia, the other in New York. Two different cities, two different teams, two different eras. One meant a trip to the World Series, the other meant reaching the first round of the playoffs. One is not related to the other. The fact that the Phillies benefited from one collapse is not offset by their utter failure in another collapse. What's more, the scars that remain from 1964 are permanent. They will never go away.

"No way that's ever going to happen," said Art Mahaffey, who suffered a 1-0 loss in the first game of the 10-game losing streak when Chico Ruiz (no relation to Carlos Ruiz) stole home with Frank Robinson at bat. "The players and the fans will never forget what happened."

On the day following the Phils' victory—the same date that the Whiz Kids won the pennant—a gala celebration was held at City Hall. It may have been a little premature, but in a city long deprived of winners, it might be considered prudent to take whatever it can get.

So, with every member of the Phillies team present, as well as club president Dave Montgomery, GM Pat Gillick and his assistants Ruben Amaro and Mike Arbuckle, broadcaster Harry Kalas, and others, a joyful victory party was held. City officials said it was the largest pep rally ever staged in Philadelphia.

A few days later, however, the season took a somewhat unexpected downturn when the Phillies met the Rockies in the first round of the National League playoffs. The Rockies had won 13 of their final 14 regular-season games to storm from behind and catch the San Diego Padres in the race for the wildcard berth. In a special playoff after the final day of the season, Colorado captured a 9-8 win in 13 innings to claim the prize.

Two days later at CBP, the Rockies scored three runs in the second inning against Hamels and downed the Phils, 4-2, despite solo home runs by Pat Burrell and Aaron Rowand. Then, fueled by a grand slam homer off Kyle Lohse by slap-hitter Kaz Matsui, the Rockies won Game Two, 10-5. Despite having distributed 95,000 free rally towels during the two games, the Phillies left for Denver in a 0-2 hole.

At Coors Field, ironically the site earlier in the season of their heroic rescue in the rain, the Phillies bowed out of the playoffs. A superb outing by Moyer couldn't keep the Phils from suffering a 2-1 loss. It was the Rockies' 17th win in 18 games.

For the Phillies, the vaunted offense, which carried the club through much of the season, had disappeared. The big hitters—Rollins, Utley, Burrell, Howard, and Rowand—went a combined 1-for-17 in the final game and 10-for-57 (a .175 average) in the three games. Overall, the Phils had a team batting average of .172.

It was a disappointing finish for a team that had ended the regular season in such spectacular fashion. Overall, though, it had been a remarkable season for the Phils, one that few people—one exception being Rollins—had thought possible when the campaign began.

After the season, Rollins, while leading the league in at-bats, runs, and triples, and becoming the first player in major league history to have at least 200 hits, 15 triples, 25 home runs, and 25 stolen bases in one season, did indeed win the MVP. Howard and Utley also finished in the top eight in the voting.

Rollins' MVP award was a fitting climax to a sparkling season. It was a season in which the Phillies overcame the improbable and put together a finish that will not soon be forgotten.

chapter 2

THE LADY WAS
A SCOUT

There was a time, long, long ago, when Edith Houghton rarely missed a baseball game. Day after day, week after week throughout the spring and summer, she drove to a ball field, stationed herself in the bleachers, and watched the players perform. Sometimes, she even saw two games in the same day.

Houghton wasn't there for the fun of it. Nor was she there simply because she was a baseball addict and couldn't live without a game. She was there because she was a baseball scout. And, like any scout, she was in search of a few good men.

But Houghton wasn't just another scout. She was something special, a pioneer, someone who made history with a feat that even today seems implausible. Houghton was a full-time major baseball league scout, the first woman ever to hold such a position.

The fact that she began the job in 1946, at a time when only a few women ever had worked for big league teams—indeed, even before baseball had become sufficiently liberated to allow African Americans to play at the game's highest level—made Houghton's achievement all the more noteworthy. Her job was as unusual as it was historic.

Houghton worked for the Philadelphia Phillies, scouting players in the Philadelphia area and in South Jersey. She held the job through the 1952 season. Since then, only a few other women have served as big league baseball scouts, most of them being bird dogs, a baseball term that refers to freelancers who get paid a commission for the players they sign.

Now, a perky 96-year-old who still drives and who lives with her bulldog in the house in Sarasota, Florida that she has owned for many years, Houghton (not to be confused with Edith Houghton Hocker, a Bryn Mawr College graduate and a leader in the women's suffrage movement in the early 1900s) talks proudly about her days with the Phillies. As she does, she displays a bulging scrapbook with dozens of pictures and articles about her career.

Former baseball star Edith Houghton was the first full-time woman scout in the major leagues.

It was a career that focused almost entirely on two things: sports and the Navy. Houghton spent her early years as a baseball and softball player and then was a member of the WAVES (Women Appointed for Volunteer Emergency Service) in the U.S. Navy for 28 years, serving as both a regular and a reserve.

Edith was born in 1912 in Philadelphia, the youngest of 10 children of William and Elizabeth Houghton. Within a few years of Edith's birth, the family moved to a new house at 25th and Diamond Streets, near where William ran a grocery store. Across the street from the house was a ball field.

For Houghton, the lure of the ball field was too powerful to resist. By the time she was six years old, she could usually be found there, playing baseball with the boys in the neighborhood, including her three older brothers, Bill, Frank, and Carlos.

"I was always there," she recalled. "I played there after school and all day during the summer. I just loved baseball. My mother would call me for dinner, but I wouldn't hear her. She'd have to send one of my sisters over to get me."

When she was eight years old, Edith became the mascot for a baseball league made up of Philadelphia policemen. Before games, wearing a uniform and carrying a bat, she led the teams to the flag pole in center field. Soon, she was also giving pregame exhibitions in throwing, hitting, and fielding.

At the age of 10, Houghton, after trying out at a nearby playground, became the shortstop and leadoff hitter for a team of 16- to 20-year-old women called the Bobbies. The Bobbies, so named because the players were required to bob their hair—the popular style of the era—were one of the top women's baseball teams in Philadelphia. They played games throughout the city, two to three games each week, often against men's teams, and occasionally traveled to other cities where the girls earned a few dollars per game.

Although by far the smallest and youngest player on the team, and wearing a uniform that was much too big for her, a cap that she had to make smaller with the use of a safety pin, and extra holes punched in her belt, Houghton quickly became one of the Bobbies' top players. She was nicknamed "The Kid." And, in a city where baseball was the biggest game in town,

Houghton was a 10-year-old shortstop with a fast-paced team called the Bobbies.

over the next few years her hitting and fielding attracted so much attention that newspapers began filing stories about her.

One article called Edith "a female Dave Bancroft," a player who a few years earlier had been the Hall of Fame-bound short-stop with the Phillies. Another newspaper said, "She could play ball. She could field and she could hit. Baseball savvy is her heritage." With incredible foresight, the lead of yet another article called Houghton "sex in the city."

Naturally, The Kid was also called a "tomboy." "She may be a tomboy," Edith's mother claimed, "but no doubt she is a crackerjack shortstop." Houghton's specialty in the field was the hidden-ball trick, which she pulled with astonishing regularity on more seasoned players.

In 1925, with Houghton now playing in her third year with the Bobbies, the team was picked to tour Japan to play a series of games against men's teams. With a Japanese sponsor agreeing to finance the trip and pay the Bobbies $800 per game, the team traveled from Philadelphia to Seattle, stopping along the way to play exhibition games in places such as Chicago; Fargo, North Dakota; and Great Falls, Montana. After reaching Seattle, the team embarked on a 13-day cruise across the Pacific Ocean to Japan.

Because they were scheduled to play men's teams, the Bobbies were joined by catcher Eddie Ainsmith and pitcher Earl Hamilton, both veteran major leaguers who would form the battery for most of the squad's games. Instead of Bobbies, the logo on the team's shirts said "USA." The schedule called for several games each week and would last for about one month.

"Ainsmith [who had caught Walter Johnson on the Washington Senators] thought I was too young to catch his throws down to second base," Houghton remembered. "So, he said he would give me a yen every time I caught the ball. I didn't miss a throw, and I collected a lot of money."

The young Bobbies were often overmatched and played only about .500 ball during their tour. Eventually, the sponsor pulled the plug, refusing to pay the team's expenses as well as its trip home. Marooned in Japan, the Bobbies spent another month trying to locate funds before finding a sympathetic businessman who paid their way back to Philadelphia via Vancouver and the Canadian Railway.

Houghton's career with the Bobbies ended soon afterward. The following season she joined the Passaic (New Jersey) Bloomer Girls, a hardball team that played throughout the state. Edith was soon being called "a female Babe Ruth."

By now, Houghton was attending Girls' High School, then located in downtown Philadelphia. There, she also played on the field hockey, basketball, bowling, and track teams. The school's playing fields, however, were located a good distance from Center City at 29th Street and Allegheny Avenue.

"I said to my father, 'How am I going to get around to all the games?' My father had been an athlete himself. In fact, they said

The Bobbies, with Houghton (lower right), then 13, get ready for a trip to Japan.

that once he swam across the Schuylkill River with a pack on his back. So, he understood my problem, and he bought me a car. It was a second-hand Ford that he paid $75 for. I might have been the only 16-year-old girl in Philadelphia with her own car."

After graduating from high school, Houghton signed to play with the New York Bloomer Girls for $25 a week. Three times a week, she rode a train from Philadelphia to New York for games played throughout the New York metropolitan area. Edith played so well that in 1931, she was invited to join the Hollywood Girls, a flashy, touring baseball team that played out of Springfield, Massachusetts. This time, she earned $35 a week, traveling with the team for games that ranged from the northeast to the southwest parts of the country. The team played virtually every day, sometimes twice a day in two different locations, and sometimes even against men's minor league teams.

Houghton, who when she was home often walked to Baker Bowl to see the Phillies or to Shibe Park to watch the Athletics, played every position on the diamond, even pitcher. "Evidently, I had the ability," she said. "At least, that's what everybody told me." One newspaper article even went so far as to call her "the greatest girl player of all time."

The Hollywood team folded in 1933 after which Edith visited the rosters of various teams. With women's baseball in a temporary decline, she played briefly on a men's semipro team in Philadelphia called Fisher AA. Then, although she had previously shunned softball, she joined a team called the Roverettes, a women's team that played its games in Madison Square Garden in New York.

"There weren't many women's baseball teams anymore, so I had to switch to softball," Houghton said somewhat ruefully. "I wasn't too happy about that, but I didn't have much of a choice. So I went to New York for a tryout, and they asked me to stay and play that night. I played first base."

Eventually, Houghton became the team's playing-manager. Meanwhile, she also talked the Renault Wine Company, located in Egg Harbor, New Jersey, to sponsor a women's softball team. The team became known as the Renault Champagne Girls, and with Houghton again serving as playing manager, it faced men's and women's teams throughout Philadelphia and South Jersey. Through the rest of the 1930s, Houghton played during the week with the Roverettes in New York and on weekends with the Champagne Girls.

In 1942, while living with one of her sisters at 7th and Allegheny Avenues and with World War II having started, Houghton volunteered for the Navy. Now 30 years old, she was accepted and sent to Bloomington, Indiana where she trained at Indiana University. Edith then served three years in the military, much of it working in supplies and accounting in Washington, D.C. She often came home to Philadelphia on weekends, and while there played on the men's baseball team at the Navy Yard. In Washington, she also managed a WAVES softball team. Before her discharge in 1945, Houghton had attained the rank of chief petty officer.

Although Houghton's age and her time in the Navy precluded her playing in the All-American Girls' League, her baseball career was far from over. Only this time, Edith's actions would not take place on the playing field.

"I'd been thinking for a while that maybe I could become a scout," she said. "I thought, I've been in baseball almost my entire life. Why not give it a try?

"Bob Carpenter was the owner of the Phillies. I figured, I'll go see him and find out what he could do for me. I called and got an appointment, and then went to see him. He was a very nice man. But he was quite surprised at what I was asking him.

"I said, 'You don't have any women scouts in your organization. But I've been in baseball for years and years, and I think I know a little about the game. Why don't you hire me?' I had my scrapbook and some other stuff with me."

With Carpenter at that meeting was Herb Pennock, the Phillies' general manager. Pennock, a baseball lifer, was already immersed in an effort to keep African American players from entering the major leagues. It stood to reason that the rigid former pitcher would also oppose the entry of women into the professional ranks.

"I think the two of them were half laughing at what I was saying," Houghton recalled. "I'm not sure they were taking me too seriously. Finally, Carpenter said, 'We'll talk it over and let you know.' He didn't say, 'no.' So, when I left, I gave them my scrapbook to look over."

Two weeks later, Houghton got a phone call from Carpenter's secretary. She told Edith that the Phils' owner wanted to talk to her again. Could she come to the office for another visit?

"When I got there, I went in to Mr. Carpenter's office and sat down," said Houghton. "He said to me, 'We've talked it over, and we think maybe it will work out. You have a job with the Phillies.'"

Houghton's hiring made national news. Not only was she the first woman ever hired as a full-time scout, she was also one of the first women hired in any position by a big league club. And, although it was widely overlooked, Houghton's hiring had once again thrust the Phillies into the forefront of the movement for women's equality. Some 14 years earlier, Mae Nugent, wife of Phillies president Gerry Nugent, had been named the club's vice president and treasurer, making her one of baseball's first female executives. (Helene Britton, president of the St. Louis Cardinals from 1911 to 1916, is generally regarded as

the first woman to hold a high-level position in organized baseball.)

Edith's starting salary was hardly staggering. As the contract she still has reveals, it was $150 a month. It was hardly
enough for Houghton to give up her regular job as a buyer for
Supplee-Biddle, then a large wholesale hardware distributor located in Center City.

"I couldn't live on what I was earning with the Phillies,"
Houghton said. "But money didn't interest me, anyway. I had
a job in baseball. That's what mattered."

Houghton joined a scouting staff that included grizzled baseball veterans such as Jocko Collins, Cy Morgan, Johnny Nee,
Eddie Krajnik, and Heinie Groh. The scouts reported to minor
league director Joe Reardon.

At the time, the Phillies were just starting to emerge from
a long, dreadful era during which they had just one first division finish in 31 years. Starting in 1918, only three years after
the club had won its first National League pennant, it had
launched an abysmal stretch from which it would not fully escape until 1949. At one point, beginning in 1938, the club had
lost more than 100 games in five straight seasons, once losing
as many as 111.

By the time Houghton joined the Phillies, the team had
started to move forward. The Phils were at long last finally
making a concerted effort to rid themselves of the stigma of
being wretched losers. Under Carpenter, who had taken over
the team at the end of 1943, the team had been reorganized,
money had become available, and good players were being
sought. Players such as Andy Seminick, Del Ennis, Granny Hamner, and Richie Ashburn had already been signed by the organization. Others such as Robin Roberts, Curt Simmons, and
Willie Jones would soon join them. Eventually, this group formed
the foundation on which the Phillies built the pennant-winning
team in 1950 called the Whiz Kids.

Edith was assigned a territory that included Philadelphia, its
suburbs, and South Jersey. She wasn't given any particular instructions. Just look at as many players as possible, she was told.

Houghton did exactly that. In a region where baseball was
then the predominant sport with teams located in virtually every
neighborhood, she watched high school games. She watched

college games. She watched sandlot games. Often, she saw two games in a single day. She worked every night of the week and on weekends, too. If someone—whether from the team, a fan, or from somewhere else—suggested that she watch a certain player, she'd do it. The lady scout became a familiar sight at baseball games throughout the Philadelphia area.

"All the teams knew me," she recalled. "I had the schedules of everybody. Each year, I scouted several hundred prospects."

Despite the still-prevailing attitude of society that a woman's place was in the home, Houghton was seldom exposed to such an unenlightened view. "Everybody was fine," she claimed. "Everybody was very pleasant. Nobody really ever said anything or gave me a hard time. But even if they had, it wouldn't have bothered me. It would have been the same as when I was playing. I just went out and focused on playing. If anybody said anything, I never heard it. "

As a scout, Houghton was always on the road. She rarely came to the team's office. "In fact, she was so busy most of us never saw her at all," said Maje McDonnell, a longtime coach with the Phillies who earlier had been a teammate of one of Edith's brothers on the Northeast High School baseball team.

Although she was a woman working in the male world of professional baseball, Edith knew as well as anybody how to size up a player's talent. "At the time," she said, "the Phillies seemed to like great, big guys. That didn't interest me. To me, what was more important was a person's knowledge of the game. I wanted to be able to put a guy on the field, and say, 'Do it.' Also, you could tell by a player's movements and his build. If he didn't have those, you didn't have to waste any more time watching him."

"She knew a ballplayer when she saw one," Carpenter said many years later in Kevin Kerrane's wonderful book, *Dollar Sign on the Muscle.*

As a Phillies scout, Houghton estimates that she signed about 15 players, although none of them reached the big leagues. Two of her top signees were 19-year-old second baseman Charlie Watson, who she plucked off the sandlots, and pitcher Eddie Zeidler from Olney High School. Both players advanced as high as Class B leagues.

"It's so hard to make the big leagues," Houghton noted. "You have to be awfully good. A lot of guys don't even make the minors."

Houghton worked for the Phillies through the 1952 season. By then, the Korean War was well under way, and having remained in the Navy reserves after World War II, Edith was called back to active duty. When discharged two years later, Houghton returned to reserve duty, but not to the Phillies. "I just wasn't making enough money," she said. "But I didn't go in and make any special demands. It was just time to move on."

Although she continued to play softball until the mid-1950s, Edith directed most of her attention toward her full-time job. After leaving Supplee-Biddle, she worked in sales for both Philco and Penn Mutual and with a pet-supply company in which she was an investor. Then, in the late 1960s, she retired and moved to Sarasota, Florida where she stayed a while longer in the Navy reserves. She also bowled, and in her one and only attempt at golf, broke 100.

Now, more than 60 years after Houghton became a baseball pioneer, and after having recently been cited by the Baseball Hall of Fame to which she has donated some of her mementos from her days with the Bobbies, she looks back on her time as a scout with both pleasure and satisfaction.

"It was a wonderful opportunity," she said. "I loved the job. I met some nice people, scouted some nice players. I just enjoyed it so much. It's hard to put a value on something like this, especially because I've lived a pretty good life. But I know that working in baseball and being the first woman scout rank as the highlights of my career."

chapter 3

16 SHUTOUTS IN ONE SEASON

*T*he *Major League Baseball Record Book* has never been something to be taken lightly.

It is jammed with facts and figures that represent virtually every documentable aspect of the game.

The book portrays both the best and the worst of baseball. Some of the records are the result of exemplary achievements. Others sprung from the dregs of excessive calamity. Regardless of the outcome, though, baseball without its record book would be like a car without tires. It could run, but it wouldn't be nearly as good.

Some of the records, of course, are more significant than others. Joe DiMaggio's 56-game hitting streak, for instance, carries considerably more weight than Gil Hodges' record of most sacrifice flies (19) in one season. Ty Cobb's career batting average of .367 is more noteworthy than Hank Majeski's mark of most two-base hits (six) in a doubleheader.

Pitching records also vary in levels of importance. Nolan Ryan's 5,714 career strikeouts certainly have a greater impact than Walter Johnson's career high of 206 hit batters. Cy Young's record of 511 career wins is a much more magnetic figure than Cy Young's record of 313 career losses.

Then there is Cal Ripken's 2,216 consecutive games played, Hack Wilson's 191 RBI in one season, Carl Hubbell's 24 straight wins. These are incomparable marks that rank among the most prestigious in the baseball record book.

Another record that commands a place at the summit of baseball accomplishments is the standard set by the Phillies' Grover Cleveland Alexander when he pitched 16 shutouts in one season. Although it is not a record that attracts much attention these days, it is, nevertheless, one of the most remarkable entries in the book.

And why shouldn't it be? Firing 16 shutouts in one season is a simply incomprehensible feat that is surely one of the most unbreakable records in the book. And in all of baseball history, going back to the days when the sport first turned professional, the only other time somebody tossed 16 shutouts was in 1876 when George Brady did it with the St. Louis Brown Stockings in an era when the mound stood 45 feet from home plate and pitchers threw the ball underhanded.

In today's game where multi-tiered pitching staffs are considered necessary and where pitch counts seem to govern how far into a game a pitcher works nearly as much as how hard he's getting knocked around, almost nobody ever throws a shutout. A shutout is a relic that is mostly gone and fully ignored. Put simply, it is something that nobody today gives a hoot about.

Whole teams don't pitch as many shutouts today as Alexander did in 1916. The league-leading team might have a dozen or so shutouts for the season. As for individual leaders, it's time to break out the champagne if the league's top guy has two or three shutouts. Over his entire 24-year career, the mighty Roger Clemens, for instance, pitched exactly 46 shutouts.

Pete, as Alexander was sometimes called, would be shocked. He set one of baseball's greatest records, and today, most pitchers wouldn't know a shutout from a zebra. In Alexander's day, though, a shutout was not only common, it was what every good pitcher was expected to throw.

By 1916, Alex had been pitching professionally since 1909. He had originally wanted to attend law school, but the Elba, Nebraska native had switched his allegiance to baseball to take advantage of the skills he had learned as a kid throwing rocks at squirrels and rabbits on the family farm. Even as a boy, Alex had uncanny control, and was often called on to load up some rocks and bring a rabbit home for dinner.

In his initial season as a pro, while earning $50 per month, Alexander got his first taste of shutout action when he pitched a no-hitter for 10 innings, then continued on to hurl an 18-inning shutout for the last-place Galesburg Boosters of the Class D Illinois-Missouri League. In less than two years, Alex was with the Phillies after the club bought his contract from Syracuse of the Class B New York State League for $750.

Alex posted a 28-13 record and at one point fired four straight shutouts in his rookie season, then won 19, 22, 27, and 31 over the next four years. He worked in more than 300 innings every season, completed more than 90 percent of the games he started, and even made seven to 12 relief appearances each year. He was usually among the league's strikeout leaders—ultimately winning five titles in six years—and his control was impeccable. In fact, the great sportswriter Grantland Rice once said, "Alexander could pitch into a tin can. His control is remarkable, the finest I have ever seen."

In 1915, Alex led the Phillies to their first National League pennant. That year, the sidewheeling righthander registered a phenomenal 1.22 earned run average, while winning 31 games, pitching in 376.1 innings, completing 38 games, 12 of which were shutouts, and striking out 241, all categories in which he led the league.

Although the team lost in five games to the Boston Red Sox in the World Series, the Phils were considered the favorite to win the NL pennant again in 1916 in a four-team race with the New York Giants, Boston Braves, and Brooklyn Robins. And the six-foot, one-inch, 185-pound Alexander was ready to pursue what would become his most spectacular season.

Manager Pat Moran's Phillies opened the season at Baker Bowl against the Giants. Before the game, the team had been presented with monogrammed gold watches, compliments of the Phils' owners. Then, after both teams had paraded to center field to participate in the traditional flag-raising ceremony, the Phillies and Alexander, who had pitched a two-inning tune-up two days earlier in an exhibition game in Washington, were ready to go. A sellout crowd in excess of 18,000 was there to watch the Phillies come from behind to win, 5-4, as Milt Stock walked, stole second, went to third on a passed ball, and rode home on a wild pitch in the bottom of the ninth inning.

Six days latter, on April 18, Alexander got his first shutout of the season with a five-hit, 4-0 whitewash of the Braves at Baker Bowl. He then won one, and lost one before bagging his second shutout of the season with a 3-0 victory over Boston on May 3 in a game in which the Braves had men on third base with one out twice, but couldn't score.

Alex then proceeded to blank the Cincinnati Reds, 5-0, on May 13, the Pittsburgh Pirates, 3-0, on May 18, and Brooklyn, 1-0, on May 26 in a game that temporarily moved the Phillies into first place. In that game, the Robins had runners in scoring position in four different innings, including the sixth when they loaded the bases with one out only to be retired when right fielder Gavvy Cravath grabbed a line drive, then threw Casey Stengel out at the plate for an inning-ending double play.

The Nebraska Cyclone, as some writers referred to him, got his next shutout on June 3 with a 2-0 win over the St. Louis Cardinals. Again, the Phillies' defense saved him. The Cards had the bases loaded with none out in the fifth, but a force out at home was followed by a sensational catch in left field by Possum Whitted, who then turned and threw the man on third out at the plate. A leaping catch by second baseman Bert Niehoff and subsequent throw to second to double up the runner, and a diving catch in center field by Dode Paskert saved Alex from damage in the seventh.

Alexander won four straight one-run games, three of them by 2-1 scores, then lost a 5-1 tilt on July 3 in six innings. His next shutout came on July 7 when Paskert's leaping grab above the wall prevented a home run in a 1-0 decision over the Cardinals. Before July was over, Ol' Pete had pitched two more shutouts, copping a 4-0 decision over the Pirates on July 15, and a 6-0 triumph over the Reds on July 20. He also won two one-run games, a 2-1 victory over the Chicago Cubs, and a 7-1 verdict against the Pirates when the only Bucs run scored on a passed ball. During July, Alex had allowed just three runs in six games.

Baseball historian Joe Dittmar points out that at that stage of the season, Alexander had a 19-6 record, while the Philadelphia Athletics, in the midst of finishing last in the American League seven straight times, were 19-64. Alex, though, went ahead of the lowly A's when he won his 20th game on August

Hall of Famer Grover Cleveland Alexander compiled a record that will never be broken.

2 with a 1-0 victory in 12 innings over the Cubs. Bill Killifer scored the winning run as Chicago first baseman Heine Zimmerman argued with the umpire about his calling batter Paskert safe at first on the play.

From August 1 to August 19, the Phillies won 13 of 15 games, including one on August 9 when Alexander pitched a three-hit, 1-0 shutout against the Reds. Then in the first game of a doubleheader on August 14, he erased the Giants, 9-0. He came back with another shutout when he beat Cincinnati, 3-0, on August 18. It was Alexander's 13th shutout of the season, and broke the National League record previously held by Reds manager Christy Mathewson.

Alex broke another record on September 3 when he blanked the Robins and Jack Coombs, 3-0, in a game in which Brooklyn had the bases loaded with two outs in the second, men on second and third with one out in the eighth, and runners at the corners in the ninth. Ironically, the shutout eclipsed the modern major league record of 13 shutouts in one season held by none other than Coombs.

The shutout over the Robins launched the Phillies on an eight-game winning streak at the end of which the team had a two-game lead in the standings. Soon thereafter, though, the Giants went on a 26-game winning streak that included a four-game sweep of the Phillies during which they committed 12 errors. In one of those games, Alex was pounded for 13 hits in seven innings.

The Phillies weren't dead yet. Both the team and the pitcher regrouped. And on September 23, the Phils, having moved back to second place, two and one-half games behind Brooklyn, met the Reds in a doubleheader at Baker Bowl. It was to be the crowning achievement in Alexander's brilliant season.

By now, starting every third day, Alex got the nod in the first game and beat the Reds, 7-3, with Niehoff's three-run homer on a ball that bounced over the wall for a ground-rule four-bagger being the deciding blow. After the game, Moran had a request. "I'll have to ask you to pitch the second game, too," he said to Alex. "We have only a little more than an hour to catch the train. Get it over fast."

Indeed, Alex did. Following his manager's orders, he recorded his 15th shutout and 30th win of the season with a

4-0 victory. Alexander allowed seven singles, walked one, and was in danger of being scored on just twice. With Cravath slamming six straight hits in the doubleheader, the game was completed in 58 minutes. After the final out, fans rushed onto the field, picked up Alex, and carried him to the center field clubhouse where upon his arrival, team president William Baker presented him with a $100 bonus check.

The win, coupled with a Brooklyn split in a doubleheader with Chicago, moved the Phillies to within one and one-half games of first. And there was still some time left in the season.

Alex won one and lost one in the ensuing days as the Phillies stayed close to the lead. Then on October 2, pitching on one day's rest, his fifth start in the last eight games, and in his final start of the season, Alex notched his 16th shutout with a three-hit, 2-0 victory over Boston in a game in which Dave Bancroft broke his ankle. The win put the Philadelphians briefly back into first place, but three straight losses to the Braves knocked the Phils out of the lead, allowing Brooklyn to win the pennant by two and one-half games over the Phils, who finished in second one and one-half games ahead of the Braves.

Although disappointingly, the Phillies failed to repeat as pennant winners, it was a magnificent season for Alexander. While getting a decision in every game he started, Alex finished with a 33-12 record and league-leading marks with a 1.55 ERA, 45 starts, 38 complete games, 388.2 innings pitched, 323 hits, 167 strikeouts, and wins. Alex's 16 shutouts were 10 more than those posted by runners-up Lefty Tyler of Boston and Jeff Pfeffer of Brooklyn. Alex also pitched three times in relief, and years later, when the statistic was introduced, was awarded a save for each appearance.

In the final tabulations, Alex had posted one shutout in April, four in May, one in June, three in July, four in August, two in September, and one in October. He fired three shutouts against Boston; two each against Brooklyn, Pittsburgh, and St. Louis; one apiece against New York and Chicago, and five against Cincinnati. The next time a pitcher would blank an opposing team that many times was in 1966 when Larry Jaster of the Cardinals did it to the Los Angeles Dodgers.

According to figures calculated by Dittmar, Alexander fired seven shutouts on the road. Nine shutouts occurred at home, which on the surface seems like an amazing feat if for no other reason than that Baker Bowl's right field wall sat 272 feet down the line from home plate and pop flies flew over it with astonishing regularity. Baker Bowl was certainly no pitcher's park, but in 1916 Alexander gave up just six home runs there, only one of which glided over the right field wall. Overall, he allowed only 33 earned runs at "The Hump" in 205 innings of work.

During the season, the man who was named for a standing U.S. president and whose life would be portrayed in a movie by a future U.S. president (Ronald Reagan) pitched in 12 games that were decided by one run, winning 11 of them. During one stretch between May 26 and June 23, Alexander won six of seven games with the Phillies scoring just 14 runs over that period. And in the seven games he failed to complete, Ol' Pete took the loss in each one.

The following year, Alexander won 30 games—his third straight 30-win season—while earning a salary of $12,000. Although he left the Phillies after the 1917 season, he would go on to pitch until 1930, completing a career that ushered him into the Hall of Fame. Ol' Pete's 373 victories tied him with Christy Mathewson for the third highest win total in baseball history, and his 90 shutouts rank second only to Walter Johnson's major league record 110.

It was his own astonishing shutout record in 1916, though, that proved to be the defining achievement of Alexander's career. Sixteen shutouts in one season, overlooked as often as it is today, ranks as one of the greatest records of all time.

chapter 4

IF ONLY THEY'D BEEN SIGNED

Every baseball team, even the good ones, has botched opportunities to sign young players who later became superstars with some other club. It is the kind of blunder that has happened often over the years, and can be a costly—and embarrassing—mistake that usually comes back to haunt the offending team.

Letting a big one get away can happen for a variety of reasons. It can result from bad scouting. The front office might be at fault. Maybe the player had a bad day during his tryout. Or there could be some other cause. Whatever the reason, though, the error is one that predictably induces endless speculation about what might have been.

One might wonder, for instance, how different Phillies teams would have been if the club had fielded a lineup that included Al Kaline, Carl Yastrzemski, and Hank Aaron in the outfield. Because each player is now positioned in the Hall of Fame, the answer is obvious.

Kaline, Yastrzemski, and Aaron with the Phillies? Unlikely as it may seem, it could have happened. And although each player wound up being a right fielder, surely the Phils would have found a way to field such a star-studded outfield (which actually included, at the time, Del Ennis and Richie Ashburn).

The Phillies in the 1950s, 1960s, and early 1970s were at best highly mediocre. Between 1951 and 1973, the team finished above fourth place just twice, one time being the fateful season of 1964. There were four eighth-place finishes, two sevenths, and four sixths. It was an era when the Phils needed all the help they could get. Kaline, Yastrzemski, or Aaron, or any combination thereof, surely would have lifted the Phillies to a higher level.

With each player, the story of his brief encounter with the Phillies is vastly different. Ultimately, however, the blame for making the unconscionable blunder of failing to sign any of them falls heavily on the Phillies front office. It had its chances but blew them.

Hank Aaron was the first possibility. With black players no longer barred from organized baseball, Aaron, who had played briefly in the Negro Leagues, was looking in the early 1950s for a chance to play in the major leagues. Then an infielder, he had tryouts with several teams, one of which was the Phillies.

At the time, the Phillies had shown no interest in signing black players. While Jackie Robinson had broken the so-called color barrier in 1947 and his Brooklyn Dodgers, as well as various other major league teams, were by then dipping heavily into the Negro Leagues to sign players, the Phillies were still embracing a racist attitude that stood in the way of their bringing black players to Philadelphia.

Although Aaron made a good impression on club officials, he was sent away with the promise that the Phillies would call if the team decided it was interested in signing him. It was a kind of "Don't call us, we'll call you" situation. The call never came.

While the Phillies did sign their first black player in 1952, it was not until 1957 when one finally appeared in an official game with the team. Meanwhile, Aaron signed with the Boston Braves, and starting in his rookie season in 1954, by which time the Braves had moved to Milwaukee, he played in 23 big league seasons while becoming baseball's greatest home run slugger until his record 755 homers was passed in 2007 by Barry Bonds. Aaron had a career batting average of .305, collected 2,297 RBI, scored 2,174 runs, and in 1982 was an overwhelming choice to enter the Hall of Fame.

Soon afterward, the Phillies had their shot at Al Kaline. An outstanding high school player in Baltimore, Kaline attracted the interest of numerous big league teams in 1952, including the Phillies.

"I never really worked out with them," Kaline told Skip Clayton, writing many years later in *Phillies Report*. "In fact, I didn't work out with any team. But I knew everybody except two clubs were watching me and wanted to sign me."

The Phillies pursued Kaline like a hawk chasing a mouse. Phils scout Jocko Collins repeatedly watched him play high school games after getting a tip from fellow NBA referee Charlie Eckman, a Baltimore resident. "He ran great, had a great arm, and was a very good outfielder," Collins said. "He had the good, level stroke, and it was just a matter of time until he got his strength. He also had a great attitude, and was a wonderful person."

Kaline was fully aware that the Phillies regarded him highly. "They were very interested in signing me," he said. "They of-

The Phillies could have signed Al Kaline, among others, but let the great outfielder get away.

fered me a lot more money than Detroit [the club with which he eventually signed] or any other club."

But, as was often the case throughout Phillies history, the team made a bad decision.

Always enamored with big, strong-armed pitchers, the Phils had a long record of signing such players. Most of the time, the pitchers were busts, and despite sometimes huge bonuses, they quickly disappeared from the scene without making so much as a minuscule contribution. Paul Penson, Tom Casagrande, and Paul Brown were just a few of these pitchers: signed for big money but hardly heard from again.

Another pitcher who fit this category was 18-year-old Tom Qualters. The Phillies had been following the hard-throwing righthander throughout his high school career In McKeesport, Pennsylvania, during which he had set 23 school records, including ones for most strikeouts, scoreless innings, no-hitters, and consecutive victories. In June 1952, they had to make a decision.

"Back in those days," Kaline said, "players paid more than a $6,000 bonus had to stay in the major leagues for two years. The Phillies didn't want to have two 18-year-olds on their major league roster, so they signed him and didn't sign me."

The Phillies, with owner Bob Carpenter personally executing the signing, gave Qualters a $100,000 bonus. And in the years that followed, the pitcher who was nicknamed "Money Bags" appeared in just eight games—all in relief—and won exactly zero games.

Kaline, on the other hand, joined the Tigers with no minor league experience, and in 1955 at the age of 20 became the youngest player ever to win a major league batting title. He went on to play 22 years with the Tigers, finishing with a .297 batting average with 399 home runs and 1,583 RBI. In 1980, Kaline was inducted into the Hall of Fame.

"Hindsight is always great," he said, "but nobody knew that an 18-year-old kid was going to sign out of high school and become a regular in the majors within a year. It was an awful large gamble [for Detroit], but it worked."

Six years later, the Phillies faced a similar situation. This time, they found themselves vying for an 18-year-old shortstop from Southampton, New York who was being hotly pursued by most of the teams on the East Coast. (He did not want to play on the West Coast.)

Carl Yastrzemski had just spent his freshman year at Notre Dame, and was being hauled from team to team by his father, who was handling the negotiations. When Yaz came to Philadelphia for a tryout, the Phillies gave him a locker with the regulars, and he was introduced around the clubhouse.

"[Manager Eddie] Sawyer patted me on the back, and Wally Moses, who was the batting coach, took an interest in me while I was in the cage," Yastrzemski recalled in his book, *Yaz: Baseball, The Wall, and Me.* "Even [Chico] Fernandez, who knew they were thinking about me as a shortstop, told me, 'Good luck, even if you think you can take my job.'"

Taking batting practice, Yastrzemski estimated he hit about one dozen balls over the wall in right field at Connie Mack Stadium. "Moses said, 'Carl, you're the finest young hitter I've ever seen,'" wrote Yaz. "And [Robin] Roberts was laughing when he told Fernandez, 'Nice knowing you, Chico.'"

Negotiating with Carpenter and Phillies executive Jimmy Gallagher (no relation to Jimmy Gallagher of the Philadelphia Eagles), Yaz was first offered a $60,000 bonus. "Everyone knows we're looking for $100,000 and the rest of his college tuition," Yaz's dad responded.

In his book, Yaz said that the Phillies raised their offer to $60,000 plus an immediate salary of $7,000. That was rejected. The offer then went to $80,000, then to $95,000, plus the $7,000 salary. When the senior Yaz again raised the issue of tuition, Carpenter said he had endowed a scholarship at the University of Delaware that Yaz could use.

"Even that wasn't enough," Yastrzemski wrote. "Dad suddenly hit Carpenter with another demand: $10,000 if I failed to finish college." This time, the Phillies refused to budge. Neither did the Yastrzemskis. And after two days of negotiations, the talks finally ended, and Yaz and his dad drove home to Long Island.

"The talks ended with Carpenter doing a funny thing," Yaz said. "As we said goodbye, he gave me his telephone credit card number and said to use it as long as I wanted, and to call anyplace I wanted."

Soon afterward, right before heading back to school, Yaz had tryouts with and fielded offers from the Tigers, Cincinnati Reds, and Boston Red Sox. The New York Yankees were also keenly interested in the young player, but his father did not want him to play with the Yanks, and would not allow any interaction between the two parties.

"If I had my choice—I knew the Yankees were out, he'd never let me sign with them—I probably would have signed with Philadelphia," Yastrzemski said. "Every time I thought of a reason to sign with a club, Dad had a good reason why I shouldn't. If I told him I liked Philly, he told me they already had Fernandez at short, and I'd just be sitting on the bench withering away."

Eventually, Yaz signed with the Red Sox with Boston giving him a $108,000 bonus, full college tuition, and a $5,000 salary in each of the next two years. And the Phillies, falling short of that package, lost out on another future superstar.

Yastrzemski spent 23 years in the big leagues, hitting .285 with 452 home runs and 1,844 RBI. He won three batting titles and a Triple Crown in 1967, a year in which he was the American League's Most Valuable Player. Yaz entered the Hall of Fame in 1989.

Aaron, Kaline, and Yastrzemski. They could have played with the Phillies.

They were, of course, not the only great players the Phillies could have signed. In 1897, the Phils sent disabled pitcher Con Lucid to a game in Paterson, New Jersey to scout a young shortstop who was drawing rave reviews for his sparkling play. After watching Honus Wagner perform, Lucid returned home with the report that "he can hit, but he's too clumsy for the National League." Lucid had much higher praise for the opposing team's shortstop, Norman Elberfield. "I believe that boy will go far," he said. "You can't go wrong investing some money in him."

The Phillies signed Elberfield, who eventually played in just 14 games for them, although he had a 14-year big league career while hitting .271. Wagner was signed a few weeks later by the Pittsburgh Pirates for $2,100. Soon after, he launched a 21-year career during which he became one of the greatest players in baseball history and a member of the first group inducted into the Hall of Fame.

The Phillies also could have signed first baseman Mickey Vernon. The future big league star had a lengthy tryout with the Phils at Baker Bowl as a 17-year-old high school senior in 1936. "I worked out every day for a week with eight or 10 other kids," Vernon said in the book, *Mickey Vernon: The Gentleman First Baseman*. "I never swung a bat, just fielded. It went all right. But they didn't offer me a contract. I only weighed 150 pounds, so I guess they didn't think much of such a frail fellow."

One year later, after a season at Villanova University, Vernon signed with the Washington Senators. That began a 20-year career in the big leagues that produced two American League batting titles and seven All-Star Game appearances for the Marcus Hook native who would have become a strong hometown favorite.

Another local favorite who was within the grasp of the Phillies was Roy Campanella. A resident of the Nicetown section of Philadelphia, Campy approached the Phils in 1942 with the hope of getting a tryout. By then, he had become a top catcher with the Negro League's Baltimore Elite Giants.

Phillies manager Hans Lobert advised Campanella to contact Phillies owner Gerry Nugent. When he did, Campy was told that an unwritten rule in baseball prevented teams from signing black players. And like so many other times, the Phillies missed out on having a superstar who turned into a three-time Most Valuable Player with the Brooklyn Dodgers and another member of the Hall of Fame.

There are other examples of similar missed opportunities. One in particular occurred in 1988. Phoenixville High School catcher Mike Piazza was available until the 62nd round when he was drafted by Los Angeles Dodgers manager Tom Lasorda as a favor to Piazza's father.

What would it have been like to have had Piazza as the Phillies' catcher? Or Campanella behind the plate in red pinstripes? Or Vernon or Wagner or what might have been one of the best outfields in baseball history—Aaron, Kaline, and Yastrzemski—playing with the Phillies?

chapter 5

CHANGES LAUNCHED A HALL OF FAME CAREER

During a Hall of Fame career, Mike Schmidt won seven home run titles outright, 10 Gold Gloves, three Most Valuable Player awards, and was named to 12 All-Star teams.

Schmidt is one of only 24 players to have hit more than 500 home runs in a career, and one of just 15 players who have hit four home runs in one game. Only Babe Ruth won more home run titles (nine), and only Hank Aaron had more seasons with 30 or more home runs (15) than Schmidt.

Also the World Series MVP in 1980, Schmidt ranks 30th on the major league all-time list in career RBI, 24th in extra base hits, and 16th in walks. He played more games (2,404) and in more years (18) with the Phillies than any other player.

The muscular slugger, who is the Phillies' all-time leader in 12 of the top 19 offensive categories, finished his career with 548 home runs, 1,595 RBI, 1,505 runs, 2,234 hits, and a slugging average of .527. Along with a career batting average of .267, he had a fielding average of .955.

As one of only eight third basemen inducted into the Hall of Fame, Schmidt is arguably the best all-around guardian of the hot corner of all time. Naturally, he has no competition as the best Phillies player of all time.

The amazing footnote to those descriptions is that Schmidt was once a switch-hitting shortstop who had knees so bad that he was forced to consider a career as an architect. While both his injured knees required surgery, thus reducing his playing time, Schmidt had as much success in football, where he played quarterback, and basketball, where he performed as a power forward, as he did in baseball.

How, then, does a kid who as a high school senior didn't draw much attention from college recruiters and in his early college days was ignored by major league scouts, reach such a lofty spot among the highest-ranking members of the baseball pantheon?

There are, of course, many parts to that answer. Numerous factors enter the equation, not the least of which was Schmidt's own single-minded determination. But viewed in the context of most superstars, it is downright amazing that a teenager with such heavy baggage could someday blossom into a player of Schmidt's stature.

A hint of that ultimate success might have been suggested when Schmidt was just seven years old. Like many small boys, Mike liked to climb trees. The big ash behind the family house in Dayton, Ohio was his favorite.

One day, however, the youngster climbed too high. Far above the ground, he lost his balance and began to fall. He reached out for a branch, but it was too small and broke. Then, as he continued to tumble, Schmidt grabbed the only thing he could reach—a high-tension electric wire. As soon as he grasped the wire, the boy was hit by 4,000 volts of electricity. Young Mike tumbled 24 feet to the ground, slamming into one limb after another as he fell.

Miraculously, Schmidt was still alive when he slammed into the ground. He even managed to climb slowly to his feet and stagger into the house where his terrified family took one look at him and raced him to a hospital. Once there, it was learned that Mike not only had escaped electrocution with the only damage being burns, but had also survived the ordeal without breaking any bones.

Two months later, fully recovered, the boy was back playing baseball and other games with his friends. It was an early sign that Schmidt was someone in possession of a strong will and the desire to overcome obstacles that stood in his way.

Such characteristics stuck with Schmidt as he became older. Although fond of other sports, he had shown an early aptitude for baseball, and at the age of eight earned a spot on a Little

League team that consisted mostly of 12-year-olds. He soon became one of the team's top players. When Mike wasn't playing with the team, he played from morning to night with his friends at a local recreation center. And he steadfastly maintained that someday he would be a professional baseball player.

A righthanded-hitting third baseman in his early baseball days, Schmidt was beginning to gain a reputation as an outstanding athlete. But in his early years as a teenager, Mike became a switch-hitter and a shortstop.

"My production was very poor," Schmidt said in an interview in 2007. "One day, I said to myself, I'm going to try batting left-handed, and I got a base hit. So I took up switch-hitting, not only because I thought I could hit the ball batting lefthanded, but mainly because I was afraid of the ball as a young kid, and as a switch-hitter you didn't have to worry about that."

With a strong arm, Schmidt was also moved to shortstop, where he still was playing when he entered Fairview High School. Not only was young Mike a baseball player, but in football, he became the starting safety as a sophomore. As a junior, he was the starting quarterback and a power forward on the basketball team.

His bad knees, however, both requiring surgery, limited his development as an athlete, although it was obvious that he had talent. In his senior year, Schmidt gained honorable mention on the all-city baseball team.

"I liked his tools, but I could tell that he still hadn't put his game together," said longtime Phillies scout Tony Lucadello, who had started watching Schmidt when he was still in high school. "He was an excellent athlete, but I felt he would be a late-bloomer. At times, he did things that truly amazed me, and other times, he did not play well."

Lucadello, who signed more than 50 players, including future Hall of Famer Ferguson Jenkins, who reached the big leagues, followed Schmidt throughout his high school days. He was about the only scout who did. Most scouts and recruiters backed off because of Mike's bad knees. By the time he graduated, only a few colleges—all in Ohio—showed any interest in him, and none was willing to offer a scholarship. Accordingly, the youth enrolled at Ohio University in Athens, about 120 miles from Dayton.

At Ohio, Schmidt played on the freshman baseball and basketball teams. Still a switch-hitting shortstop, Mike hit only .260. "He hit just one home run and wasn't spectacular in the field," Lucadello wrote in an article in 1987. Except for Lucadello, most of the other scouts who had been following Schmidt quit watching him.

Neverthless, Lucadello and Ohio varsity baseball coach Bobby Wren could see that Schmidt had outstanding ability. Wren, who kept quiet about the scout's interest in the young player, also saw something else. He didn't think much of Mike's lefthanded hitting. He felt that Schmidt had a much better swing from the right side, and suggested that he give up switch-hitting.

"In my sophomore year in college," Schmidt recalled, "my coach said, 'How about trying to hit righthanded against a righthanded pitcher?' I tried it and hit a home run."

"Stick with it, and I'll stick with you," Wren told Schmidt. "And don't worry about the strikeouts." From that day forward, Schmidt was a full-time righthanded hitter.

Wren wrangled a partial scholarship for the young player as he entered his sophomore year. Schmidt responded by hitting .310. The following season, his batting average inched up to .313, and Mike was named first-team All-American. Still, in part because of what were perceived as a pair of weak and vulnerable knees, he was ignored in the annual free agent draft. What the scouts didn't know, however, was that Schmidt had undertaken a rigid weight program that had fully restored the strength and condition of his knees.

Meanwhile, in the years that he had been scouting Schmidt, Lucadello tried desperately to hide his interest in the youngster from other scouts and teams, refusing to talk to anyone about him—even Schmidt's family. He seldom talked with Schmidt's coaches and on occasion he even delayed his reports to the Phillies with the hope that team officials wouldn't take note of his enthusiasm and perhaps let it slip out to other clubs.

"When scouts see another scout at a game, they usually know who he's there to see," Lucadello said. "So, I wound up scouting Mike from behind bushes and trees, around the corners of buildings, and I even went to a few games in a disguise. I was 'The Invisible Baseball Scout.'"

The late Tony Lucadello, a man regarded as one of the finest scouts ever to work the game, finally had to go public. In Schmidt's senior year, he hit .330 with 10 home runs and 45 RBI while again earning All-American honors and ultimately graduating with a degree in business administration. By now, every team knew about the promising slugger. The California Angels were especially interested.

But Lucadello and the Phillies had the upper hand. The scout had convinced then-Phillies farm director Paul Owens that Schmidt was a player with exceptional potential. Still, every team, including the Phillies and Angels, passed on Mike in the

Mike Schmidt went from a switch-hitting shortstop to a power-hitting Hall of Fame third baseman.

first round. Instead, with the sixth pick overall, the Phils selected pitcher Roy Thomas. The club also had the 22nd pick in
the first round, and with it chose first baseman Dane Iorg.
(Thomas never played in a single game with the Phillies, and
Iorg appeared in 12 games in 1977.) The Phils picked Schmidt
in the second round, right after the Kansas City Royals had selected another future Hall of Famer, George Brett.

Lucadello, Schmidt, and his father, Jack, then met in a Holiday Inn in Dayton to negotiate a contract. When Mike asked
for more money, the veteran scout called Owens in Philadelphia and got permission to up the offer. "Mike was shy, but he
was straightforward and honest, and knew what he wanted,"
Lucadello said.

Ultimately, the contract was signed with Schmidt getting a
$35,000 bonus. He was assigned to Reading of the Class AA
Eastern League. Although he was no longer a switch-hitter,
Mike was still a shortstop. And in his first game as a professional—an exhibition game between Reading and the Phillies—
he was asked to play in the lineup of the parent club, filling in
for injured shortstop Larry Bowa. In the eighth inning, Schmidt
smashed a game-winning home run off Reading pitcher Mike
Fremuth.

Schmidt struggled at Reading, hitting just .211 with only
eight home runs and 31 RBI in 74 games, while striking out 66
times in 237 trips to the plate. "I took some heat for that, but
I kept saying, 'The kid's a late-bloomer. He'll develop,'" Lucadello said.

Mike's hitting improved considerably the following year
when after getting moved up to Portland, a Triple-A team in
the Pacific Coast League, he posted a .291 batting average with
26 home runs and 91 RBI. Schmidt, by then almost 23 years
old, wound up the season in Philadelphia where he appeared
in 13 games.

Mike was still a shortstop when he began the season at
Portland. He was a third baseman when the season ended.

Portland Beavers manager Andy Seminick moved Schmidt
out of the shortstop spot, for most of the season playing him at
second and third bases. By the end of the season, Seminick, a
former Phillies catcher and an astute judge of talent during a
long career with the club that included scouting, coaching, and

managing, had stationed Schmidt full-time at the hot corner.

"I think his best position is third base," said Seminick at the time, having observed Schmidt's strong arm, sure hands, and quick reflexes.

And the transition was complete. From switch-hitter to righthanded hitter, from shortstop to third baseman, Schmidt had finally found a home for all his talents. And in both departments, he would ultimately realize the enormous potential that others, especially Lucadello, had predicted.

chapter 6

THE LEFTHANDED CATCHER

here are certain positions in professional baseball that a lefthander is not allowed to play. He can't play second base. He is not permitted to play shortstop. And he is barred from taking a position at third base.

He can't play any of these positions because it is generally conceded that lefthanded infielders must turn to make throws to first base (or second if he's on the left side of the diamond). And that is not only a more difficult chore than that facing a righthanded thrower, but it also gives the base runner an extra step, which on many occasions can be critical. The ban on lefthanders is furthered by the view that a southpaw's throw normally fades to the left, a condition that would be especially damaging on a double-play ball to the left side of the diamond where the third baseman or shortstop has to throw to second.

Call it sound baseball logic. Call it tradition. Call it discrimination. Whatever the case, lefthanders, especially since the 20th century began, are not considered acceptable at three-quarters of the positions in the infield. (In the outfield, it doesn't matter which hand is used to throw a ball.)

The limitations on lefthanders also extend to the catching position. You can't catch if you're lefthanded. Why? Mainly, because you can't throw to first base with a lefthander in the batter's box and you can't throw to third if a righthander is at bat. And, although the reverse of this could be said of a righthanded catcher, it is a simple fact that lefthanded catchers are not welcome in the baseball games played on this planet.

Roughly estimated, going back to the 1800s, probably more than 8,000 players have been catchers in big league baseball games. But just 33 of them were lefthanders. Of this group, 10 played in only one game—probably an emergency situation—and 16 played in five games or less, including those better known at other positions such as Chris Short, Dale Long, and Mike Squires. Most of the lefty backstops did their duty before the start of the 20th century, although even then, a southpaw catcher was considered with about the same regard as a three-headed monster at a freak show.

Of the 33 lefthanded catchers, 10 played in 50 or more games. Five of them went behind the plate in more than 100 games, and three caught in more than 200 games. One of them was Jack Clements, who caught most of his games with the Phillies.

Among all the catchers who squatted (or in the early days, stood) behind batters, none of them was in a class with Clements. He was truly in a league of his own.

Clements was a big league catcher for 17 years. He caught in 1,073 games, a record for lefthanded catchers. The southpaw catcher with the second highest number of appearances is an unknown backup player named Sam Trott, who went behind the plate in 272 games in the 1880s.

John J. Clements was no backup catcher. He played in the big leagues from 1884 to 1897, most of the time as a regular. He was the first big league catcher, lefthanded or righthanded, to catch in 1,000 games, and when the 19th century ended, only two other backstops (Wilbert Robinson and Deacon McGuire) had caught in more games.

Standing five feet, eight inches and weighing 204 pounds, Clements, who also hit from the left side, had a career batting average of .286. He finished his career with 1,226 hits of which 77 were home runs. He drove in 673 runs and scored 619.

Defensively, Clements was one of the better catchers of his era. He led the league in putouts three times, and in double plays and fielding average each once. For the decade of the 1890s, Clements ranked among the top 10 catchers in games played, putouts, assists, chances, and errors. His fielding average for the decade was .950, fourth highest among catchers of that period. Overall, he had a career fielding average of .936.

Clements is also credited with being one of the first catchers to wear a chest protector. In *Nineteenth Century Stars,* published by the Society for American Baseball Research, writer Al Glynn says that in 1884, "Clements appeared on the field with a chest protector that jeering fans and sportswriters referred to as a 'sheepskin.'"

History has not recorded why Clements became a catcher. Or where he managed to come up with a lefthanded catcher's mitt. Or how many lefthanded hitters got hit in the breadbasket with his throws to first base. What it does say is that Clements was without question the best lefthanded catcher in baseball history and one of the top backstops of the 19th century.

It can be speculated that Clements got his start as a catcher somewhere on the streets of Philadelphia where he was born on July 24, 1864. As a youth, Clements played on local sandlot teams before getting a chance to turn pro in 1884 with the Philadelphia Keystones.

At the time, three so-called major league teams resided in Philadelphia—the Phillies of the National League, the Athletics of the American Association, and the Keystones of the Union Association, a league formed in opposition to the "reserve clause" used by the two other leagues to bind a player to one team for life.

While the Union Association lasted just one year, the Keystones didn't even make it to the end of the season. When the team folded, Clements, who had hit .282 in 41 games, was picked up by the Phillies.

At that point, the Phillies, a team that has sometimes been called the Quakers, were in just their second season after having opened their first season with a disastrous 17-81 record. Harry Wright, in his first year as Phillies manager, was looking everywhere for decent players, and even a lefthanded catcher was worth considering.

With the season almost over, Clements played in nine games. He would spend the next 13 years with the Phillies, becoming the anchor for a pitching staff that during that time included such standouts as Charlie Ferguson, Ed Daly, Charlie Buffinton, Dan Casey, Kid Gleason, and Kid Carsey.

Clements' early seasons with the Phillies were a bit rocky. Although he caught more games than anyone else on the team, he hit just .191 and .205 in his first two full seasons with the club. Then in 1887, his batting average rocketed up to .280, and Clements became a fixture in a lineup that would soon include Hall of Famers Ed Delahanty, Billy Hamilton, and Sam Thompson.

Although he hit only .245 in 1888, Clements followed that with averages of .284, .315, .310, .264, .285, .346, 394, and .359. His .315 in 1890 was the third highest average in the National League. That season, while clubbing seven home runs, he ranked second in the league in slugging percentage with a .472 mark. Clements' .310 in 1891 was the league's fourth best average and his .394 in 1895 placed third and was the highest one-season average ever recorded by a big league catcher. Clements also placed second to Delahanty in home runs (17) in 1893, and second in slugging average (.612) and third in home runs (13) in 1895. (In 1894, Clements hit .346, but broke his ankle during the season and played in only 45 games.)

The Phils' regular catcher in nine of his 13 full seasons with the club, Clements, whose career high in games played in one season was only 109, was also filling in at other positions. He played in 41 games in the outfield, 18 games at first base, and four each at shortstop and third base.

He also took a turn as a Phillies manager. Early in the 1890 season, Harry Wright suffered a case of temporary blindness. Although he recovered, three others took his place as manager over a 55-game spread during the season. One was club owner Al Reach. Another was rookie shortstop Bob Allen. And the third was Clements. The acknowledged team leader, Clements was the first man to replace Wright. He held the reins for 19 games, winning 13 of them, before Reach relieved Jack of his duties and replaced him with himself.

During the 1890 season, Clements added another footnote to his colorful career by staging a one-man strike. Feeling overworked after catching two doubleheaders in a row, he informed Wright, who had returned to the team in July and wore sunglasses on the bench, that he would only work one game of a doubleheader the next day against Brooklyn. As the story goes, Clements was the team's only catcher at the time. Because of that, Wright cancelled one game of the twin bill. Clements went 4-for-4 in the lone game.

Lefthanded catcher Jack Clements spent 14 years with
the Phillies.

In another odd twist, the 1896 Phillies fielded lefthanders
at two positions usually manned by righthanders. In addition
to Clements behind the plate, Bill Hulen played in 88 games at
shortstop. Hulen was also a lefthander. In his one season with
the Phils, Hulen hit .265, fielded .874, and played in more games
at shortstop than any other southpaw in baseball history. In
1898, he appeared again, this time playing in 19 games with
the Washington Nationals.

In those days, errors by catchers were a frequent occurrence (passed balls counted as errors). Clements held his own in that department, four times committing more than 40 miscues in a season with a high of 47 in 85 games in 1888.

Apparently, none of the errors came from winging an intended throw to first into a lefthanded batter's skull. When they stood in the batter's box, southpaw swingers seldom obstructed Clements when he wanted to make a throw. "It was either give him plenty of room when he was throwing or else have the ball hurled in your face," recalled Al Maul, who pitched for the Phillies when Clements was catching.

After the 1897 season, with his career winding down, Clements was part of a blockbuster trade with the St. Louis Browns. The Phillies sent their aging catcher, pitcher Brewery Jack Taylor, and outfielder Tommy Dowd to the Browns for pitcher Red Donahue and catcher Klondike Douglass.

While wearing a Phillies uniform, Clements had hit .289 with 70 home runs. He had appeared in 953 games as a catcher, which today ranks as the fifth highest number of games played by a Phillies backstop. Only Mike Lieberthal, Red Dooin, Bob Boone, and Darren Daulton caught more games for the Phillies.

Clements spent just one year with the Browns, hitting .257 and leading National League catchers in fielding. The following year, he joined the Cleveland Spiders, but played in only four games before getting released. He finished his major league career in 1900, playing in 16 games with the Boston Beaneaters.

When he retired, Clements held the records for most home runs by a catcher in one season and in a career. Both records stood until the 1920s when they were broken by Gabby Hartnett of the Chicago Cubs.

Clements spent the 1901 season with Worcester, Massachusetts in the Eastern League, then stepped away from baseball for good. He went to work for Al Reach at the Phillies owner's sporting goods company in Philadelphia. When the plant closed, Clements moved to Connellsville, Pennsylvania in the western part of the state at the request of his brother-in-law, who needed help with the family after his wife had died. While there, Clements took a job in the machine shop of a furnace manufacturer.

In 1915, while Clements was still in Connellsville, the Phillies won their first pennant. Jack was thrilled. "They have come through in the old town at last," he told Joseph Thompson of the Philadelphia *Public Ledger*. "They certainly earned it. I tried for 14 years to help win a pennant for Philadelphia, along with Joe Mulvey, Alex McKinnon, [Jim] Fogarty, and others. Sometimes, we came pretty close, and if we didn't win, we at least had the satisfaction of knocking some other team out of the bacon."

A few years later, Clements moved back to the Philadelphia area, locating in Perkasie where he found work in what's been described as "a baseball factory." He was still living in Perkasie when he developed a heart condition. Clements was ill for six weeks before passing away at Norristown State Hospital on May 23, 1941. He was 76 years old.

Clements is buried in Arlington Cemetery in Drexel Hill in a grave that is unmarked. That's too bad. A marker could've said, "Here lies one of the most unusual players in baseball history. Jack Clements, lefthanded catcher."

chapter 7

RESCUE IN THE ROCKIES

I n an era when professional athletes don't care much about anybody but themselves, the Phillies showed that this attitude can have exceptions. To make the point, all it took was a torrential rainstorm and an uncontrollable infield tarpaulin.

It happened on a stormy July night in Denver during the 2007 season. In the midst of a heated battle for the division title, the Phillies were facing the Colorado Rockies at Coors Stadium in the final game before the All-Star break.

The night was made for goblins. Storm clouds drifted across the Rocky Mountains during much of the night. The threat of rain hung heavily over the ballpark. And as the dark and dreary night progressed, conditions became increasingly dismal.

Then suddenly in the seventh inning it happened. The clouds erupted, releasing torrents of rain on the field and the more than 25,000 people in the stands. Players, fans, and everyone else in the way of the violent storm ran for cover.

All except, of course, the ballpark's groundskeepers. As they always do in a storm, the men who tend the playing surface quickly sprang into action. Grabbing the heavy tarpaulin, the kind that all teams with unroofed stadiums use in such situations, they began spreading it out across the infield.

No one ever claimed that such a job is easy. Weighing about 1,300 pounds and measuring some 170 feet long and 170 feet wide, the bulky, waterproof cloth is a huge, cumbersome cover that takes a dozen or more men to move. Add the weight of the rain collecting on the tarp, and the job of pulling it as quickly as possible over a field in the midst of a drenching storm, wind, and perhaps lightning, and the task is one that is exceedingly difficult.

It was especially difficult for the Rockies' ground crew, and not just because of the driving rain. No sooner had they begun spreading the tarp over the grass and dirt infield, going from the third base side of the field toward the first base line, and a huge surge of wind exploded across the field. In an instant, the tarp was out of control. The men desperately tried to hold on to it, but without much success as the unwieldy cloth flapped violently in the gale.

Suddenly, what already seemed like an impossible job became deadly. The raging wind had thrown the tarp over three groundskeepers. And there was virtually no way they could escape by themselves.

"The tarp looked like a tidal wave," said Phillies shortstop Jimmy Rollins, who with the rest of his teammates had retreated to the safety of the visiting team's dugout. "There were six guys trying to pull the tarp over the field, but the wind kept throwing it back. Three guys on the one side were trying to pull it back, but they had no chance. One guy (head groundskeeper Mark Razum) was holding onto a corner for dear life Then the wind just blew him about 30 feet. He was bouncing all over the place. The three guys on the one side flew under the tarp. They tried to run, but the tarp just covered them up."

Although that happens sometimes during a ground crew's attempt to get the tarp over the infield as quickly as possible, it is always a dangerous predicament for the men swept under the tarp. And while teams such as the Phillies have a backup group of security guards and others standing by ready to pitch in, it is a scary situation that requires immediate attention.

There are many times in sports when athletes are accused of being too self-centered, of caring only about the almighty buck, of being ungrateful, often mean-spirited wretches who wouldn't know a good deed from a used car. This was not one of those times.

The 2007 Phillies were already regarded by most observers as a team of good guys. Almost without exception, they were amiable, down-to-earth fellows who got along well with each other and even with Philadelphia's often-critical working press. The Phils personified the old adage, "There's no I in team."

As the team sat in the dugout, watching what was transpiring in front of them in disbelief, teamwork once again showed itself as a strong characteristic of the '07 Phillies.

From out of the dugout they sprinted. The whole team, racing to the rescue of the trapped groundskeepers.

"It was spontaneous," said right fielder Shane Victorino, who with Rollins, Ryan Howard, and Chase Utley was one of the players who led the charge. "We saw what was happening. We saw the guys get sucked under the tarp. We just said to ourselves that we've got to go out there and help. We didn't want to see anybody get hurt. It was a very serious situation. And we just acted instinctively. Luckily, no one was hurt."

The players—stars and scrubs alike—all ran to the tarp and grabbed a part of it. Victorino snatched a corner and dug his feet into the turf. Howard pulled a side of the tarp with all his might. Utley grabbed an end. Others, including the Phillies

Phillies players rushed to save trapped groundskeepers during a violent thunderstorm at Denver.

pitcher at the time, Adam Eaton, and even players on the injured list such as Aaron Rowand, Carlos Ruiz, and Jayson Werth tried to grip the sides. Coach Jimy Williams yelled for sandbags, and Michael Bourn and Abraham Nunez raced to get them.

"Shane was the first to recognize what was going on," said Rollins, "and he ran out to help. Next thing you know, all of us were out there. We weren't there to help keep the field dry. Our whole objective was to get the guys out from under the tarp. Otherwise, they could have suffocated."

Umpires John Hirschbeck and Bill Welke helped, too. Hirschbeck said it was the first time in 32 years that he'd touched a tarp. But the only Rockies player to help was reliever LaTroy Hawkins. About 10 Colorado players watched from their dugout while the rest of the team retreated to the clubhouse.

"It probably took a few minutes to get the tarp under control," Rollins said. "At first, guys were pulling in different directions. Some guys were saying, 'Pull it this way,' and other guys were saying, 'No, you have to pull it this way.' Finally, we all pulled the same way, got the guys out, and then it took another five or six minutes to get the tarp spread out on the field and get the sandbags in place.

"When we got the tarp off the guys, they were just sitting there," Rollins added. "Their eyes were about as big as the speaker on your tape-recorder. I don't know if they were in shock, but we were looking at them like, come on, get out already, and they just sat there. I guess they had lost their sense of direction once the tarp covered them, and they were really scared."

By the time the job was finished, all of the Phillies were soaked. No one seemed to mind. A sense of satisfaction appeared to sweep over the team. There were even smiles and laughter. And as the team ran off the field, the highly partisan Rockies crowd stood and cheered its efforts.

Ultimately, the storm ended and the game resumed with the Phillies clinging to a 5-4 lead. Before the seventh inning was over, Victorino had hit a two-run homer. Another run in the ninth gave the Phils an 8-4 victory. Eaton was the winning pitcher with Ryan Madson yielding just two hits over the final three innings to record a save. As the game ended, Razum and his crew ran over to the Phillies to thank them. "It kind of changes your whole outlook on baseball players," said Razum, a veteran of 29 years on the ground crew.

In the days that followed, the Phillies' selfless act received national attention. Newspapers and radio and television stations reported the event. And the team was widely acclaimed for preventing a potentially disastrous situation.

"I never saw a whole team do what they did," said Mike DiMuzio, the Phillies' director of ballpark operations who when he first started in the baseball business in the early days of Veterans Stadium was a groundskeeper himself. "I've seen one or two players help in a situation like that, but never the entire team."

Phillies manager Charlie Manuel also took special note of his team's highly praiseworthy display. Manuel said he was enormously proud of his club. "It really showed the character of this team," he said. "They saw some people in trouble and they responded.

"I'll tell you something else," Manuel added. "I thought that kind of fired us up. We won the game, and I think all that happened that night added some energy to the team."

The evidence supporting that statement was clear. Prior to the game, the Phils had lost seven of their last nine outings and were one game under .500. After the All-Star break, the Phillies won 12 of their next 17 games, including a sweep of the Pittsburgh Pirates, and three out of four games against the San Diego Padres. Then, the Phils roared down the homestretch to overtake the New York Mets and win the National League's East Division title. After the rescue in the Rockies, the Phillies won 45 of 74 games for a .608 winning percentage.

Along with the division crown, the Phillies had clinched first place in another important category: they led the league—perhaps all of professional sports—in character and human decency. And in the morose climate of the day when all manner of blemishes taint America's athletes, there could be no feat more commendable than the one the Phillies performed on that stormy night in Denver.

"It was just a natural human reaction," Rollins said. "When you see somebody in trouble, that's the way you should react."

Whether it's in sports or in life, no one can dispute the merits of that attitude.

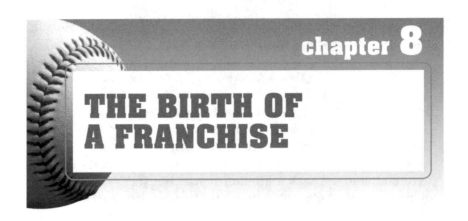

chapter 8

THE BIRTH OF A FRANCHISE

What are the three most often sung songs in America? If you said that one is the *Star-Spangled Banner*, you're right. If you said another is *Happy Birthday*, you're right again. And if you said *Take Me Out to the Ballgame*, too, go to the head of the class. You're 3-for-3.

The words to *Take Me Out to the Ballgame* were written in 1908 by a man named Jack Norworth as he rode a train in New York that was packed with people headed to, you know where— a ballgame.

It is entirely appropriate that Norworth, a songwriter by occupation, wrote the words to that extraordinarily popular song, even though he was not a baseball fan himself. That's because Norworth was a native Philadelphian. And in Philadelphia, baseball was king of all sports. It stands to reason that a song about baseball would be written by a guy from Philadelphia.

The most noteworthy element of Philadelphia baseball is, of course, the Phillies. The Phils have been around since 1883, which is not only considerably longer than any other professional sports team in Philadelphia history, but longer than all but three other current major league baseball franchises, those being originally called the Cincinnati Red Stockings, the Chicago White Stockings, and the Boston Red Caps (which is counted as one franchise even though it has passed through Milwaukee and is now in Atlanta). What's more, the name "Phillies" is the oldest continuous nickname in professional sports.

Long before the Phillies entered the world, though, baseball had been an integral part of the sports scene in Philadelphia. By a sizeable margin, it predated football, basketball, and golf in the city; the only other sports of any stature in the first half of the 19th century were boxing, rowing, tennis, cricket, and track.

Philadelphia in those days was not the only area where baseball thrived. New York, Brooklyn, and northern New Jersey were baseball hotbeds, as were parts of New England and the Midwest. In most cases, the game was called either town ball, cat ball, or base ball.

A remotely related version of baseball was said to have been played in Philadelphia as early as the mid-1700s. By 1820, there were other variations of the game being played in Philadelphia. Then in 1831, at least two club teams were known to have been formed in the city. Games were held on Sunday afternoons in Camden. The participants were men 25 years or older who rode a ferry across the Delaware River from Philadelphia, playing on the New Jersey side because local blue laws forbade their playing on Sundays in Philadelphia.

In 1833, several groups from Philadelphia came together to form the Olympic Town Ball Club of Philadelphia. The Olympic Club eventually grew to more than 1,000 members and had a clubhouse at Broad and Wallace Streets. According to most accounts, this team, which had its own constitution, bylaws, and officers, was the one most responsible for giving the impetus to baseball in the Philadelphia area.

Eventually, other clubs were formed, and by 1850, baseball was thriving in the Philadelphia area (with games often played on days other than Sundays). Numerous club teams, including ones called Keystone, Athletic, Equity, and Olympic, dotted the local landscape. In 1860, in what was recognized as the first game reported in a local newspaper, Equity defeated Pennsylvania, 65-52, at what later was known as Recreation Park, the city's first real ballpark.

Soon afterward, with the Civil War having begun, baseball became the primary form of recreation for the soldiers of both the North and the South. Recreation Park, used as an encampment by Union troops, provided a baseball field on which they played during breaks in their military duties.

Philadelphia had another defining moment in 1865 when a five-foot, six-inch, 155-pound lefthanded second baseman from England named Al Reach became the city's first professional player. Reach, jumping from the Eckford club in Brooklyn, was paid $1,000 for his first season with the Athletic team, an independent team that played in the loosely organized National Association of Base Ball Players.

By then, the Athletic team, which in 1865 averaged 49 runs per game, was the premier nine in Philadelphia. There were numerous other teams, including some made up entirely of black players—the most successful being the Pythians, Union, and Excelsior—and baseball thrived in Philadelphia. In 1866, Athletic won what was described as the "baseball championship of the United States" by defeating the Brooklyn Atlantics in a series that included a game played before an estimated crowd of 30,000 at the first Columbia Park, located at 15th Street and Columbia Avenue.

In 1871, two years after the Cincinnati Red Stockings became baseball's first all-professional team, the first league for professional teams was formed. Called the National Association, it included a team called the Philadelphia Athletics (the letter s now added to the name), a slightly altered version of the previous Athletic club and no relation to future Athletics teams. Nearing the end of his career, Reach and future Hall of Famer Adrian (Cap) Anson were two of the star players as the Athletics won the first championship of the new league.

While the Athletics won no more pennants, the National Association lasted only though the 1875 season before folding. In addition to the Athletics, the league briefly had other Philadelphia teams, including the White Stockings (or Whites), which played in 1873; the Pearls (the name had been changed to Pearls because a team in Chicago was also calling itself the White Stockings) in 1874-75, and the Centennials in 1875. In its final season, the league had three teams from Philadelphia.

A new league was formed in 1876. It was called the National League, and more than 13 decades later, it was still going strong. When the National League began, Philadelphia was one of its most important cities. Another team called the Philadelphia Athletics also represented the city, playing at Jefferson Park at 25th and Jefferson Streets. Jefferson Park had been the site of the first professional no-hitter, thrown by the Athletics' Joe Borden in 1875 in a National Association game. Then, in 1876, the ballpark was the site of the first National League game ever played. Borden, a resident of Yeadon who had jumped to Boston, got the league's first win, beating the Athletics, 6-5.

The Athletics, mired in seventh place and out of money, failed to last the full season, getting expelled from the league after refusing to make a late-season road trip. Philadelphia would not have another NL club until the Phillies arrived seven years later.

Meanwhile, a new league—the American Association—had been formed in 1882. The league included still another team called the Philadelphia Athletics. In the AA's second year of operation, the Athletics, edging the St. Louis Browns by one game, won the league championship. Although they won no more titles, the Athletics remained in the league until it folded after the 1891 season.

The Phillies' entry in the National League, coinciding with the same season the Athletics won their AA pennant, plugged a hole that had plagued the circuit since the previous Philadelphia team had been booted out in 1876. With no Philadelphia team, the league lacked a representative from one of the country's most avid baseball regions, which left its claims to big league status not only debatable, but forced it to field teams from cities out of the geographic loop and with far smaller populations.

One of these cities was Syracuse. In 1879, in an effort to add teams from the more densely populated East while eliminating teams from the midwestern cities that were not yet ready to support big league teams, NL president William Hulbert dumped clubs in Indianapolis and Milwaukee and added teams from Buffalo and Syracuse, the previous year's champion and second-place team, respectively, in the International Association, a new team from Cleveland, and one from Troy of the New York State Association.

The Syracuse Stars were failures both on the field and at the gate, playing a lineup composed entirely of minor leaguers and toward the end of the season averaging crowds of 200 to 300. At the end of the season, the team was ushered out of the league. Its spot in the lineup was filled by a newly formed team called the Worcester Brown Stockings (or Ruby Legs, as they were also called). Other than being its replacement, Worcester had no connection with the Syracuse franchise; in fact, only one player moved from the Stars to the Brown Stockings.

Worcester's roster included future Phillies manager Arthur Irwin, Philadelphia natives, catcher Doc Bushong and future five-time American Association home run champion Harry Stovey, and Lee Richmond, who pitched the major league's first perfect game in the Brown Stocking's first season in the NL. The Stockings, however, finished above last place just once in their three years in the league. In 1882, the club posted an 18-66 record while finishing 37 games out of first place, $17\frac{1}{2}$ out of seventh, and drawing crowds that would barely fill a church pew.

Again, it was time for a change. The Worcester franchise as well as the almost equally downtrodden Troy Trojans were banished from the league. The Brown Stockings' spot in the NL was taken by a new franchise in Philadelphia (Troy was replaced by the New York Gothams, later to be known as the Giants). Al Reach, the onetime lefthanded second baseman, was awarded the new franchise.

Reach had been only peripherally involved in baseball since his retirement as a player in 1878, preferring to concentrate on his sporting goods store in downtown Philadelphia. The business was highly successful, and by 1881 Reach had expanded his operation into the manufacturing of sporting goods while taking in Benjamin Shibe (future owner of the American League Athletics) as his partner. Shibe manufactured horse whips and was an expert on leather.

Although the business thrived, Reach maintained his contacts in major league baseball. And as the Worcester team disbanded, he heard the rumors that the league might want to place a new team in Philadelphia.

With that possibility in mind, Reach formed what would probably be the equivalent of a minor league team today, and bought the baseball field that sat on an oddly shaped lot bounded by 25th and 24th Streets and Ridge and Columbia Avenues. Although it had been the hub of baseball activity after the Civil War, housing both amateur games, including those of the Pythians, and serving in 1875 as the home of the American Association's Centennials, the ballpark, then called Columbia Park (the first of three Philadelphia ballparks that would use that name), had in recent years been neglected and become rundown. Weeds grew out of every corner of the field and the grandstands were in serious disrepair. In the years leading up to Reach's purchase, the ballpark had even been used as a horse market.

Reach had the weeds pulled, leveled and resodded the playing field, had the field fully enclosed, and built new grandstands that would accommodate crowds of up to 6,500. He named the field Recreation Park and his new team, the Fillies. The Fillies' first game was on April 8, 1882.

According to baseball historian Frank Vaccaro, the team played at least 120 games, including about 60 against National League teams. In games that Vaccaro found, the Fillies had a 14-39-5 record against NL clubs. All Fillies games were played at Recreation Park except those for which the team traveled to New York to meet a club that would become the Giants. The two teams met at least 41 times.

During the season, Reach was approached by an old friend and former teammate, Colonel Abraham G. Mills, the president of the National League. Would Al be interested in starting a new team in Philadelphia? Mills asked. Mills told Reach he was anxious to place new franchises in Philadelphia as well as in New York, and he hoped that his old friend would like to participate in the plan. "We've got to get these big cities back into our league," Mills said. "Both New York and Philadelphia have tremendous futures, and someday their populations will be in the millions."

Reach could hardly wait to accept. "I'm in," he said. "Let's get going."

The sporting goods tycoon wasted no time getting going. He quickly contacted Colonel John L. Rogers, a Philadelphia lawyer and member of the governor's staff, and the two brought in a group of investors who would put up most of the money to start a team. Then Reach, who was in charge of baseball and administrative operations, gave the team a name. It was "Phillies." He chose the name, Reach said, because he wanted the team to be identified with the city of Philadelphia. (Some followers ignored that name and called the team the Quakers.)

Because it was an entirely new franchise, the Phillies inherited nothing from Worcester. Reach had to form his team from scratch. And he looked everywhere for players—in local amateur leagues, in the minor leagues, and on other big league teams. He left no stone unturned.

Ultimately, Reach appointed veteran big league player and manager Bob Ferguson as the team's manager. Ferguson, whose nickname for unknown reasons was "Death to Flying Things," was also a second baseman and had piloted the Troy team in 1882. He had also been president of the old AA for four years in the 1870s.

Among the top players Reach and Ferguson found were right fielder Jack Manning, who had been in the league since it began, left fielder Blondie Purcell, who had broken into the NL in 1879 with Syracuse, and shortstop Bill McClellan, center fielder Bill Harbidge, and catcher Emil Gross, all veteran players. Only four players on the initial team had no prior major league experience.

The Phillies held their first spring training at Recreation Park. In the club's first exhibition game, played on April 2, it defeated a semipro team from Manayunk called the Ashland Club. Phillies pitcher John Coleman, a minor leaguer the previous season, tossed a no-hitter.

Coleman was again on the mound when the Phillies opened their first season at Recreation Park. The date was May 1, 1883. The opponent was the Providence Grays, managed by Harry Wright.

The Phillies had a 3-0 lead after seven innings, but Providence scored four runs in the eighth to capture a 4-3 victory. Charles (Old Hoss) Radbourne, who would win 48 games that year en route to a career as one of baseball's greatest 19th-century pitchers, got the decision. Coleman took the loss.

Despite the defeat, falling by only one run to one of the league's top teams was far from discouraging. The new team, some felt, might be halfway decent.

Al Reach (top) started the Phillies in 1883, and John Coleman lost 48 games that first year.

How wrong they were. The Phillies lost their first eight games and were barely heard from again. After their first 17 games, having won just four of them, Reach, heeding his players' complaints about Ferguson's tyrannical and bullying tactics, fired him as manager, replacing him with Purcell, a man with no experience as a skipper. Ferguson remained with the club as its second baseman while also serving as the Phillies' business manager, but his big league career was essentially over. He became an umpire two years later.

The newborn Phillies were thoroughly outplayed the rest of the season. In one game, they made 20 errors and lost to Providence, 28-0, in what still stands as the highest-scoring shutout victory in major league history. The Phillies bowed to the Boston Beaneaters, 29-4. They made 27 errors in another game (walks, wild pitches, and passed balls were then counted as errors). The Phils gave up 20 or more runs in a game eight times. And they hit a league-low .240 as a team with only one player (Gross) hitting over .300 with a .307 average.

Moreover, the Phillies drew so poorly that league officials allowed the team to drop the price of a ticket from 50 cents to 25 cents so it could try to compete with the much more popular Athletics of the American Association. The Athletics charged 25 cents at their Jefferson Street Park, and despite the Phillies' reduced ticket price, continued to far outdraw the downtrodden rivals who played a few blocks away.

The 20-year-old Coleman, the team's primary pitcher, posted a 12-48 record, yielding 544 runs and 772 hits in 538 innings while hurling 59 complete games in 65 games (the mound at the time was 50 feet from home plate and it took nine balls to issue a walk). Coleman's losses and his runs and hits allowed are major league records that will stand forever.

The Phillies finished with a 17-81 record, 46 games behind the front-running Beaneaters. In 33 of their losses, Phillies pitchers allowed 10 or more runs. Ironically, after the season ended, the Phillies played the Athletics in what could be considered the first City Series. The Athletics, prepping for a series with Boston to determine who would be proclaimed the nation's best team, were soundly trounced by the Phillies. As a result, the Athletics cancelled what would have been a forerunner of the World Series.

Although Reach was highly disturbed by his team's horrendous debut, he was determined to make amends. His first move in that direction was to lure Harry Wright to Philadelphia to manage the team. Wright, an Englishman, too, had been the playing-manager at Cincinnati in 1869 when the Red Stockings became baseball's first all-professional team. He had also been a highly successful pilot at Boston, where he won two league titles, and at Providence. Wright was regarded as baseball's premier manager.

Later described as "The Father of Baseball" on his gravestone at West Laurel Hill Cemetery in Philadelphia, the man who came up with the idea of colored stockings, knicker pants, and flannel uniforms, and who was one of the Hall of Fame's early inductees, Wright changed the entire complexion of the team. He brought in new players, most notably pitcher Charlie Ferguson, who went 21-25 in his rookie year and center fielder Jim Fogarty. Under Wright's tutelage, other young players such as first baseman Sid Farrar, third baseman Joe Mulvey, and second baseman Ed Andrews, began to develop, and with veterans Manning, Purcell, and McClellan also in the lineup, the Phillies improved considerably.

In 1884, the National League was one of three circuits touted as a major league. A new one-year entry was the rebel Union League, formed by players protesting the Reserve Clause, which tied players to one team for life unless they were traded or sold. The league had a team in Philadelphia called the Keystones. Their home field, called Keystone Park, was located at Broad and Moore Streets in South Philadelphia.

The Keystones had little effect on the Phillies—or, for that matter, the Athletics. Although the Phillies hit just .234 as a team (Manning leading the way with a .271 average) and had a fielding percentage of just .888 as McClellan made 83 errors and Mulvey committed 73, the club improved its record to 39-73 while moving up to sixth place in the eight-team league.

That was the lowest the Phillies would finish until 1896. Over an 11-year period leading up to that season, the club had one second-place finish (1887), four thirds, and six fourths. The team that had begun so dismally had become one of the National League's most important franchises. Much of that success was attributable to the astute Wright, who managed through the 1893 season and today ranks as the second-win-ningest manager (behind Gene Mauch) in Phillies history.

Another union league called the Brotherhood League or Players' League, which again was protesting the use of the Re-serve Clause, was formed in 1890 with a team called the Quak-ers playing in Philadelphia at Forepaugh Park at Broad and Dauphin Streets. That league also lasted just one year. Then the following year, the American Association disbanded, leav-ing the Phillies as the only major league team in town. They remained in that position until the American League was launched in 1901 with yet another team called the Athletics, this one headed by Reach's old partner Ben Shibe, taking the field as one of the original franchises.

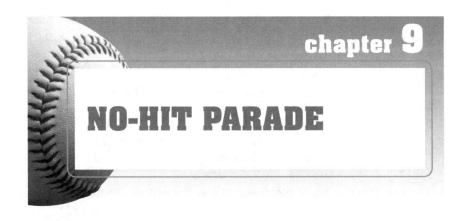

chapter 9

NO-HIT PARADE

A no-hitter is a spectacularly exhilarating event that generates enormous amounts of electricity, suspense, and tension. It doesn't matter if one is a participant or an observer, a no-hit game is a thrilling, breathtaking, spellbinding affair that holds those present in an unbreakable grip. Nothing in baseball, or for that matter in all of sports, matches the excitement created by a no-hit game.

No-hitters, of course, are extremely rare. Since the distance from home plate to the pitching rubber was moved to 60 feet, six inches in 1893, there have been just 220 one-pitcher no-hitters of nine innings or more hurled in major league baseball games. That amounts to an average of about 1.9 no-hitters per season.

Naturally, some teams have more no-hitters to their credit than others. Pitchers from the Brooklyn/Los Angeles Dodgers, for instance, have fired 20 no-hit games. Pitchers from the Boston Red Sox and the forenamed Pilgrims have tossed 18 hitless games. And 17 no-hitters have been recorded by pitchers with the Chicago White Sox.

Phillies hurlers have eight no-hitters to their credit since 1893. That is low for teams of long duration.

The first Phillies no-hitter was pitched in 1898 by Red Donahue. With three future Hall of Famers (Ed Delahanty, Nap Lajoie, and Elmer Flick) in his lineup, Donahue blanked the Boston Beaneaters, 5-0. It was just the fifth major league no-hitter hurled since the 1893 alteration.

Subsequent Phils no-hitters also had special features. Chick Frazer, who wound up losing 20 or more games for four different teams, beat the Tinkers-to-Evers-to-Chance Chicago Cubs (or Orphans as they were also called), 10-0, in a 1903 game in which the Phillies rapped 14 hits and their shortstop, Rudy Hulswitt, made three errors. John Lush was a converted infielder/outfielder when he struck out 11 and whitewashed the Brooklyn Superbas, 6-0, in 1906. The game took one hour and 45 minutes and was played before a sparse crowd of 1,500 at Brooklyn's Washington Park.

The Phillies went 58 years before recording another no-hitter. That came in 1964 when Jim Bunning fired the only perfect game in club history and the first in modern National League annuals. The unblemished game allowed Bunning, who had pitched a no-hitter six years earlier for the Detroit Tigers, to join Cy Young, Jay Hughes, and Nolan Ryan as the only pitchers to fling no-hitters in both the National and American Leagues. He used just 90 pitches (69 strikes) to lick the New York Mets, 6-0, on Father's Day at Shea Stadium. Bunning, who struck out 10, eventually had eight children of his own.

The next Phillies no-hitter occurred in 1971 as Rick Wise downed the Cincinnati Reds, 4-0, in a game that ended on third baseman John Vukovich's sensational catch of Pete Rose's searing line drive. Especially noteworthy in the game was the fact that Wise hit two home runs (and drove in three) to become the only pitcher ever to homer twice in his own no-hit game.

Another 19 years passed before the next Phillies no-hitter was hurled. It came in 1990 with Terry Mulholland pitching the club's first home no-hitter in the 20th century in a 6-0 victory over the San Francisco Giants. It was also the first no-hitter thrown at Veterans Stadium. Mulholland was the first Phillies lefthander since Lush to bag a no-hitter.

Tommy Greene tossed a no-hitter in 1991, beating the Montreal Expos, 2-0, while striking out 10 but walking seven. After the game, Greene was told he had a telephone call from the Canadian prime minister, only to find out it was a joke with a clubhouse attendant actually on the other end of the line.

The Phils' last no-hitter—and only the second one ever tossed at the Vet—came in 2003 with Kevin Millwood topping the Giants, 1-0. Coming on the Phillie Phanatic's 25th birthday

Four of the Phillies' nine no-hitters have been pitched by (top from left) Tommy Greene and Terry Mulholland, and (bottom from left) Rick Wise and Jim Bunning.

celebration, Millwood got the decision on Ricky Ledee's first-inning home run.

The no-hitters by Donahue, Bunning, and Millwood all came in their first years with the Phillies. Wise's happened in his last year with the club. Strangely, only Donahue (twice) and Fraser were 20-game winners with the Phillies, and none of the post-1893 Phils hurlers ranks in the top 10 of the team's all-time career leaders in wins. The no-hitters by Mulholland and Greene were each one of a record-tying six pitched in each of those years.

The Phillies had one other no-hitter in their history. That came in 1885 when the mound was still just 50 feet from home plate. Charlie Ferguson blanked the Providence Grays, 1-0, in the second of what would be four straight seasons in which he won more than 20 games (including 30 in 1886). Ferguson played in just four seasons in the majors before he died of typhoid fever less than two weeks after his 25th birthday.

The number of no-hitters pitched by the Phillies pales by comparison to the number of no-hitters hurled against the team.

In the last 115 years, Phillies batters have been blanked 17 times by pitchers going the distance. No other team has had that many no-hitters pitched against it.

The National League teams nearest that figure are the combined franchises of the Boston/Milwaukee/Atlanta Braves and the Brooklyn/Los Angeles Dodgers, both with 16, and the New York/San Francisco Giants with 15. Separately, the Brooklyn Dodgers and San Francisco Giants each have been no-hit 10 times.

In the American League, the White Sox and the combined entries of the Philadelphia/Kansas City/Oakland Athletics each have had 14 no-hitters pitched against them. Boston, the Cleveland Naps/Indians, and the Detroit Tigers have been victimized 12 times apiece.

The Phillies have not had a nine-inning no-hitter pitched against them since Bob Forsch of the St. Louis Cardinals did the job in 1978. Prior to that, there was one other long stretch between no-hitters. The Phils escaped nine-inning goose eggs for 30 years between a no-hitter by the Dodgers' Dazzy Vance in 1925 and one by Jim Wilson of Milwaukee in 1954.

Eleven of the 17 no-hitters tossed at the Phillies were registered within a 24-year period between 1954 and 1978. Six of them came in the disastrous decade of the 1960s, starting with Lew Burdette's gem for Milwaukee on August 18, 1960. Just 29 days later, on September 16, the next major league no-hitter occurred when 39-year-old Warren Spahn matched his roommate's game with the first no-hitter of his career.

Don Nottebart of the Houston Astros no-hit the Phillies in 1963. The Dodgers' Sandy Koufax chucked a no-hitter against the Phillies in 1964. George Culver did it for the Cincinnati Reds in 1968, and the Montreal Expos' Bill Stoneman completed the decade with a no-hitter in 1969, also one of six that season.

The Phillies have been no-hit by some pretty good pitchers. Three of them—Vance, Spahn, and Koufax—are in the Hall of Fame. With 363 career wins, Spahn is the winningest lefthanded pitcher in baseball history. Vance, the dominant pitcher of the 1920s, won 197, while Koufax, another dominant hurler of his era, won 165 while firing four no-hitters. Spahn, Stoneman, and Forsch each twirled two no-hitters during their careers.

Burdette (203 wins) and the Dodgers' Sal Maglie, owner of a 1956 no-hitter against the Phils, were also outstanding hurlers. So were Hooks Wiltse (no-hitter in 1908), Jeff Tesreau (1912), and Jesse Barnes (1922), each of whom pitched with the New York Giants.

Two pitchers who no-hit the Phillies, Burdette and Culver (1968), later played with the Phillies. Culver was also a coach in the Phils' farm system. Burdette was a Phillies moundsman in 1965, while Culver was on the hill for the team in 1973-74.

The combined franchises of the Braves, Dodgers, and Giants have each registered three no-hitters against the Phillies. Cincinnati and Montreal have two apiece.

Many unusual features accompanied the 17 times the Phils were no-hit. For instance, Noodles Hahn's no-hitter was one of 211 complete games he pitched in 243 starts during his career. Hooks Wiltse's gem, a morning game played before 10,000 at the Polo Grounds, was decided by an unearned run in the bottom of the 10th inning. Jeff Tesreau, the only rookie to blank the Phillies, gave up what was originally scored as a hit to lead-off batter Dode Paskert in the first inning. But after considerable protesting by the Giants, the scorekeeper changed the hit to an error after the game.

George Davis, a Harvard Law School student, walked the six miles from Cambridge to Fenway Park to capture his first National League win with a no-hitter. Dazzy Vance was in the midst of a streak in which he set a National League record by leading the league in strikeouts seven straight times. Jesse Barnes completed his masterpiece in one hour and 37 minutes. Jim Wilson beat Robin Roberts in his victory. Eleven days after his no-hitter, Sal Maglie was the losing pitching in the game in which the New York Yankees' Don Larsen fired the World Series' only perfect game. Lew Burdette doubled in the bottom of the eighth inning and scored the game's only run on Bill Burton's two-bagger in his 1-0 victory.

Five starts after he no-hit the Phillies, Warren Spahn hurled the major league's next no-hitter, this one coming early the following season in a 1-0 victory over the Giants. Of the major league's last eight no-hitters, Don Nottebart's was at the time the fourth one registered against the Phils. For Sandy Koufax, it was his third no-hitter in three years. In his no-hitter, George Culver lost a shutout in the second inning when the Phillies scored one run on an error by Reds shortstop and future Phillies general manager, Woody Woodward.

Bill Stoneman's no-hitter came when the expansion Expos had been in the league for just 10 days. To make sure it wasn't a hit, Bill Singer threw wildly to first for his second error of the game after Don Money was seemingly about to beat out a nubber back to the mound for a hit in the seventh inning. Five years after his no-hitter, Phillies fans got revenge against Burt Hooton when they booed him off the mound during a streak of wildness in the third game of the 1977 League Championship Series against the Dodgers. Last but not least, Bob Forsch's brother Ken tossed a no-hitter the following season, making the pair the first brothers with no-hitters. Both the Hooton and Bob Forsch no-hitters were achieved on April 16.

There have also been four no-hitters pitched against the Phillies of less than nine innings. And the Phils came up empty-handed once when the mound was 50 feet from home plate.

The list of no-hitters by and against the Phillies follows below.

By the Phillies
    August 29, 1885: Charlie Ferguson vs. Providence, 1-0
    July 8, 1898: Red Donahue vs. Boston, 5-0
    September 18, 1903: Chick Fraser at Chicago, 10-0
    May 1, 1906: Johnny Lush at Brooklyn, 6-0
    June 21, 1964: Jim Bunning at New York, 6-0
    June 23, 1971: Rick Wise at Cincinnati, 4-0
    August 15, 1990: Terry Mulholland vs. San Francisco, 6-0
    May 23, 1991: Tommy Greene at Montreal, 2-0
    April 27, 2003: Kevin Millwood vs. San Francisco, 1-0

Against the Phillies
    September 13, 1883: Hugh Daily vs. Cleveland, 1-0
    July 12, 1900: Noodles Hahn at Cincinnati, 4-0
    *September 26, 1906: Lefty Leifield vs. Pittsburgh, 8-0
        (6 innings)
    July 4, 1908: Hooks Wiltse at New York, 1-0 (10 innings)
    September 6, 1912: Jeff Tesreau vs. New York, 3-0

September 9, 1914: George Davis at Boston, 7-0

May 7, 1922: Jesse Barnes at New York, 6-0

September 13, 1925: Dazzy Vance at Brooklyn, 10-1

*June 22, 1944: Jim Tobin at Boston, 7-0 (5 innings)

June 12, 1954: Jim Wilson at Milwaukee, 2-0

September 25, 1956: Sal Maglie at Brooklyn, 5-0

*June 12, 1959: Mike McCormick at San Francisco, 3-0
  (5 innings)

August 18, 1960: Lew Burdette at Milwaukee, 1-0

September 16, 1960: Warren Spahn at Milwaukee, 4-0

May 17, 1963: Don Nottebart at Houston, 4-1

June 4, 1964: Sandy Koufax vs. Los Angeles, 3-0

July 29, 1968: George Culver vs. Cincinnati, 6-1

April 17, 1969: Bill Stoneman vs. Montreal, 7-0

July 20, 1970: Bill Singer at Los Angeles, 5-0

April 16, 1972: Burt Hooton at Chicago, 4-0

April 16, 1978: Bob Forsch at St. Louis, 5-0

* September 24, 1988: Pascual Perez vs. Montreal, 1-0
  (5 innings)

* Less than nine innings

MOST DECORATED PLAYER

During the four years of World War II, people from every corner of the country and from every walk of life served in some branch of the United States military. Ultimately, more than 16 million Americans took part in the armed forces before the war ended in 1945.

Like virtually every other field, professional baseball players were not immune to the war effort. Some 400 of them from the major leagues served in the military, and several thousand more minor league players participated.

The Phillies did their part. The first major league player inducted into military service was Phillies pitcher Hugh Mulcahy. A member of the starting rotation for the previous four years, Mulcahy was drafted on March 8, 1941—two months ahead of Hank Greenberg's drafting—and served until late in 1945.

While the Phillies were also contributing to the effort to ration gas by holding spring training once at Hershey, Pennsylvania and twice at Wilmington, Delaware, numerous other players from the team also spent time in the service. Danny Litwhiler, Danny Murtaugh, Schoolboy Rowe, and Del Ennis were among the many Phillies players who joined the fight. Among the many others who played after the war with the Phils, two of them, outfielder Johnny Wyrostek and first baseman Earl Torgeson, were wounded in action.

Another was Phillies pitcher John S. Thompson, better known as Jocko. A lefthanded hurler, Thompson had yet to join the big club before the war broke out, but by the time he returned to the system in 1946, he was the most decorated player in professional baseball.

While spending more than four years in the armed forces in North Africa and Europe, beginning as a paratrooper and eventually becoming a company commander, Thompson was awarded two Purple Hearts, a Silver and a Bronze Star, and seven battle stars. Twice wounded, he also won numerous other ribbons, citations, and awards, plus a battlefield commission, during a heroic career in the war.

Thompson was just a young minor leaguer when he entered the service. Born in Beverly, Massachusetts, he had attended Northeastern University in Boston before the Boston Red Sox signed him to a pro contract in 1939. He didn't play that year, but the following season, Thompson appeared in seven games with the Canton Terriers of the Class C Middle-Atlantic League before getting sent to the Centreville Red Sox, a Class D team in the Eastern Shore League.

The 23-year-old southpaw had a banner season at Centreville. Appearing in 27 games, he posted an 18-5 record while leading the league in strikeouts (268) and earned run average (1.56), and earning a berth on the league's all-star team.

The following season, Thompson jumped all the way up to Greensboro of the Class B Piedmont League. In a bit over his head, Thompson worked in 28 games, but his record slipped to 8-13 and his ERA to 3.56.

Thompson was scheduled to start the 1942 season with the Scranton Red Sox, then playing in what was the Class A Eastern League. But war had broken out, and Thompson never made it to Scranton. Instead, he was called into military service, and after basic training in Louisiana, became a paratrooper with the famed 504th Paratroop Regiment of the elite and highly decorated 82nd Airborne Division, one of the most famous military units in American history. Then called "The All-American Division" and under the leadership of Major General Matthew Ridgway, the 82nd was still a branch of the Army. At various times later in the war, it would come under the command of both General Mark Clark and General George Patton.

Thompson and the 82nd made jumps in virtually every major war zone from Italy to Northern Europe. After starting out in North Africa, one of his early jumps was into Sicily in 1943

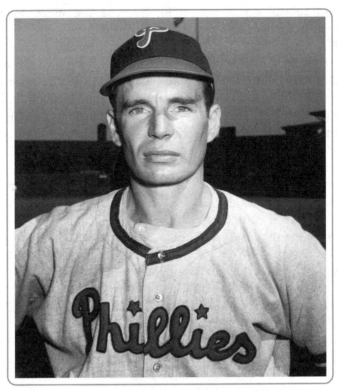

Pitcher Jocko Thompson won numerous medals as a
paratrooper in World War II.

that led to the Allies' capture of Italian dictator Benito Mus-
solini. Thompson also parachuted into Salerno and onto Anzio
Beach, an area 30 miles south of Rome that became the site of
one of the most fiercely fought battles in the war.

Some 36,000 U.S. troops landed at Anzio to engage a German army of 100,000 men under the command of Field Marshal
Hermann Goering. Catching the Germans unprepared, the
Americans quickly moved behind enemy lines. But with the
Germans holding the high ground, the U.S. troops were pinned
down and forced to retreat. A battle raged for the next four
months before the Americans claimed victory, and marched on
to liberate the city of Naples.

By then a platoon leader with E Company in the 504th—
nicknamed "The Devils in Baggy Pants," a description originally

found in a German officer's diary—Lieutenant Thompson continued to make jumps. Holland, Belgium, Great Britain, and France were among his many landing points. While on land, Thompson led 16 men who fought off the Germans and on September 17, 1944, captured the Grave Bridge over the Maas River in Holland, a highly strategic location.

Wounded in action, Thompson fought on and eventually was made a company commander. It was in that position that Thompson took part in the Battle of the Bulge, a deadly clash that occurred on the Allies' final thrust into Germany.

In the Battle of the Bulge, also known as the Battle of Ardennes, 600,000 German soldiers stormed across an 85-mile stretch to engage 500,000 American and British troops in a desperate attempt to split the Allied armies and to push them away from the German border and back into southern Belgium and Luxembourg. It was the last major Nazi offensive and the largest land battle of World War II.

Fought in snow and freezing winter temperatures, the horrific battle raged from December 16, 1944 until January 25, 1945. Eventually, the Nazis were beaten and forced to retreat, while the Allies began a march across the Rhine River that would lead to the German surrender and the end of the war in Europe five months later. At the Battle of the Bulge, Americans suffered 81,000 casualties, including 19,000 killed. Some 85,000 Germans were killed, wounded, or taken prisoner.

Thompson, now a captain serving as an aide to General James M. Gavin (who later was appointed by President John F. Kennedy as Ambassador to France), was among those who marched into Berlin where they would join Soviet troops and occupy the city as the war ended. Shortly afterward, Thompson's military career came to an end.

In the spring of 1946, the battle-scared, 29-year-old lefty reported to Scranton. The team, led by future Boston luminaries Sam Mele and Mel Parnell, ran away with the Eastern League championship, winning 96 games and finishing first by $18 \frac{1}{2}$ games during the regular season, then beating Wilkes-Barre and Hartford in the playoffs. The Utica Blue Sox, the Phillies' farm team, finished seventh under manager Eddie Sawyer, 37 games out of first.

Struggling to regain his form, Thompson finished at 13-7 with a 2.60 ERA in 26 games. But an important step in his career was about to happen.

Herb Pennock, previously the director of the Red Sox farm system, had become general manager of the Phillies in 1943. Soon after he joined the Phils, Pennock began recruiting members of his Boston staff. One of the key people was Joe Reardon, the business manager with the Scranton club, who moved to the Phillies as the club's farm director.

Both Pennock and Reardon, and, of course, Sawyer knew about Thompson. The six-foot, 185-pound pitcher may have found it hard to come back after more than four years of heavy combat, but all of them were fully aware of the guy's heart, his toughness, and his credentials as a fighter. All agreed that the Phillies should try to get him.

Prior to the 1947 season, that mission was accomplished. Thompson's contract was purchased from the Red Sox. That season, pitching with the Phillies' Triple-A farm team, the Toronto Maple Leafs of the International League, Thompson went 6-12 in 32 games with a 3.80 ERA. The Leafs finished last, their 90 losses pushing them 30 games out of first.

Toronto was again Thompson's home in 1948. This time, with Sawyer managing the club part of the season before moving up to the Phillies, the Leafs finished fifth. Thompson's record improved to 12-8, but his ERA tumbled to an unsightly 5.09 in 32 games. At the end of the season, Thompson was called up to the parent club and got to start two games. He earned his first major league victory in the second game of a doubleheader against the Cincinnati Reds, allowing just five hits in a 6-1 win.

Thompson went back to Toronto to start the 1949 season. In what would be the most dazzling season of his career, he posted a 14-5 record with a 2.73 ERA in 32 games. Along with future Phillies pitching coach Al Widmar, Thompson was named at the end of the season to the International League all-star team.

That brought Thompson another call to the big leagues, and this time he appeared in eight games at the end of the 1949 season, starting five of the games and winning one while losing three. Those who saw him, though, were convinced that he had a strong arm with an especially sharp-breaking curveball.

Thompson, who was attending Massachusetts Institute of Technology during the off-season in pursuit of a degree, had arm trouble during spring training in 1950, but that wasn't his only problem. If there was one position in which the Phillies were amply supplied it was pitcher. With a bevy of strong young arms that included Robin Roberts, Curt Simmons, Bob Miller, and Bubba Church, plus a handful of veteran hurlers led by Russ Meyer, Ken Heintzelman, and Hank Borowy, there were no open spots on the roster. Moreover, Thompson was now 33, a rather advanced age for a guy trying to join a pitching staff with little big league experience.

Still, Thompson persevered, and when the season-opening roster was determined, he was on it. But his spot on the roster was short-lived. Thompson pitched in just two games for a total of four innings. On April 17, the Phillies acquired left-handed pitcher Ken Johnson from the St. Louis Cardinals in a trade for outfielder Johnny Blatnik. It was back to Toronto for Jocko, while the Phillies, the Whiz Kids as they were known, went on to win the National League pennant in one of the team's most thrilling seasons.

If he was disappointed, the mild-mannered Thompson kept it to himself. Instead, he pitched in a career-high 35 games, posted a 10-14 record with a 4.57 ERA, and, considering that he played with a club that lost 90 games, had a respectable season.

That was enough to invite Thompson back to spring training in 1951. This time, he stayed with the club for the entire season. With Simmons serving in the National Guard and Miller sidelined much of the year with injuries, Thompson had an increased role on the staff. On April 23 at Shibe Park, he threw a slick six-hitter to beat Jim Hearn and the New York Giants, 8-4. Jocko scored the go-ahead run himself after poking a double. Six days later at Boston, he hurled a sparkling two-hitter, but lost a heartbreaker to the Braves, 1-0.

Despite his early-season promise, Thompson finished the season with a 4-8 record after getting 14 starts in 29 games. He had a 3.86 ERA.

The 1951 season would be Thompson's last in the big leagues. After seeing no action at the start of the 1952 campaign, he was shipped to the Baltimore Orioles, at the time the

Phillies' Triple-A farm club in the International League. In December, the 35-year-old hurler was handed his release.

Thompson tried without success to land a spot with the Chicago White Sox, and in 1954 retired from the game. He had given it his best shot, but the undeniable fact was that the war had taken too much out of him.

Thompson eventually moved to Maryland and took a job as the sales manager for a company in Rockville. He died in Olney, Maryland on February 3, 1988.

He would be remembered as a big league pitcher, of course. But of far greater note, he would be remembered as the most decorated professional baseball player in World War II.

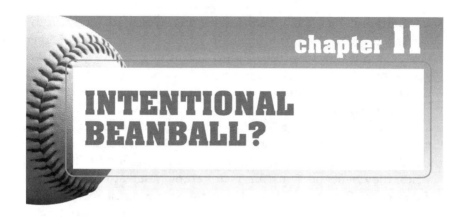

chapter 11

INTENTIONAL BEANBALL?

Throughout baseball history, there have been certain pitches that had special significance and that were remembered long after they were thrown.

Ralph Branca's pitch that Bobby Thomson hit for a home run to win a special playoff and the pennant for the New York Giants. Don Larsen's pitch that struck out Dale Mitchell to finish off the only perfect game ever thrown in a World Series. Ralph Terry's pitch that Bill Mazeroski hit into the stands in the ninth inning of the seventh game to clinch a World Series victory for the Pittsburgh Pirates. Herb Score's pitch that Gil McDougald lined off his head.

They were all memorable pitches, ones that will not be forgotten as long as there is a man standing on a little, dirt hill with a ball in his hand and another placed alongside a heptagonal piece of heavy rubber with a bat in his hands, the two separated by a distance of 60 feet, six inches.

Such a pitch exists in Phillies lore, too. There have, of course, been many noteworthy pitches hurled by Phillies pitchers or to Phillies batters. But this one was unlike the others. It came unexpectedly. It did not result in or climax a single, significant feat. It didn't even change the score of the game. Yet, to this day it remains the most widely discussed and the best remembered pitch in Phillies history.

It was a pitch that reliever Dickie Noles threw to George Brett on October 18 in the fourth game of the 1980 World Series.

Certainly, the 1980 Series was one that had many note-worthy features, not the least of which was another famous toss, the one fired by Tug McGraw that struck out Willie Wilson to end the sixth and final game. That was a pitch that will be remembered as long as there is a team called the Phillies.

Noles' pitch didn't clinch the Series. But to anyone who had any interest whatsoever in the Phillies at that time, it is credited as being the pitch that turned the Series around.

The Phillies had clinched their first pennant in 35 years when they beat the Houston Astros three games to two in what was one of the most—if not *the* most—exciting League Championship Series ever played. The Phils then went to the World Series where the opponent was the powerful Kansas City Royals, a team that had won its division by 14 games and the ALCS by defeating the New York Yankees, winners that season of 103 games.

The Phillies won the first two games of the Series at Veterans Stadium. They captured a 7-6 victory in the opener on the strength of Bake McBride's three-run homer and rookie Bob Walk's outstanding pitching. Then they won the second game, 6-4, behind Steve Carlton and a four-run eighth. But, after moving to Kansas City, the Phillies lost Game Three, 4-3, as Willie Aikens singled home the winning run for the Royals in the bottom of the 10th.

Despite their Series lead, the Phillies, in the eyes of some observers, were looking a bit lethargic. There was no pep to their steps, no pop to their bats. That view was supported as Game Four got under way in Kansas City when the Royals scored four runs in the first inning. Phils starter Larry Christenson didn't even make it through the inning, getting replaced by Noles after working just one-third of an inning.

Noles gave up a solo homer to Aikens in the second, and by the fourth inning, the Phillies were down, 5-1. It was not a good spot in which to be. KC was coming on strongly, the Phils looked like they were fading fast, and the Series seemed to be tilting in the Royals' favor.

Then in the fourth inning it happened. Noles was still on the mound. Brett was the batter.

Brett was coming off a spectacular season. For a while, it seemed during the year that he might be the first batter to hit

.400 since Ted Williams hit .406 in 1941. Brett flirted with that mark through much of the campaign before settling for a .390 average, still the highest to win an American League batting title since Williams in '41. Then, in the LCS, it was Brett who gave the Royals a 4-2 victory with a three-run, seventh-inning homer in the pennant-clinching game.

The future Hall of Fame third baseman had touched off a commotion in Game Two when he had to be pulled from the lineup and forced into the locker room after the sixth inning. It was announced later that Brett had been smitten with a violent attack of hemorrhoids and was in too much pain to continue. Brett returned to action in the third game, however, and for the second game in a row smacked two hits.

Brett had already drilled an RBI triple when he batted for the third time in the fourth inning of Game Four. Out on the mound, the 23-year-old Noles, now in his third inning of relief, was enjoying a splendid outing.

A rookie the previous year when he started all 14 games in which he appeared, Noles had been converted to a relief pitcher in 1980, and had responded by being a highly effective middle-distance member of the bullpen.

Dickie was well-suited for the role. A tough, often surly character who had a penchant for booze, brawls, and bouts with the law, Noles was a fighter who could be as mean and nasty on the mound as he could be off of it. Plus, he had a sizzling fastball and the ability to put it just about anywhere he desired.

With one out and Brett at the plate, the count went to 0-2. Then, with the suddenness of a summer thunderstorm, Noles fired a crackling, high fastball that headed straight for Brett's head, sending the Royals' cleanup hitter sprawling in all directions before crashing unceremoniously to the ground. Before Brett could climb back up, Royals manager Jim Frey had raced screaming from the dugout, bellowing to umpires that Noles should be put out of the game. Soon, Frey and Phillies first baseman Pete Rose became engaged in a heated, nose-to-nose shouting match.

After order was finally restored, both teams were warned about throwing knockdown pitches. Then Brett struck out, as did the next hitter, Aikens.

Although they scored no more runs the rest of the game, the Royals went on to capture a 5-3 victory—with Noles pitching four and two-thirds innings and yielding just the one run to Aikens—the pitch to Brett was what made the headlines. It had not only sent the Royals' biggest star sprawling in the dirt, but had, according to expert analysts, served as a wake-up call for the Phillies, and had also taken the starch out of the Royals. From that point on, it was felt by many that the Royals had been intimidated and were a different, meeker team.

With Brett getting only three singles and Aikens one, the Phillies went on to win the next two games, clinching the Series, and giving the team its first victory in the Fall Classic in its 97-year history. A 4-3 victory in the fifth game was followed by a 4-1 verdict in Game Six, which launched a celebration the likes of which have never been seen before or after in Philadelphia, with two million fans ultimately watching a parade of the new champs down Broad Street.

Mike Schmidt, Larry Bowa, Del Unser, Bob Boone, McBride, Carlton, and McGraw were all toasted for their key roles in the victory. But no one was forgetting Noles, either. After all, he had thrown the pitch that many said turned the whole Series around.

Was Dickie intentionally throwing at Brett? Did he deliberately try to knock the Royals' third sacker on his hemorrhoids? What was the real story behind the pitch that even now is vividly remembered as a key element of Phillies history?

"People ask me if I was throwing at Brett," Noles said some years later. "If I was, I tell them, I did a bad job. I was really just trying to move him off the plate. I will say, though, that day I had the best stuff I ever had."

Bob Boone was the Phillies' catcher at the time. What pitch had he called? "I called for a fastball," he said, clearly recalling the incident some 27 years later.

Was Noles aiming for Brett's head? "What happened," Boone said, "is that the ball really cut. Dickie threw it in a good spot, and the ball just ran in. I think Dickie was trying to get in there and send a message. He was never shy about that."

When asked for his version of the pitch, Dallas Green, then the Phillies' manager, smiles somewhat sheepishly. Green is not one who ever lacked for a strong opinion, but this time he tries

An inside fastball thrown by Dickie Noles may have turned the 1980 World Series around.

hard not to state what many feel was the obvious. "I don't care what he was doing," Green said. "Whatever it was, it worked in our favor. It sent a message to the other club that we weren't going to settle for second best.

"That kid [Noles] went out there and did a job," Green added. "He did it on his own, and he did what he felt the club needed at that particular time. I don't think it affected Brett that much, but I do think it affected his club. I think they took a look at what happened, and it set the tone for the rest of the Series."

Brett, himself, said in an interview that he still thinks occasionally about the pitch, but that he holds no hard feelings toward Noles. "That's the way the game is played, or it used to be played—it's not played like that anymore," he said. "I didn't take offense to it. I was swinging the bat decently at the time, but not great, and he was trying to intimidate me. But I didn't go to sleep after that. I was still swinging the bat pretty well after that at-bat."

Unlike Green, Brett is not willing to concede that Noles' pitch slanted the Series in the Phillies' direction. "I have no idea if that turned the Series around," he said. "All I know is, we lost. Someone had to lose. They were a great team. We were a great team."

Some 25 years ago—just a few years after the Series and while still in the midst of a 12-year major league career, Noles turned his own life around, dumping his bad-boy image, finding religion, becoming sober, and taking a job in the Phillies' front office in which he counsels the team's major and minor league players on drug and alcohol abuse and other unsuitable traits and speaks to school and community groups. Over the years, Noles' take on the pitch to Brett and its resulting effects have undergone some alterations.

"To say that I turned the Series around is really crazy," he said in an interview in 1990. "I'm flattered that people think that, but I don't think one pitch could have ever changed a whole World Series. We had too many good players who contributed. I am just proud to have been one of the guys on that team.

"The only effect I think that pitch had was to embarrass Brett," Noles added. "I think he was embarrassed, and his whole team was embarrassed."

Since that day, though, the pitch has remained an especially memorable one. And while Noles continued to reject the notion that it turned the Series around, he heard the opposite view so often that he began thinking differently.

"I used to think that saying that one pitch turned the Series around was absurd," Noles said. "I laughed at the theory. But I've talked to Hal McRae and Amos Otis [both members of the 1980 Royals] in recent years, and obviously it made a bigger impact than I thought it did.

"I do believe now that it was an inspiration to our team. And I think there was a change in momentum. Of course, it didn't win the Series. People like Carlton, Schmidt, Rose, McGraw and others won the Series for us.

"One thing I remember about the pitch," Noles continued, "was that George got right back up. He gave me a little look, and the whole stadium was going crazy. Frey was screaming. Then Rose came over and stood beside me, and he was saying, 'Pitch your own game. You want to knock somebody else down, go ahead.' Pete sized up the situation, grabbed it, and turned it into an us versus them thing. It wasn't me who knocked down Brett. It was the Phillies. He was saying to them, 'We did it, now what are you going to do about it?' I think that intimidated them."

Some 17 years after the now-legendary pitch, the Phillies were holding their annual midwinter carnival for fans at Veterans Stadium. Both Brett and Noles were invited to the affair to sign autographs. They were to sit together in the same booth.

"We didn't know each other, hadn't even seen each other since the Series," Noles recalled. "I was a little nervous about how it would go. I didn't know what to expect. And I felt very uncomfortable about signing my name with a great player like George Brett."

Noles' apprehension was quickly relieved. Brett arrived at the event a few minutes after Dickie. As Brett approached the booth, Noles noticed something strange. The fun-loving ex-third baseman had a baseball taped to the side of his head.

And a situation that was once deadly serious had become, at least for the moment, one that was laced with hilarity.

chapter 12

NO BLUE JAYS
IN THIS FLOCK

In the back yards and the forests of the eastern part of the United States, the blue jay is one of the more conspicuous members of the avian kingdom. And that is not only because of its striking blue, black, and white plumage.

The blue jay is a bird with a personality. Unlike other members of the flock that gather around the feeder or even some of its relatives in the jay family that reside in other sections of the country, the blue jay is a colorful character that is neither quiet nor timid.

Chances are, if it's nearby, you know it. The blue jay is noisy. It loves to whistle. It finds joy in mimicking the sounds of his fellow flyers. And it is the alarm system in the bird community that warns of lurking danger.

Known for being mischievous, the blue jay has also been labeled a pest, a scoundrel, and a rogue. It makes trouble. And it is certainly not beneath its dignity to attack other birds. Sometimes, it even takes on a neighborhood cat.

All this, of course, has given the highly intelligent blue jay a reputation as being brash, bold, and aggressive. Don't mess around with Mr. Bluejay. He is one tough guy.

With these characteristics on the table, it is, therefore, excessively misguided to consider the 1940s Phillies as blue jays. Pigeons or turkeys, maybe. Perhaps even sparrows. But blue jays? This team of losers was woefully lacking in the combative qualities of the fiery feathered flyer.

Yet, in 1944, at a time when the Phillies—having carried that nickname since 1883 when original owner Al Reach viewed it as a way to relate the team to the city in which it played— were at their all-time worst, there was an attempt to change the name of the team to Blue Jays. It happened following the purchase of the team by the Carpenter family of Wilmington, Delaware.

After William Cox, the president of a syndicate that owned the Phillies, had been banned from baseball for life for betting on his team's games, the Carpenters purchased the club for $400,000. Bob Carpenter was installed as president.

Although just 28 years old, Carpenter had a clear idea of what had to be done to make the Phillies respectable. One of the first things to do was to give the team a new nickname. A new nickname, Carpenter thought, would give the team a whole new identity, suggest a new team spirit, and help fans to forget the awful Phillies, a team that since 1917 had finished in the first division just once and that had finished in last place 14 times and in seventh seven times between 1918 and 1943. A new nickname would surely erase the stigma of those pathetic teams, as well as signal the dawn of a fresh, new era featuring a team on the way up.

This was not the first time someone had tried to give the Phillies a new nickname. In 1910, Horace Fogel, the first of two Phillies presidents to have been kicked permanently out of organized baseball—in his case, for making disparaging comments about various issues in the National League—had attempted to switch the team's name to Live Wires. As was the case later, Fogel thought this would help to project a new image for a floundering team that had never won a pennant, while at the same time instilling an invigorating spirit in his lethargic players.

Neither fans nor sportswriters, nor even the league itself paid any attention to Fogel's plan. The name Live Wires was uniformly rejected, and in a short time was forgotten by even its staunchest supporters, most of whom were named Fogel.

In 1942, after onetime Phillies third baseman Hans Lobert had been named manager of the team, another attempt had been made to change the nickname. Using the same logic as Fogel, Lobert, who among other things was noted for racing a horse around the bases before losing by a nose, convinced Phillies president Gerry Nugent that henceforth the club should be called simply the Phils with the words printed all in capital letters on the team's uniforms.

Again, the idea was to eliminate the old name, which carried with it the stigma of a loser, which in this case was about to endure five straight and six of the last eight seasons of losing more than 100 games, including a team-record 111 in 1941. Again, the name, having never been officially filed with the league, struck out, although in later years it was often used as the team's secondary nickname.

In 1945, after his team had finished eighth and lost 92 games, Carpenter added his name to the list of those who tried to make the nickname Phillies disappear. Carpenter, though, had a different way to accomplish that goal. He ran a contest among fans, offering a $100 war bond to the winner and season tickets to those who made the top three suggestions. A panel of local sportswriters, broadcasters, and team officials was selected to serve as judges in the contest, which would run from January 25 to February 27.

New Phillies owner Bob Carpenter ran a contest to rename the team.

Using advertisements in the local newspapers while claiming that a new name and logo would help to overcome the futility that the name Phillies represented, Carpenter urged fans to submit new names for his team. Ultimately, 5,064 took part. The winning entry, much to the chagrin of bird-lovers, was submitted by Mrs. John Crooks, a Philadelphia resident. Her entry, which Carpenter as well as the judges agreed reflected a revitalized team and would stimulate new interest in it because it symbolized a colorful member of the animal community, was "Blue Jays."

Carpenter wasted no time getting the new name out into public view. He had a blue jay logo developed and put it on the club's stationery. He put it on the sleeve of the team's uniforms. The logo was conspicuous on the team's 10-cent programs. It was made into a pin that sold at Shibe Park, the team's home. Carpenter even had a pennant produced that said Blue Jays and bore a large picture of the bird. It was sold for 25 cents.

Alas, with one exception, no one seemed to care. That one exception, though, was the student body at Johns Hopkins University in Baltimore.

Since 1922, Hopkins sports teams had been called "Blue Jays," an adaptation of a nickname that had previously been "The Black and Blue." That was a name that represented the team colors, and had first been used in 1907. But after a while, the name "Blue Jays" slipped gradually into the Hopkins vocabulary, eventually becoming the accepted nickname.

Some years later, when a group of Hopkins students learned that another sports team, an appallingly forlorn one at that, was using the university's beloved nickname, it signaled a call for action. The students drew up a resolution, which was then endorsed by the student council and passed around the campus for signatures. Several hundred students put their names on the resolution, and it was sent to Carpenter in Philadelphia.

At the heart of the resolution was the students' protest against the Phillies' employment of the name blue jays. The Phillies' use of the name was a "reprehensible act which brought disgrace and dishonor to the good name of Johns Hopkins University," the resolution said in part. It urged the Phillies to discontinue using the nickname "Blue Jays."

That was not a point that could be easily contested. Although the 1943 team had won more games (64) than any Phillies team since 1932, the 1944 team presented the team with its seventh last-place finish in nine years. Surely, no respectable blue jay would want its name to be used in conjunction with this sorry franchise.

Actually, neither did the Phillies fans or the sportswriters. Both groups almost completely ignored the name and continued to call the team the "Phillies." And although Carpenter persisted in using the Blue Jay logo, the name never caught on.

At the end of the 1945 season, sportswriters declared that the nickname was dead. Carpenter continued to promote it, but by 1948, he, too, gave up. There were Cardinals and there had been Orioles and Robins, but there would be no Blue Jays. The Phillies were the "Phillies" and nothing else.

Sometimes, it has been said that the team was not always called the "Phillies," that it had once been named the "Blue Jays." Yet, the team's nickname was never officially changed. Until a team was formed in Toronto in 1977, no major league team was ever officially called the "Blue Jays."

And because it was never dropped, the nickname "Phillies" is the longest, continuous, one-city, one-team name in all of professional sports.

chapter 13

THE MAKING OF A SLUGGER

I t is not hard to cast a kid as a power hitter. Watch how he swings the bat. See how quick he is with his hands. Look to see how he uses his body. Check how strong he is.

If a kid incorporates the best of these features, there's a good possibility that he has the tools to be a power hitter.

The best power hitters always have these traits—and more. Did Hank Aaron make good contact? Did the ball jump off Babe Ruth's bat? Did Mickey Mantle have good balance on his swing? Did Willie Mays shift his weight properly? Did Ted Williams have great eyesight? You bet they did. And they had these characteristics long before they reached the big leagues.

It may be true that power hitters are not born, they evolve. They start with the basic tools, and then these tools are honed and refined, and if the process is successful, eventually a power hitter emerges. It is, of course, no simple task. But if it works, and the body and brain are willing, the final product may turn out to be a remarkable slugger.

A splendid example of this evolution is Phillies first baseman Ryan Howard. He had the tools as a kid. And when he developed them, he became one of major league baseball's most spectacular long-distance clouters.

The numbers bear this out. In 88 games in 2005, Howard hit .288 with 22 home runs, including 10 in September, and, despite not playing a full season, was named National League Rookie of the Year. Then in 2006, playing his first full season,

Howard hit .313 and crushed 58 home runs, which led the major leagues, set a Phillies record, set a major league record for most home runs by a sophomore, and tied for the 10th highest single-season total in ML history. Howard's 149 RBI was the second-highest RBI total for a second-year player, trailing only Joe DiMaggio's 167 in 1937. For his efforts, Howard was rewarded with selection as the league's Most Valuable Player, only the second player in history (Cal Ripken was the first) to win Rookie and MVP awards back-to-back.

In 2007, Howard continued his heavy hitting, belting 47 homers to finish second in the league. Although his batting average fell to .268, the lefthanded swinger became just the fourth player in Phillies history to have back-to-back 40-plus home run seasons. Howard also reached 100 career homers faster than any other player in major league history.

Aaron was in his fourth season when he passed 100 homers. Jimmie Foxx was in his fourth season, too, as was Barry Bonds. Alex Rodriquez passed the century mark in slightly more than three seasons.

So what sent Howard on the road to becoming an outstanding power hitter quicker than any of the game's most noted bangers? And when did he know he was one?

"My mom started to tell me when I was a little kid," Howard said. "I was somewhere around seven or eight years old."

A few years later, Howard played Little League baseball. Eventually, he arrived in high school where he attended Lafayette High in St. Louis. He was already starting to attract the attention of local scouts. At the time, Howard stood six feet, two inches and weighed 210 pounds, compared to the six-foot-four, 256-pound stature he now commands.

"As a teenager, he was very athletic-looking," said Jerry Lafferty, who is the Phillies scout in a nine-state area in the Midwest and who first saw Howard when he was a sophomore in high school. "He had the physical skills and the baseball skills, and he handled himself very well. He had real power potential, which kind of said, 'Hey, keep an eye on me.'"

Lafferty, who had scouted future Phillies such as Darren Daulton, Jeff Stone, Tyler Green, Todd Frowirth, and Andy Ashby, wasn't the only one watching Howard. Other scouts were attracted by the powerful kid with the bulging muscles.

So were college baseball coaches, among them Keith Guttin, longtime head coach at Southwest Missouri State University.

"In his senior year in high school, he really blossomed," Guttin said. "He was very athletic, and he had good bat speed with great power. He had all the tools."

As the tools developed even farther, Howard's reputation expanded. More and more scouts and coaches came to see him play, both in high school and in American Legion ball. Eventually, Ryan decided to attend Southwest Missouri.

"At the time, I just thought of myself as a contact hitter," Howard recalled. "I knew that the power was going to come.

At an early age, it was obvious that Ryan Howard would become a big-time slugger.

But I wasn't as concerned with that as I was just trying to stay focused and meet the ball."

In his freshman year in college, Howard gave a graphic demonstration of why he had been so avidly tracked. Batting third in the order, he hit .355 with 19 home runs and 66 RBI in 57 games. His biggest game came against Indiana State when he drove in five runs on four hits, including a double and home run, and scored three times. At the end of the season, he was named the top freshman player in the Missouri Valley Conference and was picked for the All-American baseball team.

Howard didn't rest on his laurels. In his sophomore year in 2000, he hit .379 with 18 homers and 63 RBI, again in 57 games. He drove in four runs in a game four times, and once knocked home five tallies with a single, double, and home run against Wichita State. That summer, Howard was named to the U.S. Olympic team.

"He just kept getting better and better," Guttin said. "And he worked hard to get better. He had a tremendous work ethic. He also had great character and a great family. The scouts were following him all around because they could see he had big league talent."

By then, scouts were virtually tripping over each other as they flocked to the Bears' ballpark to chart every move of the blossoming young slugger. "By then, everybody knew about him," Guttin said. "Players like Ryan are in short supply, so lots and lots of scouts were following him. And they saw him hit some unbelievable shots. He hit some over the light tower. Nobody had ever done that before."

Lafferty sat in the stands and watched intently. Like the others scouting Howard, he knew that he was seeing a big league power hitter take shape.

"He looked like the real deal," Lafferty said. "He had a real good approach to hitting, and he was very mature. He had solid tools and makeup. I had a gut feeling that he would develop into an outstanding major league hitter. I said, 'This guy's going to be a good one.'"

In his third season at Southwest Missouri, however, Howard's hitting took a sharp step backward. His batting average plummeted to .271 and he hit only 13 home runs while driving in 54 in 58 games. He had five-RBI games against Kansas and Missouri Universities, but his season was considered a big disappointment.

"A lot of the scouts who were interested in him lost interest and walked away," Lafferty said. "There was no way I was going to walk away from this kid. But where he had once been projected as a first-round draft choice, he now had slipped to the fifth round."

That is precisely where the Phillies picked Howard in the 2001 draft. He was a fifth-round choice just behind third baseman Terry Jones in a draft in which the Phils selected pitcher Gavin Floyd in the first round.

While missing his final year of college ball, Howard's first summer in the pros was good but not great. In 48 games, he hit .272 with six homers and 35 RBI. He had four RBI in one game and went 5-for-5 with three RBI in another. But it was obvious that Howard was no ordinary hitter. He had all the attributes of an exceptional power hitter.

Phillies manager Charlie Manuel, who was a power hitter himself, especially when he played in Japan, and who was later a hitting coach in the big leagues, knows about such attributes. "When I was in eighth grade, I used to hit balls over the fence," he said. "I didn't know what I did, but my coach said, 'Man, you have a lot of power and you have a quick bat.' I didn't even know what that meant. Later, I figured out that the reason for that was that I had good mechanics, used all my strength, had good leverage with my swing, I was strong, and I utilized all these things.

"When a guy is young, you can watch his swing," Manuel added. "If he has good balance, a good weight shift, a quick bat with the ball jumping off the bat, you know he might be something special. As he grows, he gets bigger and stronger, and then all of the sudden, he masters all the different elements of his swing. He makes good contact, has good bat speed, and with his strength, he starts to hit the ball a long way."

That's exactly the path that Howard followed. After his first season in the minors, his numbers moved steadily forward. In 2002, he went .280-19-87 at Lakewood. That was followed by .304-23-82 at Clearwater during a season in which he led the Florida State League in batting average and home runs and was named the league's Most Valuable Player. Then came a .297-37 and a league-leading 102 RBI at Reading after which he was moved up to Scranton/Wilkes-Barre and a .270-9-29 before finishing the season with the Phillies and going .282-2-5 in 19 games.

Former Phillies star Dick Allen, one of the greatest sluggers the team ever had, remembered watching Howard at spring training when he was a minor league player.

"He was a big, strong, strapping kid who really stood out," Allen said. "You could see right away the direction he was headed. It was nowhere but up."

Howard started the 2005 season at Scranton, was called up by the Phillies, then sent down to Scranton where he was leading the International League with a .371 batting average (16 homers, 54 RBI) when summoned back to Philadelphia. From there, the powerful first baseman began his quick climb to the top ranks of baseball's power hitters.

At one point, the Phillies tried to make an outfielder of Howard in an attempt to keep power-hitting Jim Thome at first base. When the experiment failed, the Phils were forced to make a difficult decision. They couldn't keep two long-distance clouters who played the same position. One had to be traded. Thome, an enormously popular player in Philadelphia and a National League home run leader himself with 47 in 2003, wound up being the one to go. He was swapped to the Chicago White Sox in a trade that brought the marvelous center fielder Aaron Rowand to the Phillies.

Keeping Howard was a prudent move for the Phillies. While Thome battled injuries, Howard easily fulfilled the promise that all had predicted. "He has his own style," Manuel said. "He strikes out a lot [In 2007, Howard set a major league record with 199 strikeouts], and that's because he lets the ball get too deep on him. Most power hitters overswing. They try to muscle the ball. Most of the time, Howard doesn't do that. When he's going good is when he has a good approach at the plate, has good balance, good rhythm, cocks his wrists, loads his hands, and makes a good, balanced weight shift."

Strikeouts notwithstanding, 129 home runs in what amounts to less than three full seasons says that Howard has perfected the art of being a power hitter. It is an art that Howard began to learn when he was just a youngster in grammar school in St. Louis.

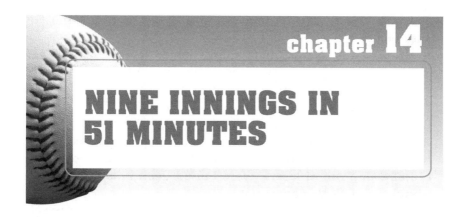

chapter 14

NINE INNINGS IN 51 MINUTES

T he way baseball is played has changed substantially in the last 50 years. Although the game is still based on the need to hit, field, run, and throw, baseball has become increasingly complex. It is a vastly different game than the one grandpa used to watch.

Aside from techniques and strategy, one of the biggest differences on the field is the length of time it takes to play a game. Rare is the game today that takes less than three hours to complete. Most modern games take an average of about three hours and 15 minutes to play. Some even take four hours.

Blame it on the rampant changing of relief pitchers. Or the constant stalling on the pitcher's mound or the fidgeting in the batter's box. Or the lengthy commercials that nobody listens to but that always have to be aired, causing long waits between innings. Whatever the case, baseball games seem to drag on and on, which, of course, has the added misfortune of turning off fans or potential fans, and sending those who come to games home early.

There was a time, though, when this was not the case. Baseball games moved swiftly through nine innings. There were no excessive delays. A well-played game could be completed in two hours or less.

Once, there was even a game played in 51 minutes. And it was a nine-inning game, too. On September 28, 1919, the Phillies and New York Giants played the first game of a season-ending doubleheader at the Polo Grounds in nine minutes less than one hour. Nearly 20,000 fans were on hand to watch the Giants win, 6-1.

It was the fastest nine-inning major league game ever played during the regular season. The record has stood for 88 years, and will surely never be broken.

The game had no bearing on the standings. The National League pennant had already been clinched by the Cincinnati Reds. The Giants were nine games behind and in second place, while the Phillies, in the second year of what would become a brutally long run of losers, were buried deep in last place and would finish 47 $^1/_2$ games out of first.

It was the year of the infamous Black Sox scandal in which members of the Chicago White Sox threw the World Series to the Reds. The Reds were managed by Pat Moran, who in 1915 had led the Phillies to their first National League pennant. (Chicago was piloted by former Phillies pitcher and second baseman Kid Gleason.)

John McGraw, who had managed the Giants since 1902, was on substantially more solid ground than the Phillies' skipper. That would be Gavvy Cravath, who had taken over the reins in early July after Jack Coombs, in his first season after replacing Moran, had been fired by Phils owner William Baker. Under Coombs, a former pitcher with the Philadelphia Athletics, the Phillies were mired in last place with an 18-44 record.

Cravath was on his way to winning his sixth and last home run title when he was named manager despite no prior experience (Coombs didn't have any, either). Gavvy, who would manage the Phils again in 1920 before he, too, was replaced, was one of baseball's premier sluggers, having hit more home runs than anybody in major league history until Babe Ruth passed him in 1921.

Cravath led a lineup that was filled with solid hitters, including first baseman Fred Luderus, center fielder Cy Williams, left fielder Irish Meusel, and shortstop Dave Bancroft, a future Hall of Famer. The Phillies, as was so often the case in that era, had good hitting but no pitching. The club's top hurler was Lee (Specs) Meadows, who led the Phils with eight wins after joining the team at midseason following a trade with the St. Louis Cardinals. Future Hall of Famer Eppa Rixey was one of four pitchers who won six games as the Phils staggered to a 47-90 final record.

The Giants, meanwhile, had won the pennant in 1917, and were in the middle season of three straight second-place finishes. McGraw was in the process of building a team that would soon win four pennants in a row and two World Series. The New Yorkers, led by future Hall of Famer and right fielder Ross Youngs and left fielder George Burns, not only had the best hitting team in the league, but also fielded an outstanding pitching staff featuring Jesse Barnes and Rube Benton.

Barnes and Meadows were the opposing moundsmen as the game got under way. The righthanded Barnes, in his fifth big league season, had won 20 for the first time and took a 24-9 record into the fray. Meadows, the first big leaguer to wear eyeglasses while playing, was on the way to a 12-20 record overall.

The Phillies scored their first and only run in the opening inning when Lena Blackburne doubled to left and came all the way around on a grounder by Williams on a play in which Giants shortstop Art Fletcher (a future Phillies manager) made a bad throw to first for the game's only error. The Giants then retaliated with a run in the second on a single by Larry Doyle, a double by Fletcher, and a groundout by Frankie Frisch.

New York came back with three more runs in the third inning. A walk to Burns and a double by Young put men on second and third. Both scored when Benny Kauff bounced a hit off Luderus' glove at first. After singles by Doyle and Frisch loaded the bases, Kauff scored on a single to left by George Kelly. Doyle also tried to score, but was thrown out at the plate by left fielder Bevo LeBourveau.

The Giants added two more runs in the sixth. Kelly doubled to right and scored on a single by Earl Smith. Barnes followed with a double, but when Smith tried to score, LeBourveau also threw him out at the plate. Barnes went to third on the play, then scored on a sacrifice fly by Burns.

Although the game was moving quickly, no one was really paying attention to the clock until the ninth inning. When the Phillies came to bat in the top half of the frame, the men on the field suddenly realized that they were on the verge of a special record. "At that time," reported the *New York Times*, "it became apparent to the players that they could do something unusual, and for a half inning they hustled."

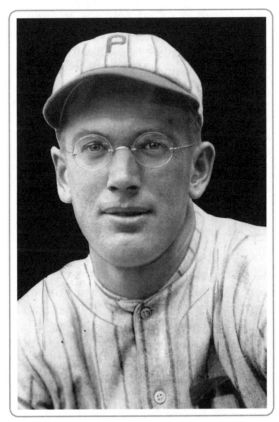

Lee (Specs) Meadows was on the mound for
the Phillies in baseball's fastest game.

Williams and Meusel made outs, but Luderus singled. He could have gone to second and been thrown out to end the game, but he didn't. But the next batter was Bancroft, and he took a half swing at a ball that rolled to Doyle at second. Doyle easily threw Bancroft out at first, and the game was over.

"Bancroft's effort with two down in the ninth was the only part of the game in which real effort was lacking," said the *Times* article.

The final line for the game had Barnes allowing five hits, striking out two, and walking none while picking up his league-leading 25th win of the season. Meadows yielded six hits, fanned one, and walked three. The Phillies left six men on base;

the Giants stranded seven. The Phillies reeled off two double plays. Kelly laced three hits, and Doyle, Fletcher, and Luderus collected two hits apiece.

According to the *Times* story, "The second game was considerably slower than the opener, but much faster than the average major league contest." With Wilbur Hubbell on the mound for the Giants, George Smith toeing the rubber for the Phillies, and McGraw playing most of his reserves, the Giants won easily, 7-1.

The Giants scored all their runs in the first three innings. The Phils' lone run came in the top of the eighth when Blackburne doubled to right and came around on two groundouts. Blackburne and Gene Paulette, who after the following season would be banned for life from baseball for consorting with gamblers, each poked two of the Phils' eight hits, while Burns, Frisch, and Doug Baird, a Phillies player earlier in the season, did likewise to lead a 10-hit Giants attack.

Although that game ended the season for both teams, the main focus was on the record-setting first game. One week earlier, fast games had entered the consciousness of the baseball community when the Brooklyn Dodgers and Cincinnati Reds played a game in 55 minutes. But both sub-60-minute games paled by comparison to an exhibition game the Phillies and Giants played in 1913.

The Giants had won the pennant, but needed some friendly competition to get ready for their upcoming date with the Philadelphia Athletics in the World Series. The Phillies, in New York to complete the season, volunteered. And in a game at the Polo Grounds, the teams played nine innings in 31 minutes. There were just 500 people in the stands.

The Giants won, 4-1, but that was beside the point. By previous agreement, both teams tried to swing on the first pitch, and ran at will, taking as many bases as possible on hits. Each inning, both teams raced to and from their positions on the field. While the Phillies kept the same lineup in the game, McGraw freely shifted his players, moving them in and out of the game while using 16 men. With all these factors in effect, it was no wonder the game was so short.

While the game had all the appearances of a fiasco, the best part of the afternoon actually took place in pregame activities.

Speedy Phillies third baseman Hans Lobert opposed Giants out-fielder Jim Thorpe, a fleet runner who had dominated the 1912 Olympic Games in Stockholm, in two races. Lobert won both a 100-yard dash and a race around the bases. In a fungo-hitting contest, Thorpe smacked a 404-foot drive to beat all hitters.

It was a highly entertaining afternoon at the ballpark. But it was only an exhibition. The real deal would come six years later when the Phillies and Giants took part in a regular-season game that was played in the astounding time of 51 minutes. It was a game that will never be duplicated.

chapter 15

DURABILITY PERSONIFIED

There was a time, seemingly long, long ago, when a complete game was like a badge of honor, a meritorious act that ranked as one of the most commendable marks on a pitcher's record.

Complete games, of course, weren't unusual. Years ago, they happened all the time. In fact, a starting pitcher was expected to go the distance whenever he took the mound.

For the better, more durable hurlers, it could almost be said that complete games were taken for granted.

During a season, the top pitchers always registered multiple complete games. Walter Johnson, who led the American League in complete games six times, hurled 531 of them during a 21-year career, at one point going below 30 only once over an eight-year stretch. A few decades later, Warren Spahn, while leading the National League in complete games nine times, averaged more than 21 CGs during a 17-year span of his 21-year career. And Steve Carlton completed 30 games as recently as 1972.

In the next decade, though, complete games began to vanish from the baseball landscape, eventually becoming as scarce as ballparks without restaurants. The complete game lost its luster, replaced by pitchers who were celebrated for lasting six innings and throwing 100 pitches, and bullpens the size of small armies that were stuffed with relievers whose specialties ranged from those who could pitch to one batter to those who could pitch for one inning.

So rare had a complete game become that league leaders often didn't even reach double figures. A team's entire pitching staff often didn't get that high, either. Indeed, whole staffs sometimes went entire seasons without a single CG. The National League's 2007 Cy Young Award winner, Jake Peavy, started 34 games, won 19, and didn't pitch a single complete game. And there were frequent instances when a pitcher had a shutout after eight innings only to find himself replaced by the ubiquitous closer, a one-inning species who seldom entered a game unless he could record a save.

All of which makes the record compiled by Robin Roberts between 1952 and 1953 particularly astounding. While a pitcher, manager, or a fan seldom comes face to face with a complete game in the present era, Roberts' 28 consecutive complete games rank as one of the greatest but often overlooked pitching performances in Phillies history.

Although it is not a league record—the St. Louis Cardinals' Jack Taylor's 39 straight CGs in 1904 stand as both the National League and the major league mark—Roberts' feat came during a stretch when the future Hall of Famer was winning 20 or more games in six straight seasons enroute to compiling 286 lifetime triumphs.

Roberts threw 305 complete games in 609 starts during his 19-year career, leading the National League five times. So it was not a particularly daunting feat for the strong righthander to hurl a game of nine innings or more. What was remarkable, though, was that he did it 28 times in a row.

"In those days, you just went out there and pitched," said Roberts, giving an untold analysis to his feat some 55 years after it happened. "You started the game, and just kept going. I never wanted to be taken out. I always wanted to pitch the whole game. I was either a rock head or a strong guy, but I never considered coming out until the manager came and took the ball away from me."

It helped, Roberts said, that the Phillies had a lead in many of the games in which he went the distance. "That made it easier for me to stay in the game a lot of times," he noted, "because they didn't have to pinch-hit for me. If you were behind by a run or two, they'd pinch-hit for you. But during that streak, we weren't behind very often. Plus, I could hit a little bit, so they left me in a lot of games instead of sending in a pinch-hitter."

The feat placed a major premium on stamina. "I developed very early in my career as a guy who could pitch the whole game," said Roberts, who in 1950, as the Phillies headed toward their first pennant in 35 years, had started three of the team's last five games of the campaign and had won the flag-winning game on the last day of the season with a gritty 10-

In one of baseball's most amazing achievements, Robin Roberts completed 28 straight games.

inning performance. "I had good strength, and I could just keep going. I always stayed in very good shape. And I didn't get tired much. Along with that, I had a good, easy delivery that didn't wear me down, and I usually had pretty good stuff. I really had more trouble in the early innings than I did in the later innings, but once I got settled in and got myself organized, I got stronger as the game went on."

The streak began August 28, 1952 and ended July 9, 1953. Over that period, Roberts won 21 games, including four against the Chicago Cubs and three over the Pittsburgh Pirates, lost six, and tied one. He worked 264 innings, even pitching one and two-thirds innings of relief along the way.

Prior to the streak, Roberts had posted his ninth straight win in a 10-5 victory over the Pirates, and then dropped a 3-0 decision to the Cubs in a game in which he was lifted for a pinch-hitter in the eighth inning. In the first game of the streak, Roberts beat the St. Louis Cardinals at Sportman's Park, 10-6, despite a three-run, seventh-inning home run by Red Schoendienst. Four days later at Shibe Park, Jackie Robinson hit a first-inning solo homer, but Roberts prevailed with an 8-2 victory over the Brooklyn Dodgers.

Then came the most memorable game of the streak. It happened on September 6 in the first game of a doubleheader against the Boston Braves at Shibe Park. An eighth-inning home run by Eddie Mathews helped to send the game into extra innings with the score tied at 6-6. The outcome wasn't decided until the 17th inning when the Phillies slipped away with a 7-6 win on a home run by Del Ennis. Incredibly, Roberts pitched all 17 innings, allowing 18 hits. The game was played in three hours and 50 minutes, the time it often takes to complete a nine-inning game today.

"I knew I had pitched a long time," Roberts remembered, "but it was no big deal. Pitching 17 innings wasn't that impressive then. But as I look back, that has become some ballgame."

The amazing marathon was followed on September 11 with a 3-2 triumph over the Cardinals at Shibe Park. Next up was a September 16, 4-2 victory at home over the Cincinnati Reds. Four days later, in his last home start of the year, Roberts beat the New York Giants, 3-2. He then beat the Brooklyn Dodgers, 9-7, on September 24 at Ebbets Field, and the Giants, 7-4, on September 28 at the Polo Grounds.

The win over the Giants gave Roberts a record of eight straight victories and a final mark for the season of 28-7. No National League pitcher has won that many games since then. Although the Phillies finished in fourth place, Roberts was expected to win the National League's Most Valuable Player Award, but lost in a controversial vote to the fifth-place Cubs' Hank Sauer. For the season, Roberts completed 30 of the 37 games he started, working 330 innings and posting a 2.59 ERA.

Roberts' winning streak ended in the season's 1953 opener on April 14 at newly named Connie Mack Stadium when he surrendered 11 hits, including a two-run, first-inning homer by Bobby Thomson, and lost to the Giants and Larry Jansen, 4-1. Six days later, Roberts hurled one of his best games of the streak, firing a three-hitter to beat Jansen and the Giants at New York, 2-1.

With only two days rest, Roberts returned to the mound and bested the Dodgers, 6-1, at home with only Pee Wee Reese's first-inning home run keeping him from a shutout. Then, again working with just two days rest, Roberts downed the Pirates, 7-6, at CM Stadium, despite yielding two-run homers to Ralph Kiner and former teammate Eddie Pellagrini. Roberts ended the month at home on April 30, but got no decision in a game that was called because of rain after five innings with Ray Jablonski's second-inning homer giving the Cardinals a 1-1 tie.

On May 3, Roberts stopped the Cubs with a six-hitter, 5-1, at Connie Mack Stadium. Six days later at Brooklyn, Roy Campanella's two-run homer with two outs in the bottom of the ninth gave the Dodgers a 7-6 victory over Robbie. On May 15, Roberts pitched another six-hitter to beat the Cubs and Warren Hacker, 1-0, at Wrigley Field. Four days later, he defeated the Reds in Cincinnati, 6-3, despite fourth-inning home runs by Willard Marshall and Ted Kluszewski. Back in Philadelphia on May 23, he allowed just four hits, one a home run by Campanella, but lost to Preacher Roe and the Dodgers, 2-0. Then Roberts completed the month on May 27 with a 14-2 rout of the host Pirates while hurling his third six-hitter in the last 24 days.

By now, Roberts' streak had reached an already remarkable total of 18 games. "But it was no big deal," Roberts recalled. "Nobody gave it much thought. I never heard anybody talking about it. And I certainly wasn't thinking about it. In fact, I had no idea that the streak was happening."

It was, though, and on June 2 it continued when Roberts fired his second shutout of the season, a 5-0, seven-hit blanking of the Cardinals at St. Louis. On June 6, he won the 100th game of his career, with a 6-2 victory over the Milwaukee Braves that was kept from being a shutout by Harry Hanebrink's two-run homer, his only four-bagger of the season and one of just three hits for the home team. Four days later, Kiner, just traded to the Cubs, homered to prevent another shutout as Roberts beat visiting Chicago, 9-1, while yielding seven hits.

Roberts was back on the losing end in his next start, bowing on June 14 at home, 2-1, to the Reds who got a solo homer in the first by Grady Hatton. Two days later, Robbie was amazingly used as a reliever at Milwaukee, working one and two-thirds innings while giving up three walks, one hit, and one run in a 6-5 Braves victory. Back as a starter on June 19, he beat the Reds, 10-3, at Crosley Field. That was followed on June 23 by a 6-1 win over the Cubs at Chicago.

In his next two starts, both on the road, Roberts lost, 7-4, to the Cardinals on June 27 in a game in which he surrendered 14 hits, and 5-4 to the Dodgers in 10 innings on July 1. He returned to the win column on July 5 with a two-hit, 2-0 victory at Pittsburgh in 10 innings. It was Roberts' 20th complete game of the season and his 28th CG in a row, the last one of the streak.

In the next game on July 9 at Connie Mack Stadium, Roberts faced rookie Johnny Podres and the Dodgers. After the Phils had taken a 2-0 lead, Campanella's two-run homer in the fourth tied the score. The Dodgers then went ahead, 3-2, before the Phillies regained a 4-3 lead with two unearned runs in the fifth.

Roberts' magnificent streak finally ended in the eighth inning when the Dodgers scored twice to regain the lead at 5-4. After a one-out triple by Gil Hodges, Phillies manager Steve O'Neill, who had replaced Eddie Sawyer during the previous season, replaced Roberts with Bob Miller. Miller retired the side, then got the win as the Phillies scored twice in the eighth to capture a 6-5 victory.

"I remember going back to the clubhouse," Roberts recalled, "and one of the radio announcers said, 'Roberts has been relieved by Bob Miller. The last time he was relieved was'...and he started looking back and back and back, and finally he said, 'It was last July.' Nobody could believe it was a whole year ago."

Roberts had gone an entire year without being removed from a game. And even after he was, he came back to pitch four more consecutive complete games. He finished the 1953 season with 33 complete games in 41 starts while working in 346.2 innings. Six losses in his last eight starts dropped his final record to 23-16. Over a two-year period, Roberts had a 51-23 record while completing 63 of his 78 starts.

Although his record makes today's starting pitchers look like coddled weaklings, Roberts is not quick to criticize. "I didn't throw a whole lot more pitches than today's starters," he said. "We didn't have pitch counts then, but my average for a whole game was probably 120 to 130 pitches. That's because I threw strikes and didn't walk many batters. I probably threw only about 12 to 15 pitches per inning.

"When he managed us, Sawyer would let some guys throw only so many pitches because they didn't keep their good stuff and wore out a little as the game progressed. Eddie could pretty much tell when a guy had had it, and he'd take him out.

"Paul Richards was the one who really started pitch counts when he was manager of the Baltimore Orioles," Roberts added. "He had four or five young pitchers, and when they first came to the big leagues he didn't want them to throw too much. So he started counting their pitches. After 60 or 70 pitches, he'd take them out.

"Of course, there were always relievers, but like Jim Konstanty on our club, they could come in a pitch three or four innings. That's different today. The game has changed. And people don't realize how much pressure the starters are under. It's not an easy thing being a starter. So often, though, when a pitcher is really going good and has good rhythm, they still take him out in the sixth or seventh inning. I really question that.

Unless a guy gets to the ninth and you have a really good reliever, it doesn't make much sense to take him out."

That, of course, wasn't an issue with Roberts. Get him to
the ninth, good relievers or not, and most of the time he was
still going to finish the game.

Such was the case during those remarkable days of the early
1950s when Roberts pitched 28 complete games in a row. It
was an astonishing streak then, and is even more astonishing
in the context of today's game.

chapter 16

THE FIRST AFRICAN AMERICAN PHILLIE

The name Chuck Randall is not one that holds a conspicuous spot in Phillies history books. It cannot be found among the pages that retell the deeds of the team's most significant achievers. It does not even appear with the names of any of the club's mediocre functionaries.

On the team's all-time roster of players who performed during the regular season with the Phillies, there is, of course, a Chuck Klein. There's a Chuck Essegian. And a Chuck Harmon, a Chuck Malone, and a Chuck Hiller. But nowhere to be found on that list is anybody with the name Chuck Randall.

And yet, Chuck Randall commands an important place in Phillies history. Maybe, it could be argued, it is one of the most important places. That might seem like an unusual claim to make about a man with such an unfamiliar name and obscure background. But consider the implications.

Long before there was Dick Allen; long before there was Dave Cash and Garry Maddox and Doug Glanville; and long before there was Jimmy Rollins and Ryan Howard, there was Chuck Randall. He was the one who paved the way for all of them.

Charles (Chuck) Randall, you see, was the first African American player ever to wear a Phillies uniform and to draw a Phillies paycheck.

For those who thought that honor belonged to John Kennedy, let's clarify the point. Kennedy, a shortstop signed off the roster of the Negro League's Kansas City Monarchs, was the first African American to appear in a regular season game with the Phillies. But that happened in 1957, two years after Randall had joined the organization as a third baseman from Glassboro, New Jersey.

The Phillies' role in accepting African American players in organized baseball had for many years been a contentious issue that would tarnish the team's image long after the arrivals of Randall and Kennedy. The issue first surfaced in the early 1940s when the Phillies rejected Roy Campanella when the future Hall of Famer sought a tryout with his hometown team. In the years that followed, the team continued as a key participant in the attempt to block the paths of black players to the majors.

When Jackie Robinson joined the Brooklyn Dodgers in 1947, no team gave him a rougher time or displayed more ugly, racist behavior than the Phillies, led by their Alabama-born manager, Ben Chapman. During the first meeting of the teams at Ebbets Field, vicious taunts and racial slurs streamed from the Phillies' dugout. Later, before the Dodgers' first series in Philadelphia, Phils general manager Herb Pennock tried to discourage Brooklyn GM Branch Rickey from bringing Robinson to town, even going so far as to block the team's hotel reservations.

With such a history, it was not surprising that the Phillies, who were then and for many years afterward, much more noted for their bigotry than for their tolerance, were the last National League team and the next-to-last major league team (preceding only the Boston Red Sox) to place an African American player on the field. That happened an incredible 10 years after Robinson had broken the "color barrier" when Kennedy appeared as a late-inning defensive replacement early in the 1957 season.

Kennedy, then 22 years old, had originally signed with the Phillies that February after spending one season with the Monarchs. At spring training in Clearwater, Florida, he drove an old 1950 Ford and, barred from the team's swanky, downtown hotel, lived with a black family near Jack Russell Stadium. Although the Phils were desperately in need of a shortstop and had hoped that Kennedy would fill the bill, it soon became apparent that the young South Carolinian was not the answer. Just before the end of spring training, the Phillies made a trade with the Dodgers, landing shortstop Chico Fernandez, a dark-skinned Cuban. After Fernandez arrived, Kennedy was relegated to the bench. He appeared in only five games with the Phillies, batting just twice, before getting sent back to the minors from which he never returned.

While Kennedy pioneered one aspect of the integration of the Phillies, Randall's story had a vastly different twist. He was really the team's original African American pioneer.

Although it was such an obscure event that even today few know about it, the Phillies actually signed their first African American player in 1952. His name was Ted Washington, and he had been an outfielder with the Philadelphia Stars, the last of the area's Negro League teams.

The Stars, owned by legendary Philadelphia sports entrepreneur Eddie Gottlieb, were in their final year of operation in 1952 after playing in the city for 20 years. After the season, Washington, a native of Camden, New Jersey, signed with the Phillies. But he never reported the following year to spring training. At the time, the United States was engaged in the Korean War. Washington was drafted into military service and ultimately sent to Korea before ever having set foot in a Phillies clubhouse.

While eight of the 16 major league teams had black players on their major league rosters by 1953, the Phillies signed no other African American until 1955 when Randall put his name on a contract after graduating from Glassboro (New Jersey) High School. A football and baseball star at Glassboro High, Randall was one of the top athletes in the area. The school yearbook said his future was in baseball and rated him the "most versatile" and the "most athletic" male in the senior class. The yearbook also rated Randall as "most courteous" and "most popular."

A third baseman and pitcher in baseball, Randall was an exceptional hitter. He was often described as one of the best natural hitters ever to play in South Jersey, and it was his fluid, powerful, lefthanded swing that attracted the attention of Phillies scout Jocko Collins. Collins, who doubled as an NBA referee, signed Randall to a contract that called for a salary of $200 a month.

Signing with the Phillies raises a critical question. Why would an up-and-coming young black player join an organization with such an unforgivable background in race relations?

"There was certainly some naiveté involved on my part," Randall reasoned. "But it was close to home. I originally wanted to sign with the Baltimore Orioles as a pitcher. The Detroit Tigers and Kansas City Athletics [newly moved there from Philadelphia] were also after me as a third baseman. But Jocko Collins was a very close friend of my high school coach, Ray Rollins. They convinced me that I should sign with the Phillies. I knew about their reputation with not having black players. I thought I could handle any problems that created."

Randall's signing was not elaborately noted in the local press. A few papers made mention of the event. But otherwise there was no fanfare. About the most attention paid to it occurred when Randall was invited to a dinner sponsored by a civic organization in Philadelphia. There, he and Eddie Bell, a member of the Philadelphia Eagles and a former University of Pennsylvania All-American, were saluted as African Americans who had cracked the world of white sports. (Philadelphia professional sports teams were slow in signing African Americans—the Athletics had not signed their first black, pitcher Bob Trice, until 1954, the same year Jackie Moore joined the Philadelphia Warriors.)

The Phillies sent Randall to Bradford, Pennsylvania, where the team had a Class D farm club in the Pennsylvania-Ontario-New York (PONY) League. The team was managed by former Philadelphia Athletics pitcher and Media, Pennsylvania native Lew Krausse Sr.

Soon after he arrived in late June, Randall was installed in the lineup at third base. And when he took the field for the first time, Charlie, as he was then called by most of his teammates, became the first African American ever to play in the Phillies organization.

As special as that distinction was, Randall did not cloak himself in the clothes of a hero or paint himself as a specially ordained pioneer. "I knew that I was doing something that no one else had done in the Phillies organization," Randall said, "But I had done this kind of thing before—playing with white teams in Glassboro. So, there was no extra pressure on me. I may have been a pioneer in some ways, but that wasn't my agenda. I just wanted to play ball."

Today, Randall lives quietly in Willingboro, New Jersey in a comfortable house where he and his family have resided for more than 30 years. At 70 years old, he is retired now after spending 42 years working in special events for Pepsi Cola in the company's office in Pennsauken, New Jersey.

A soft-spoken gentleman with a keen sense of humor and deep religious convictions, Randall vividly recalls the circumstances that led to his historic debut with the Bradford Phillies, a team that had been in the Phils' farm system since 1944.

Randall's professional debut did not draw any special attention. And even though he was the only African American player on the team, he was not subjected to the same abuse players before him had encountered. "The people in Bradford were completely okay with me," he said. "There was some racism displayed in some of the other towns in the league, but overall it wasn't too bad."

Randall had a banner rookie season. In one game, he set a league record with eight RBI, driving in the runs with a single, two doubles, and a home run. During the season, he appeared in 76 games, finishing with a .351 batting average with eight home runs and 66 RBI. Bradford, meanwhile, finished in second place behind Hamilton (New York) while leading the league in hitting with a .285 average.

In 1956, Randall went to spring training at Clearwater with the big club. He, too, lived in a private home, sharing a bedroom with future Phillies first baseman Juan Francisco (Pancho) Herrera, at the time a hot prospect from Cuba.

"They made a pretty big deal out of my being there," Randall recalled. "A lot was written in the papers about it. I wasn't paying too much attention to that, though. I was just trying to play ball."

Although he didn't appear in any games with the parent club, Randall spent many days in the company of the major leaguers. Most of the time, he was getting instructions, learning the finer points of the game. It was all part of the learning process for the 19-year-old youngster.

Before camp broke, Randall had his next assignment. The Phillies sent him to Matoon (Illinois) in the Class D Midwest League. The manager was former big league infielder Benny

South Jersey native Chuck Randall was the first African American player to wear the Phillies uniform.

Zientara. One of Chuck's teammates was Art Mahaffey, a young righthanded pitcher from Cincinnati playing in his first professional season.

"I remember him very well," recalled Mahaffey, who became a star hurler with the Phillies in the 1960s. "He was a pretty good ballplayer. He could sure hit. Kind of reminded me of Smoky Burgess. It seemed like every time he hit, it was a line drive.

"Everybody really liked him personally, too," Mahaffey added. "In fact, I don't remember anybody ever being any nicer than Charlie. He was a very friendly guy. I've never forgotten him."

Two other teammates at Matoon were Eddie Logan and Nate Dickerson. Both were African Americans, the former having been a huge football and baseball star in suburban Philadelphia at Ridley Township High School. As was now becoming apparent, the Phillies were finally starting to sign more black players.

Playing in 96 games and batting 350 times, Randall hit .309. The power that he had displayed the previous season became more conspicuous as he blasted 19 home runs while collecting 81 RBI.

The following spring, Randall was back in Clearwater with the Phillies when he met Kennedy. "He was a very pleasant guy, very easygoing," Randall said. "He was rather quiet, and he never talked about the role he might be playing."

At the end of spring training, Randall was assigned to High Point-Thomasville in the Class B Carolina League. But after hitting .270 in 17 games with no home runs and just three RBI, Randall, much to his disappointment, was shipped back to Class D ball and another stint in the PONY League. This time it was with Olean (New York), which had replaced Bradford in the Phillies' farm system. Getting sent to Class D for the third straight year bothered Chuck so much that he wrote a letter to Phillies president Bob Carpenter.

"I was wondering if they even knew I existed," Randall recalled. "So I wrote to Carpenter and told him that I had hit .300 in the preceding years and I thought I was a better than adequate hitter. But I wasn't going anywhere. I wasn't progressing the way I thought I should be. I was a young kid, and I guess I didn't understand the dynamics of baseball. Carpenter wrote back and said, 'We know you, but we have Willie Jones at third base.' He told me they didn't have a spot for me right then, but that I should hang in there."

Randall's new team in Olean was managed by Paul Owens, then on his way to becoming the most successful nonplayer in Phillies history as a farm director, general manager, and manager. Owens also played first base for Olean.

"I really liked playing for him," Randall said. "He was a very good manager and a very intelligent man. He was gentle and very likeable, but he could be forceful and had a quick temper. Sometimes, he could get really angry."

Appearing in 79 games, Randall hit .308. While playing both third base and in the outfield, he slugged eight home runs and collected 61 RBI.

In 1958, Randall was moved back to High Point. Frank Lucchesi, who 12 years later became the manager of the Phillies and who Randall said often "threw things around the clubhouse," piloted the team. Mahaffey and Chris Short were members of the pitching staff, and Tony Curry (a dark-skinned native of the Bahamas), Jacke Davis, and Al Kenders, each of whom played briefly with the Phils a few years later, were in the starting lineup.

Another member of the team was none other than John Kennedy. Having failed to stick with the Phillies the previous season, he was now in the midst of an extended minor league sojourn. Ironically, Randall and Kennedy were cast as roommates and lived all season together in a rooming house in High Point. Although Randall could sense Kennedy's disappointment at not having stayed in the big leagues, he said that the man who made Phillies history never talked about it. "He didn't seem bitter or angry," Randall said. "He just never brought up the subject."

That season, Randall got his first real taste of the racism that polluted the South. "People in the stands called us names," he said. "We couldn't eat in the same places as the white players. Usually, we had to stay in different hotels. It [racism] was all around us. The only thing you do about it was to stay positive and tell yourself, 'I'll show them.'"

After hitting .251 with six home runs and 27 RBI in 72 games at Olean, Randall opened the 1959 season in the Class A Eastern League with the Phils' farm club in Williamsport, Pennsylvania. But he hit just .167 in nine games, and was sent back to High Point.

By 1959, there were 27 African American players in the Phillies' minor league system. Former Negro League stars Judy Johnson and Bill Yancey had been scouts with the team for several years. Two black players—infielder Chuck Harmon and pitcher Hank Mason—had made brief appearances with the parent club. Clearly, the Phillies had finally moved beyond the days when they considered African American players unwelcome.

But Randall would not be part of the Phillies' long-overdue process of integration. After the 1959 season, he was released.

"They never gave me a reason," Randall said. "I guess they just didn't want me anymore. I thought I still had a lot of talent. But when I asked the farm director, Gene Martin, he never gave me a direct answer."

Randall was picked up by the Tigers and went to spring training with the club in Lakeland, Florida. Then he was assigned to Raleigh, back in the Carolina League, but played in just a few games. After spending most games on the bench, Chuck decided that he had little future in baseball. It was time to move on.

He came home to New Jersey for good. Randall eventually got a job with Pepsi Cola and began attending night classes, first at Burlington County Community College, then at Temple University. After a while, he stopped going to school and focused on his full-time job, ultimately rising to the position he had when he retired in 2005.

If, as it is sometimes said, a picture is worth 1,000 words, the one in Randall's living room certainly qualifies for that designation. Nestled among the collection of family photos is one taken in 1956 that shows four young players wearing Phillies uniforms. One of them is Randall.

The look on Randall's face is that of a man who is confident, content, and happy with the hand that fate had dealt him. And the letters on the front of his uniform say that fate had dealt him a hand that gave him an enormously significant place in Phillies history.

chapter 17

THE OFFICE BOY WHO BECAME PRESIDENT

I t can never be said that the Phillies were lacking in unusual characters. After existing for 125 years, they might even lead the league in that category.

Among the major contributors to that distinction are the team's managers. This is a group that includes a manager, Hans Lobert, who as a player once raced a horse around the basepaths (losing by a nose). Another skipper, Red Dooin, was a vaudeville singer in the off-season. Yet another pilot, Doc Prothro, was a practicing dentist. George Stallings was a former medical school student, Arthur Irwin was an alleged bigamist, Harry Wright created knickered pants, flannel uniforms, and colored stockings, and Hugh Duffy held the all-time major league record for highest batting average (.440). Eddie Sawyer was an off-season college professor, Danny Ozark once claimed during a losing streak that "even Napoleon had his Watergate," Jim Fregosi and Larry Bowa were all-star shortstops, and Terry Francona couldn't win with the Phillies but took his Boston Red Sox team to two World Series victories in four years.

Then there was Billy Shettsline. He might have been the most unusual character of all. At the very least, he was certainly the biggest.

Weighing in at more than 300 pounds, Shettsline was one of three Philadelphia natives who were full-time managers of the Phillies (Jimmie Wilson and Lee Elia were the others). Shetts, as everyone called him, spent five seasons as Phillies manager, in the process turning around a bad team and straightening out a bad situation.

In those five years, Shetts' teams posted a combined 367-303-7 record. Only five of the 51 men who have managed the Phillies won more games than that. And only six of them skippered the Phils in more games than Shettsline's 677.

But Shettsline was more than a manager with the Phillies. He began with the team as an office boy. Then, he became a ticket-taker. Eventually, he became the team's president. He might be the only person in baseball history who went from office boy to team president with stops along the way as ticket-taker and field manager.

Altogether, Shetts spent 43 years with the Phillies. During that time, he became the first executive to take his team south for spring training, survived three baseball wars, and helped to oversee the Phillies' move into its new ballpark at Broad Street and Lehigh Avenue. He also briefly coached a football team.

Born in 1863 the son of a man who painted coaches and was a respectable amateur pitcher as a youth, Billy got his start in pro baseball in 1884, running errands and working in the office of the Philadelphia Keystones of the short-lived Union League. When the Keystones folded late in the season, Shettsline was hired by the Phillies as an office boy by the club's part owner, John Rogers. Shetts had been a law school student doing work in Rogers' Center City law office prior to his joining the Phillies at the age of 21.

Shettsline's new job with the Phillies coincided with the club's second year of operation. Launching a new franchise had not been an easy process, and despite the wisdom and experience that principal owner Al Reach brought to the club, the Phillies had a sluggish beginning. That was amplified by the team's having to play in an old ballpark that dated back to the Civil War and for a while had been used as a horse market. Worse yet was the 17-81 record with which the Phils finished their first season.

Among his early duties, Shetts did odd jobs around the club's office and served as Rogers' secretary. The youth impressed his superiors with his intelligence and his enthusiasm, and soon he was appointed the team's business manager. Part of that job was keeping the books and handling the sale of tickets.

When Recreation Park's 6,500-seat capacity became too small to hold the team's growing number of fans, it became necessary to find a new ballpark. Reach and Rogers decided to build one. The site they selected had been a dump with Cohosksink Creek running through it. The new park, originally called both Philadelphia Base Ball Park and Huntingdon Street Grounds, initially sat 12,500 fans. It was opened in 1887.

"Our opening was the most wonderful thing I've ever seen," said Shettsline, who as one of the Phillies' few front-office employees, played a major role in the planning and development of the ballpark.

In the Phillies' first season at the new park, Shetts handled the sale of 253,671 tickets, nearly five times the number of seats that had been sold in Recreation Park's first year. Although ticket sales after that fluctuated from season to season, the figure leaped all the way up to 474,971 in 1895, the year after the Phils' Hall of Fame outfield had all hit above .400.

Shettsline's job was never easy. The team finished higher than third only once, and at one point wound up in fourth place four straight years (1891-94), despite the presence of a sizeable array of outstanding players. In 1890, he had to contend with a long-simmering salary dispute in which numerous players from around the league, including seven key Phillies (one being future Hall of Famer Ed Delahanty), quit their jobs and formed the Brotherhood or Players' League. One of the teams in the new league was placed in Philadelphia in direct competition with the Phillies. Although the revolt lasted just one year, the Phillies, as well as the other teams, had to struggle to get through the year, and permanently lost some players.

The biggest challenge Shetts faced came in 1894 when a fire destroyed much of the ballpark and some of the surrounding area. Billy and his cohorts had to oversee the construction of a new ballpark, which as it turned out, resulted in a vast improvement over the one that had burned down.

A challenge of a different kind surfaced in 1898 following another player revolt. This one occurred when Phillies players, led by center fielder Duff Cooley, went on strike in protest of what they called the abusive and tyrannical tactics of manager George Stallings. "We are fed up with the way Stallings has been riding us and we decided we had enough of him and would regard him as our manager no longer," said a statement released by the rebels. "For weeks, he's been handling us like a lot of cattle. We may not be the best team in the league, but we don't intend to put up with Stallings' tactics."

Management responded to the uprising by firing Stallings and replacing him with Shettsline. Billy, of course, had no managerial experience, but as a good and faithful employee with a happy, likeable personality, he was considered the right man for the job.

Shettsline quickly restored order. From a last-place spot and a 19-27 record the unhappy team had logged under Stallings, the Phillies posted a 59-44 mark under Billy, finishing in sixth place. And Shetts had earned himself a new job.

In 1899, with 20-game winners Wiley Piatt, Red Donahue, and Chick Fraser, NL ERA leader Al Orth, batting champion Ed Delahanty, and two other future Hall of Famers, Larry (Nap) Lajoie and Elmer Flick, Shettsline led the Phillies to a third-place finish with 94 wins, a number the team would remarkably not top until 1976. The '99 Phils were undoubtedly the club's best team in the 19th century, and many consider it one of the top Phillies teams of all time.

As a new century dawned, Shettsline drove the Phils home to another third-place finish (75-63-3). Then in 1901, Shetts showed his innovative side when he took the Phillies to Charlotte, North Carolina for spring training. Neither the Phillies nor any other big league team had ever gone south before to get ready for the coming season. (The Phils had always held spring training in Philadelphia.) "I'll never forget the stir we made," Billy said.

During the Phils' stay in Charlotte, the ponderous Billy, who during games wore a suit and tie rather than a uniform, demonstrated his lack of agility after an 11-6 victory over St. Mary's College. "Manager Shettsline was so pleased at the playing of his regulars that he fell out of the carriage and got a mud bath," the Philadelphia *Evening Bulletin* reported.

That season, Shettsline had to contend with yet another problem, this being the formation of the American League, which again took players from the National League, including the brilliant second baseman Lajoie, Fraser, Piatt, and several others. Despite the losses, Shettsline led the Phils into second place with an 83-57 record.

But the American League, especially Connie Mack and the Philadelphia Athletics, whose primary owner ironically was Reach's former partner in the sporting goods business, Ben Shibe, continued to plague the Phillies in 1902. By then, Dela-hanty, Flick, Orth, Donahue, and other stars such as pitcher Bill Duggleby, shortstop Monte Cross, and third baseman Harry Wolverton had jumped to the new league. For the Phillies, the season was a disaster. Attendance plunged to 112,066—with the exception of 1883 and 1884, the lowest in team history— and the Phils finished in seventh place with a 56-81-1 record.

That fall, Shettsline coached a football team in a short-lived Philadelphia professional league. Then during the winter, Reach and Rogers sold the Phillies for $170,000 to a syndicate headed by Main Line socialite James Potter, who became the team's president. With the sale went Shettsline's job as manager.

How good a manager had Shetts really been? "Judge for yourself," he said years later. "Del and Larry and those boys

During a long career with the Phillies, Billy Shettsline held jobs as office boy, ticket-taker, manager, and president.

never called me anything but Bismarck. That's how tough I was...The Iron Chancellor."

Fortunately for Shettsline, he still had a job with the Phillies. He was reappointed the team's business manager. But Shetts still couldn't avoid problems. In his first year on the job, a balcony at Philadelphia Park collapsed, resulting in the deaths of 12 people and injuries to 232 more. Billy, who was also in charge of ballpark operations, was "so badly prostrated by the shock," said a report in the *Inquirer*, "that he could scarcely tell a coherent story."

Although Reach and Rogers had retained ownership of the ballpark, leasing it to Potter and his group, the disaster took such a heavy financial toll that eventually the group was forced to reorganize. Potter was relieved of his duties as president. And Shettsline was named as his successor.

Billy took over late in 1904. During his presidency, he landed hard-hitting Kitty Bransfield in a trade, signed a brash young semipro outfielder named Sherry Magee, and hired Bill Murray to replace Hugh Duffy as manager. During Shetts' reign, the Phillies finished fourth three times and third once. In 1908, the team drew 420,660 fans, the second highest attendance up to that point.

In 1909, however, a new syndicate headed by Philadelphia political bosses Israel W. Durham and James P. McNichol, bought the Phillies from the Potter group. Durham made himself president. Once again, Shetts was out of a job.

Mysteriously, Shettsline chose voluntary retirement, although he was just 45 years old. But it didn't last long. Soon, the ever-resilient Billy was back on the Phillies' payroll when he was again named the team's business manager.

Once again, Shetts showed his pioneering spirit. He insisted that the Phillies ride trains wherever they traveled. And to accommodate that desire, he memorized every train schedule the team might need.

Not only did Shettsline, who by then resided in Glenolden in Delaware County, have an uncanny knack of memorizing train schedules, he saw to it that no Phillies player ever missed a train. What's more, he always went on the road with the team. Players called him "the travel nurse." Shetts was an early version of what is now called a traveling secretary.

It was once estimated that during his career in the big leagues, Shettsline traveled 800,000 miles. That might not be a huge total today, but in Billy's time that distance was staggering.

Shettsline held down the job as the Phillies' business manager until 1926. During that time, he encountered another baseball turmoil when the Federal League was formed in 1914, saw the club win its first pennant in 1915, and watched extraordinary players such as Grover Cleveland Alexander, Gavvy Cravath, Dave Bancroft, and Cy Williams perform with the team. He also worked for four more presidents and saw the demise of a franchise that would collapse into the dregs of the National League, not to arise again until the late 1940s.

That collapse was accompanied by a financial debacle that extended from World War I to well beyond World War II. In that period, the Phillies were so financially depleted that the team had to take every possible shortcut to stay alive. That included keeping just one groundskeeper to maintain the field at Philadelphia Park, which in 1913 had been renamed Baker Bowl by team owner William Baker.

Groundskeeper Sam Payne could hardly do the job by himself. So, he brought in three sheep—two ewes and a ram—to help keep the grass trim. The sheep ate grass by day and slept under the left field bleachers by night.

One day, Shettsline was strolling across the outfield when the ram decided to attack him. The overweight Shetts, running with the ram in hot pursuit, presented a picture never to be forgotten by those who saw it. Fortunately for Billy, he reached safety before the ram could do any damage. Unfortunately for the ram, he was given his unconditional release the next day.

After the 1926 season, Baker replaced Shettsline with Gerald Nugent, husband of his secretary, Mae Nugent, and a man who would later became the team's primary owner. Shetts left the Phillies after having served 43 years with the team. He left knowing that it had been a great run, one that far exceeded his expectations when he first joined the team as an innocent young man.

"I have seen all the great teams, survived three baseball wars, and seen all the great players," he said at the time. "I can tell you that Delahanty was one of the greatest hitters the game has ever known."

Shettsline worked briefly for the Philadelphia Athletics. He succumbed in 1933 at the age of 69. At the time of his death, he was employed by the city's Department of Highways in the street maintenance division at Chew Street and Chelten Avenue. He lived at 3313 North 15th Street in North Philadelphia.

Shetts' obituary pointed out that he knew Philadelphia baseball history as well as anybody ever did. "He was inseparably identified with Philadelphia," the article added.

He was also one of the most interesting and unusual characters the Phillies ever had.

chapter 18

NOW PITCHING,
THE BEAST

I t is commonly known that Babe Ruth began his major league career as a pitcher. Not so well known is the fact that a number of other future Hall of Fame sluggers appeared on the mound during their big league careers. Ty Cobb was one of them. So was Ted Williams. And during their days in the majors, Honus Wagner, George Sisler, Stan Musial, Tris Speaker, and Sam Rice were among others who toed the rubber in regular-season games.

Some appeared just once or twice. Others pitched more frequently. But no matter how many games they pitched, it was—and still is—highly unusual for a position player to become even a temporary hurler. It's even more unusual if that player is a future Hall of Famer.

The Phillies had one such player. The great slugger Jimmie Foxx went to the mound nine times with the 1945 Phillies. Of 28 nonpitchers who faced hitters since the club was formed in 1883, Foxx's nine appearances represent the second-highest total, trailing only outfielder Earl Naylor's 20 games in 1942.

At the time, Foxx was in the final year of what had been a magnificent career. Beginning in 1925, the man who became known as "Double X" had been one of baseball's most renowned hitters. Appearing in 11 seasons with the Philadelphia Athletics and in slightly more than six with the Boston Red Sox, Foxx, by then a first baseman, had won four home run titles and two batting championships.

During one 12-year stretch, he had never hit less than 30 home runs, reaching a high of 58 in 1932, then second only to Ruth's record 60 homers. In that same period, Foxx had hit under .334 only three times, once getting up to .364. He also drove in 100 or more runs 13 years in a row, setting a personal record in 1938 with 175.

Foxx, sometimes called "The Beast" because of his powerful bat, led the Athletics to three straight American League pennants and two World Series victories. But his greatest year overall came two seasons after the A's last pennant when he won the American League's Triple Crown in 1933 with a .356 batting average, 48 home runs, and 163 RBI. Remarkably, that achievement was matched in the National League by the Phillies' Chuck Klein (.368-28-120), which made Philadelphia the only city in big league history ever to have Triple Crown winners from each league in the same year. That year, Foxx also won his second straight Most Valuable Player award while earning a salary of slightly more than $16,000.

A native of Sudlersville, Maryland, Foxx and pitcher Johnny Marcum were traded after the 1935 season by the Athletics to Boston for two unknown players and $150,000 in cash. He enjoyed more sparkling years with the Red Sox, although no pennants were forthcoming. In 1938, Double X won his third MVP after leading the league in batting (.349) and RBI (175) while stroking 50 home runs.

As his career began an abrupt slide downhill, Foxx was released by Boston during the 1942 season and signed by the Chicago Cubs. According to *Jimmie Foxx—Hall of Famer*, written by W. Harrison David, after appearing in 70 games with the Cubs, Foxx, who was 4-F and hence not eligible to be drafted into military service, did not play at all during the following season. He was back in a Cubs uniform in 1944, but in midseason, after just 20 at-bats, retired as a player and became a coach. Less than two months after becoming a coach, however, Chicago released him from that duty so he could take a job as manager of the team's Portsmouth club in the Class B Piedmont League. Foxx was then released as the team's manager in December.

Foxx took a job with an oil company and moved to Short Hills, New Jersey. But, although 10 pounds above his playing weight and with his splendid ability as a hitter perceptibly diminished, Foxx wasn't through with baseball. Hoping to stay in the game, broke, and out of a job, he convinced Phillies general manager Herb Pennock that he could still play, and signed a one-year contract on February 10, 1945 with the National League team. The idea was that Jimmie might help the team as a pinch-hitter, fill in a little at first and third bases, and maybe render some useful advice to the club's ragtag band of players.

In March, with World War II limiting what was considered nonessential travel, the Phillies trained for the second straight year at Wilmington, Delaware. With only 17 players in camp, the 37-year-old Foxx's presence on the roster swiftly became more significant.

The 1945 season, of course, was far from being one of baseball's—or the Phillies'—finest. Although nearing the end, the war was still being waged, and with legions of baseball players still serving in the armed forces, the rosters of major league teams fell far below big league caliber. Most of the players in the majors were either too young or too old to be in the big leagues during regular times, or they were unfit for military duty and not in the best of physical condition.

The Phillies' roster as the season began was no exception. The team had five players under 21 years of age, and nine over 35. It included 17-year-old Ralph (Putsy) Caballero, 18-year-old Granny Hamner and his brother Garvin, the least of the DiMaggio brothers, Vince, plus a combination of washed-up veterans, stopgap wannabes, and minor leaguers in way over their heads. Only shortstop Granny Hamner, catcher Andy Seminick, and pitcher Ken Raffensberger went on to successful big league careers.

The 1945 Phillies were symbolic of the club's long-term incompetence. Except for two years in seventh place, the Phils had been last every year since 1936, and in six of those years, including five in a row between 1938 and 1942, the team had lost 100 or more games every season. As it would turn out, the 1945 season fit right into the mold, with the Phillies losing 108 games and finishing 52 games out of first place and 15 behind the seventh-place Cincinnati Reds.

Clearly, it was one of the worst teams in club history. It was so bad that even manager Ben Chapman, named to succeed Freddy Fitzsimmons near midseason, called upon himself to pitch in three games.

It was no wonder, then, that Foxx was summoned to the mound. Although he was not exactly knocking down the fences—he would hit .268 with seven home runs and 38 RBI while appearing in 89 games—Jimmie was certainly one of the club's better hitters. But with a staff that didn't include a single pitcher who would win more than eight games, there was a place for him on the mound, too.

Foxx had always felt he could pitch. According to baseball historian and Philadelphia Athletics authority Norman Macht, Foxx "fooled around on the sidelines, practicing various deliveries" after he reached the big leagues. Even in high school, although he was a catcher with a rifle arm, Foxx sometimes took the mound, and was known for his overpowering pitches.

Although he had broken into the majors as a catcher, and would also appear during his career in games at third base, the outfield, and in one at shortstop, Foxx was primarily a first

Hardly known is the fact that one-time slugger Jimmie Foxx (left with coach Merv Shea, Hall of Fame outfielder Al Simmons, and manager Freddy Fitzsimmons) pitched in 1945 with the Phillies.

baseman. But in the early weeks of the season, he was used mostly as a pinch-hitter and at third base. Then, after a prolonged cold forced him out of the lineup for two weeks, Foxx was moved to first base when he returned in late May.

As the season wore on and the Phils' pitching staff crumbled, however, the club was desperately in need of someone—anyone—who could throw the ball over the plate. Foxx had pitched in one inning of one game with Boston in 1939 and set the opposing Detroit Tigers down in order in the ninth. But he had never thrown a single inning anywhere else in a regular-season game, except for a complete game victory in 1944 with Portsmouth. With the Phils' pitching staff in shambles, however, Foxx got another chance to toe the rubber. He had one game to get ready, a July 10 exhibition against the Athletics. He started the game and pitched three scoreless innings before tiring and getting knocked out in the fourth as the A's scored six runs in what eventually became a 7-6 Phillies victory.

"The Beast" was approaching his 38th birthday and was no longer the imposing physical specimen he had once been. But generally speaking, there weren't many hitters to be feared in the National League at the time, and if a guy could get the ball over the plate with even a little bit on it, he could be useful. Chapman told Foxx that his best way to remain in the big leagues was as a pitcher.

On the way to using 19 pitchers during the season, Chapman handed the ball to Foxx for the first time on July 15 in a game at Crosley Field in Cincinnati. Working the last two and two-thirds innings, Foxx allowed no hits and no runs, but walked four. The Reds, behind the seven-hit pitching of former Phillie Bucky Walters, won, 6-1.

One week later, Foxx was back in action on the mound at Wrigley Field in Chicago. He replaced Phils starter Charley Schanz with none out in the second inning and wound up working two frames, allowing two hits, striking out two, and walking one. Despite two home runs by DiMaggio, the Phillies lost to the Cubs, 8-5.

On August 19, with the Phils buried in last place with a 31-81 record, Chapman stunned the minuscule crowd of Phillies followers—the club drew just 285,057 for the entire season—by naming Foxx as the club's starting pitcher in the second game of a doubleheader against the Reds at Shibe Park. Dick Mauney had pitched a shutout to give the Phillies a 5-0 win in the first game.

Chapman beseeched Foxx to give him five innings. Mixing a fastball, a screwball, a change-up, and a knuckle ball, Foxx, who had driven in one run in the opener, allowed no hits in the first five innings, at one point retiring 12 batters in a row. Then, although Foxx was tiring rapidly, Chapman left him in the game. Foxx was finally replaced with a 4-1 lead by reliever Andy Karl. As Jimmie left the field, he got a loud ovation from the appreciative fans.

Foxx wound up pitching six and two-thirds innings, giving up four hits and one run, striking out six, walking four, and hit-

Ex-slugger Jimmie Foxx hurled in nine games.

ting one batter. Lo and behold, Jimmie got his only win as a pitcher as the Phillies prevailed, 4-2. The losing pitcher was future Phillie Howie Fox.

"I never did so much throwing in a game," Foxx said in the winner's clubhouse. "I'm beginning to realize a pitcher earns his money."

Foxx said he relied mostly on fastballs, change-ups, and a few screwballs. "I was supposed to throw a curve, too," he said. "But the trouble is, it don't curve."

By then, Foxx was being used mostly as a pinch-hitter with Jimmy Wasdell playing regularly at first base. But as the season mercifully wound down, he would get an increased amount of playing time on the mound.

Jimmie worked the ninth inning of a 4-0 loss to the New York Giants in the first game of a doubleheader on August 27 at Shibe Park in a game in which Bill Voiselle tossed a three-hitter. Foxx allowed no hits and walked one.

Foxx's next opportunity came on September 2, again in the opener of a twin bill at Braves Field. Chuck Workman homered twice to lead Boston to a 6-3 victory, while Foxx worked two innings, allowed three hits and one run, struck out one and walked one.

Four days later, Foxx relieved Izzy Leon in a 4-1 Reds win at Cincinnati, and in one of his best games of the season, pitched four innings and yielded no hits or runs while fanning four and walking four.

On September 14, Foxx hurled the final one and one-third innings in the second game of a doubleheader at Chicago. Former Phillie Claude Passeau fired a four-hitter to lead the Cubs to a 6-0 decision. Foxx allowed one hit and struck out one.

The Phillies, who would lose all but one of the games in which Foxx pitched, bowed on September 16, 10-3, to the St. Louis Cardinals in the second game of yet another doubleheader. The home team got four hits from both Augie Bergamo and future Phil Emil Verban, who also drove in three runs. The line on Foxx went: one inning pitched, no hits, no runs, one strikeout, and one walk.

Foxx hurled again the next day at Sportsman's Park. Jimmie took the mound for the eighth and ninth innings, surrendered four hits and one run, and issued one walk in a 7-3 Cardinals victory. Bergamo again slammed four hits and Verban three behind the eight-hit pitching of future Phillie Blix Donnelly.

The outing was the last one on the mound for Foxx. On September 23, he made his final big league appearance, playing first base in a 4-3 victory over the Brooklyn Dodgers. Soon afterward, his career ended when the Phillies gave him his release. "Jimmie has done everything we have asked of him, and more," Pennock told the *Inquirer.*

In 20 seasons in the big leagues, Foxx compiled a batting average of .325, and with 534 home runs he became only the second player (behind Ruth) ever to surpass the 500 mark.

Although it was undeniably one of the more obscure phases of Foxx's career, the 1945 season also has a special place in baseball history. It was the year one of baseball's greatest sluggers pitched for the Phillies.

Tallying up the box scores, the final line on Foxx's Phillies outings read like this: nine games, 22 2/3 innings pitched, 14 hits, two runs, 15 strikeouts, 17 walks, and one hit batter. His earned run average was 1.59.

Not bad for a guy who wasn't a pitcher.

chapter 19

PHILLY GUYS WITH THE PHILLIES

D ating back to the 1800s, the Philadelphia area has always been known as a baseball hotbed. High school, college, kids, and sandlot teams have blanketed the area in huge numbers over the years, many of them producing top-level players who went on to perform professionally.

Thousands of players who were born in the greater Delaware Valley—Philadelphia, the four surrounding counties, South Jersey, and northern Delaware—have signed pro contracts. Of these, more than 350 have appeared in the major leagues.

Some of them have been Hall of Famers. Some of them were Most Valuable Players, home run kings, batting champions, 20-game winners, no-hit pitchers, or Rookies of the Year. Some of them have been good, everyday players. And some of them only made it to the bigs for the proverbial "cup of coffee." But whatever levels they reached or lengths of time they played, all contributed to the indisputable claim that when it comes to baseball, the Philadelphia area ranks at least on a par with any metropolitan area in the country.

So, how many of these homegrown players have worn the uniform of the hometown Phillies since the team began in 1883? The answer might surprise you. More than one-fourth of all local players who appeared in the major leagues played at some point during their careers with the residing National League club. (To qualify as a "local" player, one had to be born in the greater Philadelphia area. The group does not include those who were raised locally, but were born elsewhere.)

The actual number is 96. Of this group, 49 were born in Philadelphia and 29 made their initial arrival in one of the four suburban counties (Bucks, Chester, Delaware, and Montgomery). Eighteen others either came from South Jersey (12) or northern Delaware (six). In the overall group, 30 players appeared in 10 or fewer games in the majors.

The list is impressive. It includes pitchers Bucky Walters (Philadelphia), Bobby Shantz (Pottstown), and Jamie Moyer (Sellersville), catchers Jack Clements and Jimmie Wilson (both Philadelphia), infielders Monte Cross (Philadelphia), Hans Lobert (Wilmington), and Danny Murtaugh (Chester), outfielders Del Ennis (Philadelphia) and Roy Thomas (Norristown), and pitcher-

Probably the foremost Philadelphia-area native to perform with the Phillies was outfielder Del Ennis.

turned-infielder Kid Gleason (Camden). Of this group, Wilson, Murtaugh, Ennis, Thomas, and Gleason began their big league careers with the Phillies.

Del Ennis is the most decorated of this collection of home-grown products, having been National League Rookie of the Year in 1946, led the league in RBI with 126 in 1950, and been selected to three All-Star teams. A graduate of Olney High School, Ennis hit .286 in 11 years and 1,630 games with the Phillies, eventually batting .284 during a 14-year career. Over-all, he collected 288 home runs, hitting 30 or more in one sea-son twice, and drove in more than 100 runs seven times. He hit .285 or above in eight different seasons. Ennis is among the top 10 in 10 of the Phillies' all-time hitting categories, includ-ing second to Mike Schmidt in home runs, and third in RBI and total bases.

Jimmie Wilson, who grew up in the Kensington section of the city, was another longtime Phillies player. He hit .288 in two stints covering a little more than nine seasons with the Phils, and .284 overall during a career that spanned 18 years from 1923 to 1940. He ranks as one of the top five Phillies catch-ers of all time.

As manager of the Phillies, a job he held from 1934 to 1938, Wilson also played a major role in the conversion of Bucky Wal-ters from third base to pitcher. Walters was a mediocre hitter during his early years with the Boston Braves and Red Sox, but after the former Germantown High student came to the Phillies, Wilson noticed his strong arm and suggested he try pitching. The switch worked, and although Walters pitched in only three-plus seasons with the Phillies, he became a three-time 20-game winner with the Cincinnati Reds and the league's Most Valu-able Player in 1939.

Roy Thomas, a University of Pennsylvania graduate, was a center fielder and leadoff hitter who led the National League in walks seven times during a little more than 11 seasons (1899-1908, 1910-11) with the Phillies. He had an overall batting av-erage of .290 (.291 with the Phillies), hitting over .300 five times, including a high of .327 in 1903.

Danny Murtaugh, a Chester High grad, spent his first three seasons as the Phillies' second baseman, and led the league in stolen bases in 1941 with the whopping total of 18. He played five more years in the majors, hitting .254. Monte Cross played from 1898 to 1901 with the Phillies, hitting .230 (.234 overall during a 15-year career that included his last six years with the Philadelphia Athletics). Hans Lobert broke into the majors in 1903, and played 16 years, including four (1911-14) with the Phillies, hitting .274 overall and .292 with the locals. Jack Clements spent nearly 14 of his 17 big league seasons with the Phillies, joining the club late in the 1883 season.

Jamie Moyer came to the Phillies during the 2006 season after breaking into the majors in 1986. In his first start with the Phils, he became the oldest pitcher (43) in team history to win a game. At the end of the 2007 season, the Souderton High alumnus had reached 230 career wins, which included 20 or more wins twice and double figures 12 times.

Kid Gleason began his career with the Phillies and in his third season (1890) posted a 38-17 mark, still a club record for most wins. That was followed by a 24-22 record. Gleason left the Phils after that season, and three years later arm trouble ended his pitching career. He stayed in the game as a second baseman, returning in 1903 to the Phils with whom he started for four years as his 22-year career wound down.

Bobby Shantz, out of Pottstown High, pitched the final 14 games of his 16-year career with the Phillies. After beginning in the majors in 1949 with the Athletics, he posted a career record of 119-99, which included a 24-7 season and the Most Valuable Player award in 1952.

The Phillies had some other local pitchers with special notoriety (Phillies records and years in parentheses). Among those from Philadelphia, Hal Kelleher (4-9, 1935-38) allowed 12 runs in one inning in a game in 1938; Frank Hoerst (10-33, 1940-41, 1946-47) was a La Salle College basketball star before choosing a baseball career; Al Maul (6-5, 1887, 1890) returned from a 15-year big league career to serve for many years as a ticket-taker for the Phillies at Baker Bowl; and Jack Meyer (24-34, 21 saves, 1955-61), while at Penn Charter, was one of the greatest hurlers in the rich baseball history of the Inter-Academic League.

Another local Phillie, infielder Lena Blackburne (.199, 1919) from Clifton Heights, became famous as the man who developed a concoction from the mud in Rancocas Creek in New Jersey—the exact location he kept secret—to rub on new base-balls, which he supplied for many years to all major league teams. A variation of the process is still being used.

Other players of note who have spent time over the years with the Phillies were pitchers Dallas Green (20-22, 1960-64, 1967) from Newport, Delaware, Rawly Eastwick (5-7, six saves, 1978-79) from Camden, Johnny Podgajny (20-33, 1940-43) from Chester, Lew Richie (22-28, 1906-08) from Ambler, and Lefty Weinert (14-30, 1919-24) from Philadelphia, catcher Mike Grady (.330, 1894-97) from Kennett Square, and infielder Rick Schu (.243, 1984-87, 1991) from Philadelphia.

In recent years, other local players such as outfielder Ruben Amaro (.241, 1992-93, 1996-98) from Philadelphia, infielders John Mabry (.286, 2002) from Wilmington, Jeff Manto (.056, 1993) from Bristol, Ramon Martinez (.268, 2005) from Philadelphia, and Gene Schall (.252, 1995-96) from Abington, and pitchers Andy Carter (0-2, 1994-95) from Philadelphia and Steve Frey (0-1,

Future Pittsburgh Pirates manager Danny Murtaugh (left) and catcher and manager Jimmie Wilson were Phillies from the Philadelphia area.

1995-96) from Meadowbrook have appeared with the Phillies during careers in the majors.

For many years, mostly between the 1950s and 1970s, Phillies management was opposed to signing local players. One of the main reasons that the club avoided local athletes was because it was felt that appearing in front of the home fans would put too much pressure on a player. And so, for a time, a local player in a Phillies suit was rare, although once in a while it did happen.

Of course, while the Phillies did sign local players during most of the franchise's 125 years, the club also failed to sign numerous local players. Collectively, this group of players was considerably more talented than the overall assortment that did play with the Phillies.

The club missed out on four future Hall of Famers—pitcher Herb Pennock (Kennett Square), a career 240-game winner; catcher Roy Campanella (Philadelphia), a three-time MVP; and outfielders Goose Goslin (Salem, New Jersey), a batting champion, and American League MVP, four-time home run king and owner of 563 career homers, Reggie Jackson (Wyncote). It also could have signed but didn't future Hall of Famer Mike Piazza (Norristown), who has hit more home runs than any catcher in baseball history, and one who should be in the Hall, first baseman Mickey Vernon (Marcus Hook), a two-time American League batting champion.

Among many other outstanding players who got away were a load of top-drawer pitchers, including Ray Caldwell (Croydon), Lew Krausse Jr. (Chester), Jon Matlack (West Chester), Ray Narleski (Camden), Barney Schultz (Beverly, New Jersey), John Smiley (Phoenixville), Edgar Smith (Columbus, New Jersey), and Bill Dietrich, Mark Gubicza, and Walt Masterson (all from Philadelphia). Caldwell, Gubicza, and Smiley were each 20-game winners, Caldwell and Dietrich both threw no-hitters, Matlack was a Rookie of the Year, Smith won the 1941 All-Star Game, and Narleski and Schultz were two of the top relief pitchers of their eras.

The list also includes catcher Mike Scioscia (Upper Darby); infielders Wid Conroy (Camden), Eddie Miksis (Burlington), Buck Weaver (Pottstown), and Tom Daly, Harry Davis, Jimmy Dykes, Brook Jacoby, Danny Murphy, and Eddie Stanky (all from

Philadelphia); and outfielders Bris Lord (Upland), Dave May (New Castle, Delaware), and Dion James, Pat Kelly, Jeff Leonard, and Amos Strunk (all Philadelphians). All were top players. Of this group, Scioscia was one of the finest catchers of his era, Davis was a two-time home run leader, Weaver hit .272 before getting involved in the Chicago Black Sox scandal, Leonard was a Rookie of the Year, Stanky was one of the fiercest competitors in baseball, and Strunk hit .284 during an illustrious 17-year career.

In recent decades, the Delaware Valley has not been regarded as an especially productive baseball area. The focus on finding players with major league potential has switched to areas in warmer climates such as California, Arizona, and Florida where teams play many more games and some take to the field throughout the year. Players in those sections of the country are considered more suitable for professional baseball.

That view, however, has exceptions. While it may be true that more players are signed out of the South, it cannot be said that the North—and in this case, the Philadelphia area—is without talent. Far from it. Witness what has happened locally in recent years.

It may come as a surprise, but since the start of the 21st century, no less than 29 players who were born in the Philadelphia area appeared in the major leagues. The list includes players such as Piazza, Moyer, Mabry, Manto, and Martinez mentioned above, plus others with varying lengths of time spent in the big leagues.

Among the more notable of these players are outfielders Kevin Mench (Wilmington) and Bobby Higginson (Philadelphia); infielders Sean Casey (Willingboro) and Joe McEwing (Bristol); catchers Ben Davis (Chester), Mike DiFelice (Philadelphia), and Chris Widger (Wilmington); and pitchers Taylor Buckholz (Lower Merion), Casey Fossum (Cherry Hill), Mike Koplove (Philadelphia), and Scott Schoenweiss (Long Branch, New Jersey).

Others who have appeared in the majors since 2000 are outfielders Cliff Brumbaugh and Pedro Swann (both from Wilmington); infielders Shawn Gilbert and Mike Moriarity (both from Camden), and Kevin Orie (West Chester); catcher Jesse Levis (Philadelphia); and pitchers Bob File and Scott Forster (both from Philadelphia), Wayne Franklin (Wilmington), Brett Laxton

(Stratford, New Jersey), Blaine Neal (Marlton, New Jersey), Dan Meyer (Woodbury, New Jersey), and Bryan Ward (Bristol).

To add one more category, of the 17 men from the area who have managed major league teams, two—Scioscia and Joe Kerrigan (Philadelphia)—did it in the 21st century. Two others—Tommy Lasorda (Norristown) and Joe McCarthy (Philadelphia)—are in the Hall of Fame, and five more—Lee Elia, Billy Shettsline, and Wilson (all Philadelphians), Green, and Lobert—piloted the Phillies.

In other words, the Philadelphia area has made a substantial contribution to major league baseball, both recently and in the past. And some of the players who have helped to do that have even made substantial contributions to the Phillies.

To reiterate, the lists above include only those born in the Philadelphia area, and do not include players who were only raised in the area. Among those raised but not born here are Hack Wilson, Orel Hershiser, Andre Thornton, Len Barker, Howie Bedell, Bob Sebra, Earl Rapp, and most recently David Bush.

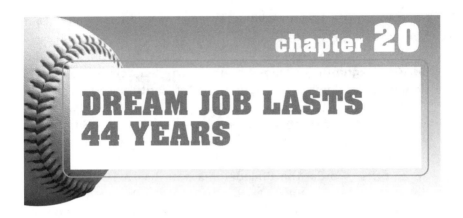

chapter 20

DREAM JOB LASTS 44 YEARS

In the ever-changing world of professional sports, very few jobs in the front office are for life. With rare exceptions, the majority of posts switch occupants fairly frequently.

Job changes are almost a given when new ownership arrives. Promotions, demotions, opportunities elsewhere, plus burnout, in-house politics, and, of course, firings rank among the major reasons people leave jobs where long hours and heavy pressure are unavoidable byproducts of the sports business.

And then there's Larry Shenk. Check the directory of baseball jobholders, and "The Baron," as he's widely known, doesn't have much competition for longevity. And he doesn't have *any* competition among the public relations directors of major league teams. That's because Shenk has served in the Phillies' public relations department for 44 years, and there isn't anybody, not a soul, who has handled PR for a major league baseball team for that long. Matter of fact, there isn't anybody on the Phillies, either, who has been with the club that many years in succession.

The unflappable, friendly, and astute Shenk, who retired in 2008 as vice president, public relations, goes back to a time when baseball was played almost entirely on grass, when Sunday doubleheaders were common, and when ballparks were where people came solely to watch games. Back when Shenk broke in, batters knew how to bunt, pitchers knew not to stall, and even umpires knew to avoid arguments.

The Baron was a rookie the same year as Dick Allen. When Shenk began with the Phillies, Gene Mauch was the manager and John Quinn was the general manager. Mike Schmidt was just 14 years old. Jimmy Rollins was 14 years away from being born.

Since he began in October 1963 as the Phils' director of public relations, Shenk has worked under four team presidents and two ownership groups. During his tenure, the Phillies have played in three ballparks in Philadelphia and two in Clearwater. They've had 17 managers. Six general managers. And the team has won one World Series, played in two others, and appeared in postseason playoffs eight times.

Shenk has been on the scene for 22 winning seasons. He's seen the Phillies win 90 or more games in a season seven times and lose 90 or more games in a season 10 times. He was around for the Phils' infamous 1964 collapse and the team's spectacular 2007 finish. And he's seen the club draw more than three million fans one year and barely more than 500,000 another.

There is precious little Larry Shenk hasn't seen during a rewarding career in which he has been one of the most respected and best-liked PR people in sports. It has been a career that has lasted 15 years longer than the next-longest current baseball PR person, and over the years has earned for him numerous honors and awards, not the least of which is the Robert O. Fishel Award presented in 1983 by Major League Baseball for "excellence in the field of public relations."

And to think, it took the "Dean of Major League PR Directors" three tries before he got the job.

Shenk is a native of Myerstown, Pennsylvania, where he attended the local high school before graduating in 1961 from Millersville State College with a degree in elementary education. His first job was as a reporter for the Lebanon (Pennsylvania) *Daily News*. While there, the job as the Phillies' director of public relations opened. Shenk applied, but was turned down.

One year later, the job opened again, and again Shenk sent in his application. Once more it was rejected. Soon afterward, he was hired by Wilmington *News-Journal* sports editor Al Cartwright as a sportswriter covering high school and some University of Delaware games.

Incredibly, about 10 months later, the Phillies job became vacant again. First Mort Berry, then Bob Chandler had left the job. Now Charlie Beck was departing.

"I was working nights with Hal Bodley, and he said, 'Why don't you apply?'" recalled Shenk. "I said, 'Well, I did apply the last two years in a row and didn't get the job. I think I'm learning good journalism under you and Al. I just got married, I'm living in Wilmington, so I don't think I'll apply this time.' And Hal said, 'I think you could do a good job. You ought to apply.'

"I realized these jobs aren't going to come along very often, so I sat down to type out a letter. I used that brown newspaper copy paper they used to have. Along the way, I had to switch typewriters. The second one had a different font. But I sent the letter in."

This time, Shenk was called in for an interview. And at the tender age of 25, he was offered the job on the spot. "I called my wife Julie," Shenk said. "She was concerned about becoming a baseball widow. We only had one car. She would be stuck in an apartment on the other side of Wilmington, while I had to drive all the way to Connie Mack Stadium. But I took the job. When I look back, I don't know how we did it."

To say that Shenk began the job under trying circumstances is putting it mildly. In his first full year, the Phillies, on the way to their first National League pennant in 14 years, lost 10 straight games late in the season and blew a six and one-half game lead with 12 games left to play. It was a horrifying disaster that ravaged the psyche of the whole city.

"That was the low point of my career," Shenk said. "We were so busy planning for a World Series, and then, before you knew it, it was over. It didn't sink in at the moment. Everything was a real blur. But as time went on, it became bigger and bigger."

Over the years, there were some other tough times. Bad teams, bad seasons, bad players, some of whom got in trouble with the law. "It was difficult," said Shenk, "because you had a job to do. I always said that if you had a bad team, you had to work twice as hard to get exposure. If you had a great team, you had to work twice as hard to keep up with the demand for players. The one good thing was that every year you got to start over."

The PR department has grown considerably since Shenk joined the Phillies. Originally, he and a secretary were the only people in the office. In recent years, he managed a group of 13 people, each with specific duties that include public relations, dealing with the media, producing the team's publications, creative services, and handling community affairs.

At first, Shenk went on the road with the team. Although he stopped doing that many years ago, he always worked every day. He spent from nine to five at the office when the team was away and throughout the off-season. When the team was playing at home, he usually worked from nine in the morning until an hour or so after the game.

"The hours were deadly," Shenk remembered. "Sometimes you'd come back from a road trip in the wee hours of the morning, and have to be in at nine that morning. I remember one time, I saw my kids Sunday night, and the next time I saw them was the following Saturday. I'd get home when they were sleeping, and I'd be sleeping when they'd go to school in the morning. Fortunately, I had a great wife. She raised our two kids [Andy and Debi].

"When Bill Giles joined the team in 1969, I thought I would be gone because he might bring in his own people," Shenk added. "But he kept me, and he opened the doors for a lot of different things."

The main part of the job always involved dealing with the media on an everyday basis. But over the years, even that changed dramatically.

When Shenk joined the Phillies, the team was covered locally by the three Philadelphia daily newspapers, two wire services, a couple of radio stations, and an occasional television station. Eventually, daily papers from the suburbs and from more distant places such as Allentown, Lancaster, Reading, Trenton, and Atlantic City began covering the team, along with increasing numbers of radio and television stations. At one time, at least 15 members of the print media, plus another dozen or so broadcasters, regularly covered home games. While those numbers decreased in recent years—particularly because some papers, as their circulations dropped, stopped covering the team—other characteristics of the press box changed, too, especially after the Phils left Connie Mack Stadium and moved to Veterans Stadium.

Typewriters eventually were replaced by computers. A press dining room was added. More writers traveled with the visiting teams. The numbers of people in the broadcast booth expanded. More pregame information was made available. Instead of calling every member of the press with new information such as a trade, the PR department first faxed, then in later years e-mailed the latest developments. Even the ways articles were written and news was broadcast changed.

"It used to be, the print media just wrote game stories," Shenk recalled. "They didn't write notes columns. There were more radio stations covering games a couple of decades ago. TV rarely came around. Then instant news came along and changed things drastically."

TV stations want to put stories on the air immediately. They also push their own web sites with stories a viewer can no longer get on the evening news. Other organizations, such as Major League Baseball with its own writers, also have web sites. There are national publications, specialty writers, talk show hosts, cable TV stations, and statistical organizations flocking to the ballpark. Because of all this, as well as the race against the clock and the need to write something that hasn't already appeared somewhere else, the newspaper guys have to do their pieces differently.

"This is a very competitive town," said Shenk. "It's competitive between print and broadcast media, between one newspaper and another, even between the beat writer and columnist on the same paper. It's been challenging to stay one step ahead. You learn what the media is looking for. You learn where the potholes are. And you learn where the hot buttons are. I've always said that do to my job, you need round shoulders so the stuff can roll off your back."

The media sometimes doesn't portray things quite the same way Shenk sees them. But he reacts calmly. "If there's a fact that's incorrect, I can correct it," he said. "But if it's a writer's own opinion, there's nothing I can do about it. I don't scream and yell. And I don't expect to be screamed and yelled at. We're in the business of communications, and I try to treat people the way I'd want to be treated."

But, while it's not always easy dealing with the press, there are times when dealing with Phillies players has not been easy, either. Some have gotten into trouble. Some, like Steve Carlton, refused to talk with the media.

"Lefty was different, but he was pretty smart," Shenk recalled. "He was a very interesting character. He had his own mind, but he could be a lot of fun. After he was here a couple of years, there were some things written about him that he didn't like. He said, 'Why do I need to spend my time with the media? I gave my answers. Then I picked up the paper the next day, and they've taken what I've said out of context. So if they can't quote me accurately, why should I spend my time with them? If I don't talk to them, that's to their benefit. Now, they can be more creative.'"

On the other hand, Shenk said, "Pete Rose was a media delight. Schmitty [Mike Schmidt] was hot and cold with the media, [Curt] Schilling was always there for the media. So was

No public relations director in baseball served longer for one team than Larry Shenk did with the Phillies.

Mitch [Williams]. John Kruk was the biggest pain in the butt I dealt with as a player. Most of the time, he wouldn't do interviews. Now, he's a guy who's making his living in the media.

"Darren Daulton was my savior with the 1993 club. That was a really difficult team. You'd have a clubhouse full of media, and the players are all in the trainer's room [off limits to the media]. After every game, Darren would go in to get ice on his knees. I'd need him for an interview, and I'd go in to get him. He'd say, 'Give me five minutes and I'll be out.' Or, if I needed somebody else, he'd say, 'Mul [Terry Mulholland], get out there,' or 'Dude [Lenny Dykstra], get out there.' He was just great."

Shenk said that the foremost character during his stint was Jay Johnstone, a prankster who was known for his sense of humor. Roger Freed was another unforgettable character. And Del Ennis was a special favorite of Shenk's.

"I didn't really know baseball until I was about 12 years old," Shenk remembered. "That was the Whiz Kids era. I went to games, tried to get autographs. I identified with that team. Ennis was my hero."

One night, long after Shenk had joined the Phillies, he went to the Warwick Hotel where the team was entertaining a gathering of Whiz Kids who'd returned to Philadelphia for a reunion. "I saw the sun come up," he said. "I never went to bed. And now, I'm writing obituaries about those guys."

Shenk's fondest memories on the job focus on two events. "One was the parade down Broad Street to JFK Stadium after we won the World Series in 1980," he said. "The other was the closing of Veterans Stadium. That was our home. We lived there for 33 years. That final day was a very touching experience."

Phillies president and CEO David Montgomery asked Shenk to put together a program to commemorate the stadium at the final game. Shenk checked into the ways other teams had closed their stadiums, and came up with a plan that would far surpass the others. One of the highlights of his plan was the on-field participation of 120 former players. In addition, Carlton pantomimed a pitch, Schmidt did the same with a swing, and an ailing Tug McGraw rode in from the bullpen. At the end, as the present team converged on the diamond, the 120 Phillies alumni spontaneously did a final lap around the field. It was a magnificent show that took more than six months to assemble, and even the most hardened individual had trouble keeping a dry eye.

The event ably demonstrated The Baron's talents as a master innovator. During his career, he produced a highly informative publication called *Phillies Phan-O-Gram* that for many years was mailed to season ticket holders and others. He wrote a column for small newspapers that didn't cover the team called "The Baron's Corner." He devised a collection of facts, figures, and anecdotes called "Newsy Notes" that was regularly passed out to the media.

Then there was Shenk's creation of the *Phillies Media Guide*. It was a project with which he is inexorably linked.

When Shenk joined the club, many teams had media guides, but not the Phillies. Shenk felt that they should have one, too. So before the 1964 season, he went to top management with a proposal.

"I had come across a media guide that Lebanon Valley College had for its football team," he recalled. "I said, 'Look, even a tiny place like Lebanon Valley has a media guide. We should have one, too.' But they said, 'No, no, it's not necessary. And it's too expensive.' So without asking anybody's permission, we did one ourselves, Julie and I."

Larry, who had found some long-forgotten team records in a dusty old filing cabinet, produced the inside material. Then, the Shenks mimeographed each page, and, spreading them all over their living room floor, collated them. Julie drew and colored each cover individually. Finally, they came up with a guide that was 58 pages with no pictures. They had 300 copies printed. It was a crude, low-budget project, but the Phillies had their first media guide. Today, the team's book-sized media guide is in excess of 350 pages. And the original one is an extremely rare and valuable collectors item that has sold for as much as $600.

Over the years, Shenk launched the Phillies' Caravan, a two-week, midwinter event in which the team takes players to functions in outlying areas. He built a dreary Phillies game program into a slick, glossy magazine. He took writers to the Instructional League and out to dinner each spring with the team's manager. He set up midwinter luncheons where the media could interview players and the manager. He addressed the entire team each year at spring training about how to deal with the media. Overall, he began or directed more projects than this chapter has room to mention.

In December 2007, then 69 years old, feeling like he had done as much as he could, and wanting to spend more time with his wife, two children, and two grandchildren, Shenk decided it was finally time to retire. Actually, he was still on the job at spring training the following year.

"I remember one spring, Jim Fregosi was giving me a hard time," Shenk reminisced. "I said, 'Jimmie, just remember one thing. I will outlast you.' We fired him that October. We had a press conference, and when he was leaving, he put his arm around me and said, 'Well, you were right.'

"This has been a job where you just worked all the time. If you don't want to work in this business, you don't succeed. I had a dream and I was able to live it. Sure, the media threw in some nightmares. And I realized early that I wasn't the smartest guy in the business. But I made a vow to myself that I would do a little bit more. And I did, and it was the right thing to do. Now, all of the sudden, I've been here 44 years. Where did the time go?

"When I took this job, it was a dream come true," Shenk added. "It was something I always wanted to do. I was able to live my dream. And I feel blessed that I could do that."

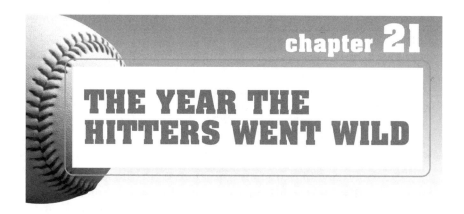

chapter 21

THE YEAR THE HITTERS WENT WILD

hat happens when one of the best offensive teams of all time is combined with one of the worst pitching staffs ever?

The answer should be obvious: The team loses 102 games and is buried so deep in last place that it not only finishes 40 games out of first, but seven games behind the team right above it.

That, of course, confirms the ageless belief that good pitching is far more important to a team than good hitting. Or, as Connie Mack, also known as "The Tall Tactician," once said, "Pitching is 75 percent of the game."

The 1930 Phillies certainly did not contradict that perceptive pronouncement. In fact, they might be one of the staunchest supporters of that theory ever assembled.

This was a club, after all, that had a team batting average of .315, third highest in National League history. It also had a pitching staff that posted the highest earned run average (6.71) of all time, while giving up more runs (1,199) and more hits (1,993) than any collection of flingers ever did since the game, as we now know it, began.

The end product of this almost unimaginable dichotomy is that in 1930 the Phillies had one of the worst teams that ever embarrassed the good name that Al Reach had bestowed on it. In a franchise fraught with woeful teams, the inglorious record of 102 losses (with 52 wins and two ties) of the 1930 Phils is exceeded in number of losses by only 11 other Phillies teams. And only 12 other teams in the 125 years of the franchise had a worse won-lost percentage than the 1930 club's .340 mark. But they had no pitching *and* no hitting. The 1930 Phils had no pitching, but spectacular hitting.

Obviously, it wasn't the pitching that the 299,007 fans who attended games at Baker Bowl that season came out to see. Along with its other exploits, the staff struck out just 384 hitters in 1,373 innings that year. And three of the Phils' top six hurlers had earned run averages over 7.50.

The only ray of sunshine (all games in those days were played in the afternoon) on the staff was a guy whose nickname was Figety Phil. Miraculously, Phil Collins posted a 16-11 record while completing 17 of the 25 games he started. He also made 22 relief appearances and finished the season with what could be considered a remarkable 4.78 ERA.

Ray Benge also won in double figures with 11 wins against 15 losses. But he had a 5.69 ERA and gave up a whopping 305 hits in 226 innings. After Benge, only one pitcher won as many as seven games, and that was Les Sweetland, whose 7.71 ERA in 34 games gives pause to wonder how he ever compiled a record as good as 7-15.

The great future Hall of Famer, Grover Cleveland Alexander, was also on the staff, returning to the Phillies for his final year in the big leagues. Before getting released in June, Alex worked in nine games and was 0-3. Others with highly forgettable nicknames and even more forgettable records were Snipe Hansen (0-7, 6.75), Hap Collard (6-12, 6.80), and Weeping Willie Willoughby (4-17, 7.59). Another pitcher, Hal Elliott, added a 6-11 record with a 7.69 ERA, but trudged to the mound 48 times to lead the league in appearances.

Weeping Willie (real name Claude) was featured in a rare bit of Phillies humor during the 1930 season. One day team captain Fresco Thompson was filling out the lineup card to deliver to home plate umpire Bill Klem. Willoughby was slated to be the starting pitcher. But mindful of the Phils' hapless mound corps, Thompson had a burst of whimsy. In the pitcher's spot on the lineup card, he wrote, "Willoughby and others."

There was little comedy for manager Burt Shotton. He had joined the Phillies in 1928, and immediately lost 109 games. Shotton kicked the team all the way up to fifth place in 1929, posting an amazing 71-82 record. Other than in 1932 when the Phils finished in the first division for the only time over a 31-year period, the 1929 team posted the best record for the Phillies between 1917 and 1949.

But the Phils had fallen back on hard times in 1930, thanks to their pitching staff. Once, a writer asked Shotton, "How can you finish last with such a hitting club?" To which Burt replied, "Have you looked at my pitching by any chance?"

Pitching, though, wasn't the only disaster area on the club. Phillies fielders played as though they had holes in their mitts. They had the worst fielding average (.962) in the league, they made more errors (239) than any other team, and the keystone combination of Thompson at second base and Tommy Thevenow at shortstop made 88 errors between them with the later contributing 56 of them.

In the interest of full disclosure, however, it must be stated that both Thevenow and third baseman Pinky Whitney led the league in putouts and assists for their positions, and right fielder Chuck Klein set a modern (since 1900) National League record for outfielders with 44 assists.

Ah, but the offense—it was sensational. Although the New York Giants that same season set an all-time National League record with a team batting average of .319 (while remarkably finishing in only third place), the Phillies' .315 mark wasn't far behind. What's more, it was one point ahead of the team average of the St. Louis Cardinals, that year's World Series winner over the Philadelphia Athletics.

Phillies batters had some splendid seasons in 1930. Klein hit .386 while clubbing 40 home runs, driving in 170, setting a modern league record with 158 runs scored, hitting in 26 straight games two different times during the season, and reaching base safely in 135 of the Phils' 156 games. Left fielder Lefty O'Doul, who had set a National League record the year before with 254 hits, swatted the pill for a .383 mark with 21 homers and 97 RBI. Whitney hit .342; Barney Friberg, who rotated around the infield, hit .341; first baseman Don Hurst hit .327, and catcher Spud Davis hit .313. The lowest average among regulars was the .280 compiled by center fielder Denny Sothern. And two utilitymen, catcher Harry McCurdy and first baseman Monk Sherlock, hit .331 and .324, respectively.

The Phillies' offense that year had more hits (1,783) and more at-bats (5,667) than any other NL team. In fact, no other team in major league history has ever had that many hits in one season. The Giants' Bill Terry with his .401 average and NL record-tying 254 hits kept Klein and O'Doul from the batting title, but Klein led the league in total bases, runs, and doubles, while finishing second to the Chicago Cubs' Hack Wilson in home runs, RBI, and slugging average. The Phils' only weakness on offense seemed to be its lack of speed. The entire club stole just 34 bases—Thompson was the leader with seven— and poked only 44 triples, 23 below the next lowest team and 75 behind the league-leading Pittsburgh Pirates.

There were, of course, attempts to explain the Phillies' astounding offense. Although the ball had become much livelier, spitball pitchers had been outlawed, and a batter was not charged with an at-bat if he advanced a runner with a fly ball, these charitable donations to a hitter's average had been around for a while. No, they were not the reasons.

The reason for the last-place Phillies' robust hitting was largely attributable to the club's oddly shaped ballpark, an aging dump known as Baker Bowl that was set on a rectangular city block instead of one that was square. It was 341.5 feet down the left field line and 408 feet to center. Respectable distances. But the distance down the right field line was in another category. The tin wall that ran from right field to dead center was just 280.5 feet down the line from home plate. The wall was 40 feet high, above which was a 12-foot screen that Phils owner William Baker had added in 1929 in an unfathomable attempt to decrease Klein's—his own player, for crying out loud—home run production so he couldn't demand a higher salary. "Home runs have become too cheap at the Philadelphia ballpark," alibied Baker, who in 1913 had named the ballpark after himself.

The height of the wall was almost irrelevant. What mattered was the wall's proximity to the batter's box. Just like the nearby right field fence at the Giants' Polo Grounds, Baker Bowl's right field wall was little more than a pop fly away, and balls flew over and against it with frightening regularity.

Baker Bowl's right field wall was so close to the basepaths that future Pulitzer Prize-winning sportswriter Red Smith, then

When the Phillies hit .315 as a team in 1930, two of the
top hitters were Lefty O'Doul (left) and Chuck Klein.

covering the Phillies for a Philadelphia newspaper, once said,
"If the right fielder had eaten onions for lunch, the second baseman sure knew it."

"If you hit a line drive down the right field line," said Phillies'
right fielder Johnny Moore, "you had to run like hell to first
base. If you didn't, you were liable to get thrown out because
the right fielder was playing so close."

Often, line drives that would've been home runs in any other
park clanked against the wall—sometimes even puncturing
holes in its rusted façade—and went for singles or doubles. And

balls that would have dropped harmlessly into right fielders' gloves flew over the wall and onto Broad Street for home runs, frequently breaking the windshields of passing cars. That happened so often, in fact, that the Phillies had a standing policy. Drivers with broken windshields could come around to the front gate and get reimbursed for the damage.

The damage was done mostly, though, to any poor soul who had the misfortune of standing on the mound at Baker Bowl and throwing balls to hitters. Doing it with any degree of success was a virtual impossibility.

In 77 games played at Baker Bowl in 1930, the Phillies scored 543 runs (944 overall), which was more than even the mighty 1927 New York Yankees of Babe Ruth and Lou Gehrig—the best team in baseball history—tallied at Yankee Stadium. Opponents scored 644 runs. The average score of games was 8-7 in favor of the opposition. There wasn't a single shutout pitched all season at the ballpark that was often called a "bandbox."

Whether playing at home or away, though, there were times when the opposition was especially brutal. During the Phillies' season of woe, opposing teams scored 20 or more runs 10 times against the Phils. The Cardinals and Giants each belted 26 hits in games. In those batting sprees, St. Louis won, 19-16, with the Phillies slamming 16 hits, and New York triumphed, 19-8.

Among other slugfests, the Phillies blasted 21 hits—five by O'Doul—in a 13-3 win over the Cards, and 22 hits in a 13-12 loss to the Giants. Klein's four hits led a 20-hit, 18-14 win for the Phils over the Pirates in a game in which the losers clubbed 14 hits. With Wilson hitting for the cycle, the Chicago Cubs took down Phils pitching for 24 hits in a 21-8 win, the Brooklyn Dodgers collected 23 hits in a 14-3 victory, the Giants collared an 18-5 triumph while getting 25 hits, and the Dodgers punched out 24 hits to capture a 22-8 verdict.

The Phillies set a club record with 27 hits in a 16-15 win over the Pirates, who had 23 hits. The next day, the Phils lost to the Cubs, 19-15, with each team pounding 17 hits. The Phillies also beat the Pirates, 15-14, while collecting 16 hits to the Bucs' 22.

Amazingly, shutouts were not totally absent when the Phillies were on the road. Willoughby and Sweetland combined to blank the Cincinnati Reds, 18-0, at Crosley Field in a game in which the Phils jabbed out 21 hits, none being a home run. The Phils also played in three 1-0 shutouts during the season, including a 1-0 victory for Sweetland on opening day against the Dodgers at Ebbets Field.

Such well-pitched games, however, were highly unusual. In a year when Phillies hitters went wild while Phillies pitchers took early showers, high-scoring games with a multitudinous number of hits were the norm. It was a year like no other in Phillies history.

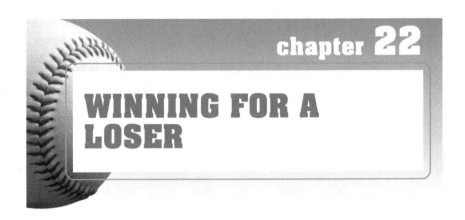

WINNING FOR A LOSER

Hardly anything in baseball is more riveting than a lengthy streak. It's exciting, it's something that creates widespread interest, and it's closely followed on a day-to-day basis. Often, streaks command as much attention as any other part of the game.

There are, of course, all kinds of streaks. Some are more riveting than others. But depending on their length and importance, streaks are a major part of the baseball landscape.

Naturally, teams, including the Phillies, have their own lists of streaks. Among the more imposing Phillies streaks, Jimmy Rollins hit safely in 38 straight games, Mike Schmidt played in 18 straight years with the club, Danny Litwhiler went 187 straight games in left field without committing an error, and Grover Cleveland Alexander pitched 41.2 consecutive scoreless innings.

Another especially noteworthy Phillies streak was the one accomplished in 1972 when Steve Carlton won 15 games in a row. That feat broke a club record that had stood since 1886 when a brilliant hurler named Charlie Ferguson won 12 straight games for the fourth-place Phillies during a season in which he won 30 games, including two complete-game victories on the same day.

Carlton's streak fell short of the major league record of 19 straight wins shared by two New York Giants pitchers, Tim Keefe in 1888 and Rube Marquard in 1912. But it was an extraordinary streak, nonetheless, one major reason being that it came during a season in which the Phillies had one of their poorest teams. The '72 Phils won just 59 games (losing 97) while finishing in last place, 37 $1/2$ games out of first. Not only did Carlton win 15 straight games, he posted a remarkable 27-10 record, which in terms of wins represented nearly 46 percent of the team's total victories.

The streak by the Phillies' slender lefthander was achieved in his first season with the club. Carlton had joined the team as the result of a rather bizarre trade, the last one made by Phillies general manager John Quinn during a career than began with the team in 1959.

As the story goes, Carlton was in the midst of a contract squabble with the St. Louis Cardinals' general manager Bing Devine. Steve had joined the Cards' regular rotation in 1967, and in a little more than five seasons had won 77 games, including 20 in 1971.

Likewise, Phillies top pitcher Rick Wise was in a salary dispute with Quinn following a season when he had pitched a no-hitter and hit two home runs in that game and won 17, which ran his win total in the previous three seasons to 45. Neither hurler could get the money he thought he deserved. Both were reportedly looking for $65,000 salaries, Carlton having earned $45,000 the previous year and Wise having received $32,000.

When Devine suggested to Quinn that the teams trade their star pitchers, the Phils' GM quickly placed a call to Paul Owens, the club's farm director and soon-to-be GM. "I have a chance to trade Wise for Carlton," Quinn said, "What do you think?"

"Run as fast as you can to the nearest phone" was one version of Owens' reply.

Quinn also consulted with Phillies owner Bob Carpenter and manager Frank Lucchesi, each of whom strongly supported the deal. On February 25, 1972, the swap was made. Wise went to the Cardinals where he continued a career that lasted for 18 years and would see him finish with an 188-181 record. And Carlton came to Philadelphia where he spent 14 $1/2$ seasons during a 24-year career that led him to the Hall of Fame as the second-winningest lefthander in baseball history with 329 victories (244 losses).

Although initially, the trade was extremely unpopular because Wise was a fan favorite and the top hurler on the pitching staff, Carlton soon won over hardened Phillies followers with his marvelous talent. Possessing a lazer-like fastball and a virtually unhittable slider, Carlton on the mound was a menacing figure that not even the heartiest hitters cared to face.

"Hitting him is like trying to drink coffee with a fork," said Pittsburgh Pirates slugger Willie Stargell.

In 1972, Bob Boone was a catcher recently converted from a third baseman and on his way up through the Phillies system. Later in the '72 season, he was brought up to the parent club and earned a starting role that he held for the next nine years of an 18-year career. He got a chance to be Carlton's battery mate that year in spring training.

"I was still in the minor leagues then," Boone said, "but I got the chance to catch him in a couple of games. The first time I did, it was like, wow, this guy is unbelievable. It was like going from a Volkswagen to a Mercedes. Later, I became the team's regular catcher, and I can tell you, he was the best I ever caught. I never saw anyone throw as hard or with a slider that dropped off like his. He was awesome."

Carlton was never more awesome than in the 1972 season. On April 15, he was the starting pitcher in the first of what would be 14 opening-day starts with the Phillies. Pitching just after a two-week players strike had ended, Carlton allowed four hits in eight innings to beat the Chicago Cubs and Ferguson Jenkins, who was coming off a 24-win, Cy Young season, 4-2, at Wrigley Field.

Three weeks later on May 7, Carlton notched his fifth win in six decisions as he bettered the San Francisco Giants, 8-3, at Veterans Stadium, which was starting its second year of operation. After that game, however, "Lefty," as he was called, fell into a funk, losing five games in a row. He went into a June 7 game with the Houston Astros carrying a 5-6 record. The Phillies had won just one game in their previous 20 outings. Carlton beat the Astros, 3-1, at the Vet, working seven innings, yielding five hits, and striking out 11. Four days later, still in Philadelphia, Carlton entered the victory column again, topping the Atlanta Braves, 3-1, hurling his first complete game since May 7 while giving up eight hits and fanning nine. During the streak, Carlton would hurl 14 straight complete games.

In Carlton's next outing on June 16, he got no decision, but fired one of his best games of the season. After 10 innings in a game against the Astros at Houston, the score was 0-0. Carlton left for a pinch-hitter in the 11th inning after yielding just six hits. Houston scored in the bottom of the 11th to win, 1-0.

Then on June 25, he blanked the host Montreal Expos in another 1-0 game in a raucous affair that included a 46-minute rain delay and a free-for-all that began after Carlton hit Tim Foli with a pitch. While the Expos' shortstop was being carried off the field on a stretcher and taken to a nearby hospital, a brawl erupted when Montreal manager Gene Mauch charged out of the dugout and up to the mound where he took a punch at Carlton. About 10 more Expos tried to get to Carlton. By the time order was restored, Carlton had been kicked in the side of his head, which produced a sizeable bruise, and had slightly injured his arm. He stayed in the game, however, and went the distance, allowing just four hits and striking out eight. Afterward, Lucchesi was so pleased that he awarded $10 extra dinner money to each player.

Carlton went on to beat the New York Mets, 9-4 (seven hits, 13 strikeouts), the Giants, 4-2 (six, seven), the San Diego Padres, 4-2 (nine, eight), the Los Angeles Dodgers, 4-1 (five, eight), the Padres, 3-2 (seven, eight), the Dodgers, 2-0 (five, six), the Cubs, 2-0 (three, seven), and the Mets, 4-1 (five, five) for his 11th straight win. Along the way, Carlton almost saw his streak ended when on July 15 at Candlestick Park, he gave up five hits and four runs in five innings, and left for a pinch-hitter in the sixth with the Giants winning, 4-0. But the Phillies exploded with 11 runs in the seventh to get Carlton off the hook en route to an 11-4 triumph.

Unlike today's starters who pitch every fifth or sixth day, Carlton was working virtually every game on four days rest. "It keeps you sharp, strong, and eager," he told reporters.

On August 5, Carlton tied Ferguson's club record with a 5-0 (five, seven) victory over his old team, the St. Louis Cardinals, at Busch Stadium. "Beating the Cardinals before the home folks was a pleasant experience, but I really didn't get any more satisfaction than I would have against any other club," said Carlton, who after the trade had retained his residence in St. Louis.

In one of the Phillies' top pitching performances of all time, Steve Carlton won 15 straight games and 27 games for a club that totaled just 59 victories.

Carlton won his 13th straight with a 12-strikeout, three-hit, 2-0 victory over the Pirates, then the best hitting team in baseball. The victory, coming August 9 at Three Rivers Stadium, marked Lefty's seventh shutout of the season. Then, his 14th win in a row came August 13 at the Vet on a 2-1 win over the Expos in a game that was played in one hour and 45 minutes.

The big southpaw captured his 15th win on August 17 with a cheering, foot-stomping crowd of 53,277 jamming into Veterans Stadium. Allowing seven hits but striking out only two, Carlton captured a 9-4 victory over the Cincinnati Reds, at the time the leaders in the West Division by five and one-half games and on their way to building a powerhouse known as "The Big Red Machine." It was Carlton's 20th win of the season, making him only the seventh hurler in big league history to win that many games for a last-place team. It also marked the first time a National League hurler had won 15 or more games in a row since 1962 when former Phillie Jack Sanford won 16 straight for the Giants. (In the American League, Dave McNally of the Baltimore Orioles won 15 in a row in 1969.)

After the game, in response to the relentless cheers of the fans, Carlton left the clubhouse and returned to the field where he spent 15 minutes waving and signing autographs. Ironically, the win came on the birthday of Carlton's wife, Beverly.

The streak ended four days later on August 21 at the Vet when Carlton bowed to the Braves, 2-1, in 11 innings on a broken-bat single by Mike Lum. Although Carlton allowed only seven hits and struck out 10 while going the distance, it was his first loss since May 30 when he was beaten by the Mets.

"It was too bad I couldn't keep it going. It was a lot of fun," he told the media.

At the time, Carlton was still speaking to the media. About one year later, he began to limit his contact with members of the press, eventually breaking off all communications by 1978.

The reasons Carlton went silent are varied. "It was a combination of things. I don't think it was any one thing," said Larry Shenk, the Phillies' director of public relations. "People had been writing a lot of negative things. Other articles were written that quoted him as having said things he claimed he hadn't said at all. 'If they get it all wrong, why should I waste my time talking to them,' he told me."

Philadelphia Daily News sportswriter Bill Conlin, in his book, *Batting Cleanup*, said that Carlton stopped talking to him well before he clammed up to others. Conlin attributed the pitcher's silence to an article he had written about him that Carlton didn't like. The situation magnified, and eventually Carlton stopped talking to all media members. Tim McCarver, who became the pitcher's designated catcher, emerged as his spokesman, too.

When asked years later about that role, McCarver bristled at the description. "I was never his spokesman," said the catcher turned television broadcaster. "I spoke for myself."

For the most part, over the years, Carlton seldom strayed from his muteness. But in the summer of 2007, he gave a rare interview about his streak for this chapter.

How was he able to maintain the streak? "You just go out and be a regular pitcher on a day-to-day basis," he said. "You can't get caught up in the moment. You have to be prepared on the particular day you're pitching and dedicate yourself to that day. Right then, that's the only day that matters, and you have to get through it.

"I didn't get involved in the momentum of the streak," he added. "I didn't worry about what happened yesterday or what was going to happen tomorrow. Before each game, I went over the pitches I normally threw. Then I'd go out and build on that, and try not to make any mistakes."

The result was one of the most amazing achievements in baseball history: 15 straight wins and seven victories in his final 10 decisions to give him 27 wins overall with a team that had the third worst record that year in the major leagues. An 11-1 victory over the Cubs at Wrigley Field gave Carlton his final win of the season on October 3.

Carlton went on that year to win his first of four Cy Young Awards. He also broke Jim Bunning's single-season record for most strikeouts by a Phillies pitcher (268 set in 1967) by fanning 310 batters in 41 starts. He finished the season with eight shutouts—the most for a Phillies pitcher since Grover Cleveland Alexander registered 16 of them in 1916—and 30 complete games, a figure that has been reached only once (by Jim Hunter in 1975) since then. And along with wins, strikeouts, and complete games, he also led the National League in earned run average (1.97) and innings pitched (346).

For Carlton, who would become the first Phillies player to earn a $100,000 salary, who was the highest-paid pitcher in baseball when he signed in early 1973 for $165,000, who won more than 20 games with the team five times, and whose 241 victories are the highest total for a Phils pitcher, the 1972 season ranks as one of the best any hurler ever had.

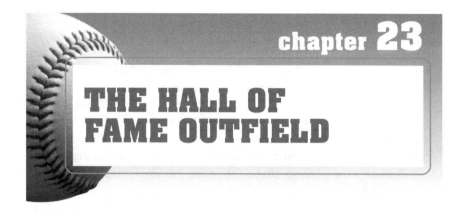

chapter 23

THE HALL OF FAME OUTFIELD

When it comes to major league outfields, there is no question which one ranks as the greatest of all time. The winner by a landslide is the Phillies' outfield of 1894.

This was an outfield in which a player named George (Tuck) Turner hit .416. And he wasn't even a regular.

How in the world could that be, you ask? Simple. The three regular outfielders all hit above .400, too. Each one was destined for a berth in the Hall of Fame.

Their names were Ed Delahanty, Billy Hamilton, and Sam Thompson. While they may not be household names in the minds of today's Phillies fans, the three rank among the top 10 Phillies players of all time.

Left fielder Delahanty is arguably the greatest hitter in Phillies history. Center fielder Hamilton is certainly the club's top base-stealer. Right fielder Thompson was the team's first power hitter. And all three were superb fielders, ranking among the best in the National League.

"The pride and delight of the Philadelphia crowds," famed sportswriter Fred Lieb once wrote, "was the crack outfield."

In 13 seasons with the Phillies, the righthanded-hitting Delahanty led the National League in home runs twice, in slugging average and doubles four times, in RBI three times, and in triples, stolen bases, and batting average once when he hit .410 in 1899. Delahanty hit above .400 three times while playing with the Phillies. He is either first or second in nine all-time Phillies offensive categories.

Ed Delahanty came out of Cleveland, Ohio, the oldest of five brothers to make the big leagues. Bought by the Phillies for $1,900 from a minor league team at Wheeling, West Virginia, Big Ed joined the Phils in 1888 at the age of 21. For most of the next 14 years—including one season in the Players' League in 1890—Delahanty was as fearsome a hitter as there was in the big leagues. Wielding one of the heaviest bats in the league with his huge, brawny arms, he was a notorious bad-ball hitter, but still hit ferocious line drives as well as towering swats.

Owner of a strong throwing arm, he was originally a second baseman—and later played all infield positions—before becoming a regular outfielder. His salary with the Phillies never went above $1,400. Known as a hard-drinking fun-lover who craved the night life and had legions of fans who followed him around, Delahanty's career was jammed with special achievements. He once had 10 straight hits. He went 6-for-6 twice. And in 1896, he became the second major leaguer to hit four home runs in one game in a 9-8 Phillies loss to the Chicago White Stockings. The feat so impressed Chicago pitcher Adonis Terry that he came to the plate and shook hands with Big Ed as he scored on the fourth homer. After the game, Delahanty was awarded a special bonus for his achievement. He was given four boxes of chewing gum—one for each home run.

During his six years with the Phillies, Billy Hamilton, a left-handed batter, won two batting titles—in 1891 with a .340 average and in 1893 with a .380 mark. His 1891 crown was the first for a Phillies player. Hamilton also led the league in hits, on-base percentage, and walks three times each, and in stolen bases four times. His 111 steals in 1891—coming one year after he'd swiped 102 bases—stood as a major league record until Lou Brock broke it in 1974.

A native of Newark, New Jersey, the electrifying Hamilton had arrived in Philadelphia in 1890 after the Phillies paid $5,000 for his services to the Kansas City Cowboys, a team that was dropping out of the fading American Association. Hamilton had stolen 117 bases for KC the year before.

Unlike Delahanty and Thompson, Hamilton was not a power hitter—with the Phillies he never hit more than seven homers in one season. The club's leadoff hitter, his forte was speed. It was said that he was "fast as a deer" yet "slippery as an eel" when he slid into base. Sliding Billy is the Phillies' all-time career stolen base king with 508, which ranks 96 above second-place Delahanty. Once, he stole at least one base in 13 straight games.

The lefthanded Sam Thompson played in 10 seasons with the Phillies and led the league in hits three times, in home runs and doubles twice apiece, and in RBI and slugging each once. Thompson's league-leading 20 home runs in 1889 were the most ever hit in the big leagues up to that point. He was also the first player to get 200 hits in one season and 300 total bases in one campaign.

Born in Danville, Indiana, Thompson, a quiet, modest man who never complained about an umpire's call, was an established star when the Phillies bought him for $5,000 from the Detroit Wolverines, a team that was going belly up in the National League. In 1887, he had led the league with a .372 batting average, while also topping the circuit with 166 RBI and 203 hits.

A solid outfielder who batted second in the Phillies' lineup, Thompson was the league's premier home-run hitter during his 10 years with the Phillies. Before the turn of the century, he hit more home runs than any other player. He also won the HR title in 1895 with 18 four-baggers, the same year his 165 RBI also led the league. And in 1893, he laced a league-leading 222 hits.

From 1892 to 1895 when they all played together and all had spectacular years, this trio ravaged National League pitching like no one has ever done before or since. During that time, one of them led the league in batting, hits, runs, RBI, home runs, doubles, triples, slugging average, total bases, walks, or stolen bases. Over that period, they had a combined batting average of .370.

The Phillies were one of the league's top clubs in those days. In a 12-team league, they finished fourth three times and third once between 1892 and 1895. Only once did they win more than 80 games, however, capturing 87 decisions in manager Harry Wright's next to last season in 1892.

The 1894 season, though, was the one that earned a special place in baseball history. It was the year that the Phillies' outfield has never been matched.

Major league baseball had undergone a colossal change the previous season when the distance between home plate and the pitching mound had been moved from 50 feet to 60 feet, six inches. Especially for pitchers, the difference was uncomfortable and required a difficult adjustment.

Pitchers had to change the way they threw. They had to alter their deliveries, adjust the breaks and bends of their pitches, and learn to throw the ball farther. Ten feet might not seem like much, but to pitchers in 1893, the additional distance represented an immense change. And big league pitching suffered because of that change.

The increased distance was an advantage to hitters, and they adjusted quickly to the change. Whereas National League hitters had hit a combined .245 in 1892, their average increased to .280 in 1893 and to .309 in 1894.

Nowhere was this improvement more pronounced than in Philadelphia. In 1892, the Phillies had a team batting average of .262. It jumped to a league-leading .301 the following year. Then in 1894, it exploded to .343, the highest mark in major league history. For the fourth-place Phillies (71-57), who finished 18 games behind the front-running Baltimore Orioles, that figure is 24 points above the modern ML record of .319 set in 1930 by the New York Giants.

The Phillies' record was in large part due to the spectacular seasons of the three outfielders. Delahanty and Thompson each hit .407, and Hamilton hit .404. And Tuck Turner, unable to crack the starting lineup except when he filled in for Thompson, who was sidelined for a time with an injury to his left hand, hit .416 while driving in 82 runs and scoring 91 in 80 games. The .405 combined average of the Phillies outfield set a major league record that far surpasses the modern mark of .367, set in 1925 by the Detroit Tigers' outfield led by Ty Cobb, Harry Heilmann, and Al Wingo.

Hamilton led the Phillies with 220 hits, followed by Delahanty with 199 and Thompson with 178. While neither Delahanty nor Thompson led the league in a single category, Hamilton topped the circuit in walks, on-base percentage, and in runs scored. His 196 runs rank as the all-time major league record, an astounding total that will never be challenged. Add that figure to the runs scored by Delahanty, Thompson, and Turner,

The 1890s Phillies outfield of Ed Delahanty (top left), Billy Hamilton (top right), and Sam Thompson (bottom left) all made the baseball Hall of Fame.

and the Phillies' quartet tallied an amazing 551 runs while collecting 441 RBI.

Never before and never since has one team had three players hit over .400 in a season. But then, never before and never since has a team had an outfield like Big Ed, Sliding Billy, and

Slugging Sam. Amazingly, in the season of their unparalleled achievement, the three were surpassed in the batting race by the Boston Beaneaters' Hugh Duffy, who set an all-time major league record with a .438 batting average. In the final figures, Delahanty and Thompson tied for second, and Hamilton placed fourth.

At a time when the Phillies' maximum salary was $1,800, there were other high achievers in the club's starting lineup. Third baseman Lave Cross hit .386, second baseman Bill Hallman hit .309, and first baseman Jack Boyle stood at .301. Although they played abbreviated seasons because of injuries, catcher Jack Clements carried a .346 average and shortstop Joe Sullivan hit .352, while reserve catcher-infielder Mike Grady swatted at a .363 clip.

The 1894 season was also one in which a fire of unknown origin destroyed much of Baker Bowl, the Phillies' home park at Broad Street and Lehigh Avenue. Starting in the grandstand, the fire quickly spread to other parts of the ballpark, and eventually to several stores and homes and a nearby transit company. The damage was estimated to be $250,000. While the ballpark was being repaired, the Phillies played their next six home games at a University of Pennsylvania ballfield at 37th and Spruce Streets. When the team returned to Baker Bowl, 9,000 temporary seats had been installed for the fans.

While there were fireworks in the stands, there were days when the Phillies were also blistering hot. In one game, with Thompson hitting for the cycle and lashing six hits in seven trips to the plate, the Phils smashed 36 hits, rolled up 49 total bases, and bludgeoned the Louisville Colonels, 29-4. Astoundingly, losing pitcher Jack Wadsworth pitched the entire game.

In another game, Delahanty went 6-for-6. Thompson bunted for only the second time in his career in another skirmish and once slammed eight hits in a doubleheader. Hamilton had a 27-game hitting streak, tied an all-time record with seven stolen bases in one game, and over one 24-game stretch scored 35 runs. And good old Turner got to pitch in one game, hurling six innings in relief while giving up five runs. He never pitched again. While Turner's big league career was limited to four seasons—none as a regular—the three titans of the Phillies outfield all went on to additional glory.

Delahanty won a batting title in 1899 with a .410 average while also finishing first in hits (238), doubles (55), and RBI (137). Two years later, he jumped to the new American League where he joined the Washington Senators. In 1902, Delahanty became the only player ever to win batting titles in both leagues when he topped the American League with a .376 mark. Tragically, Big Ed died during the 1903 season when after being put off a train for unruly conduct, he either fell, jumped, or was pushed off a bridge over the Niagara River. His body was found one week later at the bottom of Niagara Falls. In 16 seasons, Delahanty had compiled a .346 batting average, the fourth highest in big league history. He also hit 101 homers, and had 2,596 hits, 1,599 runs, and 1,464 RBI.

Hamilton was traded to Boston after the 1895 season for Billy Nash, who became the Phillies manager for one year in 1896. Sliding Billy spent six seasons with the Beaneaters, leading the league in slugging percentage twice, and hitting above .300 (reaching a high of .369) in five of his half-dozen seasons. He retired after the 1901 season. Then, starting in 1903, he managed in the minor leagues for the next 14 years. Also playing in 14 big league seasons, Hamilton finished his big league career with a .344 batting average, 40 home runs, 2,159 hits, 1,691 runs, 739 RBI, and 912 stolen bases.

Plagued by a bad back, Thompson retired while still wearing the Phillies uniform after the 1898 season. He had led the National League in home runs (18) and RBI (165) in 1895. At first, Thompson took a job in Detroit as an advisor to Tigers owner Frank Navin. Later, he became a U.S. Marshal and a court bailiff while playing amateur baseball. In 1906, when the Tigers suffered a series of injuries, Thompson was pressed into service and played eight games before retiring for good. He finished his 15-year big league career with a .331 batting average, 1,979 hits, 126 home runs, 1,256 runs, and 1,299 RBI.

Delahanty was elected to the Hall of Fame in 1945. Hamilton entered the baseball shrine in 1961. And Thompson made it to Cooperstown in 1974.

chapter 24

THE HARDEST JOB IN BASEBALL

They can usually be seen sitting in clusters in the lower stands behind home plate, their eyes riveted on the playing field as they intensely watch all that is happening. They have piles of papers, books, and charts, and they constantly make notes. Some have radar guns, too.

They are major league advance scouts, performing what could be one of the hardest and most important jobs in baseball.

Being a major league advance scout is no job for the fainthearted. Nor is it a job for anybody who insists on working regular hours. And certainly, it is not a job for those who dislike constant travel, hotel rooms, and being alone much of the time.

No, a job as a major league scout takes a special kind of person. But most of all it takes a person who is extremely observant and focused, and who knows the game of baseball backward and forward. Being a major league scout means that the complexities and nuances of the game must always be recognized.

No one knows that better than Hank King, the veteran major league advance scout of the Phillies. King has held that position for 24 years, a term that is longer than that of any other current advance scout in baseball.

"You really have to like what you're doing to handle this job," King said. "Nothing about it is easy. And you have to know what you're doing because if you don't give your team good information, you're not much use to it."

King is a local guy who grew up in the Philadelphia area, graduated from Upper Merion High School, and still resides in one of the northwestern suburbs. He has been with the Phillies since 1975 when he joined the club as a batting practice pitcher. A minor league pitcher for seven years in both the Baltimore Orioles and Chicago White Sox farm systems, King made his daily 200 to 250 batting practice pitches for nine years for the Phillies before taking the scouting job in 1984.

Even when he was still a batting practice pitcher, King, who refereed basketball games for 42 years and in recent years has operated a highly successful baseball school that he runs in a large facility behind his house, sat in uniform on the bench during games and kept charts on the tendencies of other teams and players. When he took the job as a full-time scout, his first mentor was Hugh Alexander, the fabled veteran scout who worked for many years with the Phillies and Paul Owens.

"When I first started the job," King recalled, "I went with Hughie to Pittsburgh. At the game, I figured he'd sit next to me and I could ask him questions. But he sat eight seats away. I had to put something together on my own. Afterward, I asked him to come to my hotel room and check my report. He looked at it and said, 'Too much writing, kid,' and then left the room. I was left to learn on my own. I knew what the team wanted and what I had to do, but at first it was kind of overwhelming."

Quickly, King devised his own system. It is elaborate and highly complex. He carries 20 pens with him when he's at work, hoping all the while that it doesn't rain and make his pens run, which would ruin his charts. And he spends long hours afterward, preparing reports that he will send in the wee hours of the morning to the Phillies, wherever they are. King is the Phils' only major league advance scout.

So what does a major league advance scout actually do? To differentiate, a major league advance scout is a man who watches his team's upcoming opponents. That's not the same as a pro scout who mostly critiques players on opposing major and minor league teams that his club may want to acquire in a trade or as a free agent. The Phillies have four of them.

Altogether, the Phillies employ 30 full-time scouts. The number includes supervisors, coordinators, and area scouts, whose main job is to find, watch, and report on potential draft choices and other players in which the club may have an interest. A relatively new category, global scouts, is also in the mix. The Phillies have four such people who scour the world in search of foreign talent. That job is doubly difficult because when it's time to sign a player to a contract, there are differences in money values between his country's currency and the U.S. rate. In addition, teams, including the Phillies, have a wide array of people known as bird dogs, essentially part-timers who scout young players.

In the case of a major league advance scout, the short answer to what he does is that he reports on every single detail he can learn about the team he is watching. He looks at tendencies. He learns if any parts of a team's game have changed since the last time he saw it. He spots strengths and weaknesses. And he makes countless other observations, all of which he reports as quickly as possible to his employer. The bottom line is that a major league advance scout sees and reports on everything he possibly can that will help his team win games. Every team has a major league advance scout. Every team needs a major league advance scout.

As one of his many jobs, an advance scout looks at the opposing pitchers. What does his fastball do? Does it sink or cut or rise or tail? Does his fastball have varying speeds? How does his curveball or slider break? Does he throw strikes? What kind of command does he have? What does he throw when he has 2-0 or 3-1 counts on the batter? What does he throw when he's ahead in the count? How long does it take for his pitches to go from his hand to the catcher's mitt? What kind of move does he have to first base? Does he fall into some kind of pattern on that each time? Does he tip off his pitches? Can you see his wrist going into the glove when he's about to throw a curve? Can you see more white when he's throwing a fastball? Do you see less white when he's throwing a change-up? All these and many more questions are among the observations an advance scout makes when he is watching the other team's pitchers.

But he also has to watch all the other players, too. He scouts outfielders to learn what kinds of routes they take to get to balls, what kinds of arms they have, if they catch a fly ball on one side or over their shoulders, and how fast they release the ball on a throw. With infielders, a scout will try to learn what kinds of range they have, what kinds of arms they have, do they wind up to throw when they get the ball, and what instincts they have.

Watching a catcher closely will reveal his release time on a throw, his accuracy on throws, the number of runners he has thrown out, whether or not a player can run on him, if he stays low when catching a breaking ball and rises to catch a fastball, and if he gives away the location of a pitch by moving in a way that the hitter can hear him.

Scouts look for hitters' tendencies, too. Does the batter like fastballs better than breaking pitches? How does he react to change-ups? Is he a low-ball or a high-ball hitter? Is he a first-pitch hitter or does he usually go deep in the count? On what counts will he take and on what counts does he like to swing away? What locations does he best like pitches to be in when he hits them? Can he be crowded at the plate? Can a pitcher get him out with off-speed pitches? Does he hook the ball? Does he turn his hands over? How fast does he get out of the batter's box?

Even the patterns of teams themselves and the ways they play the game, the strategies they use, and the manner in which their managers operate don't escape a scout's scrutiny. Under what circumstances does a team like to hit and run? When does it like to steal? What pinch-hitter does it use when it needs two runs or is facing a lefthander or needs somebody to get on base? And who is injured, where is the injury, can he play or is he on the disabled list, is the team trying to hide an injury, and why did a guy play Friday night, but not Saturday or Sunday?

All of these questions and hundreds more are the kinds of riddles a major league advance scout needs to explore when he goes to the ballpark. Once he gets the answers, he writes a daily report and relays it quickly to his team so that the information can be digested before his club meets that opponent.

In King's case, he watches an opponent for two series before it meets the Phillies, which allows the team ample time to digest fully the material he has prepared. After each game, he returns to the hotel room, dissects the information he's compiled, and then fills out a complicated report that's accompanied by what are called "spray charts." These are color-coded charts that show the interior of the ballpark he's working and log each hitter's at-bats in the game—what count did he have when he hit the ball, where did he hit it, how hard did he hit it, who was pitching, and various other pieces of information.

The information is sent to a designated coach—right now it is Milt Thompson; it used to be John Vukovich—on the parent club. The spray charts, done on the road by hand and transferred later to a computer, are sent by overnight carrier, not only so King can get the material to the team quickly, but so he can track it if necessary. The regular reports are sent via computer.

When the coaching staff receives the material, it devours even the most minute details. Reports on hitters are distributed to the pitching staff. When a pitcher who's been scouted is working, King's reports on him are posted in the dugout for that game so hitters can refer to them.

"I try to report anything that will allow us to get a jump on the other team," King said. "Of course, the information is only as good as the success the players have executing it. I try to keep my reports simple, just three or four lines to make the point. The coaches don't want to spend a lot of time reading. But I write something every night. Sometimes, I'm working on it at one or two o'clock in the morning and have to get up at five or six to catch a plane.

"Basically," he added, "I try to write what I see. Let's say I watch Dontrelle Willis and then I see Derrick Lowe. They're as different as night and day. One guy throws a sinker, one guy has a high leg kick and is very deceptive. I tell the team what I think and how I would do something against them. Naturally, that could change the next time you see those guys. But if somebody else tells me something and I haven't seen it, I'm not going to guess. So I don't depend on what other people say. Most of the time, you're not going to get the right answer, anyway."

Unlike some scouts, King doesn't use a radar gun, mainly because the speeds of pitches are posted on the scoreboards at most ballparks, and he uses those figures. Similarly, he doesn't pay attention to the opponent's signs, not only because he's too busy watching other elements of the game, but also because some Phillies players and coaches are quite adept at picking up the other team's signs. He also avoids critiquing umpires because every ump has his own technique and his own strike zone, and most players already know what they are.

East Division teams fall under King's watchful eye either four or five times each season. At the other end of the scale are American League clubs that the Phillies will meet during the season in interleague play. "That's the biggest nightmare for scouts," King claimed. "I might have to go see Seattle, and I don't know three players on that team. So about two weeks prior to watching them, I try to pick up some games on the dish and tape them. Then I have some idea about the team by the time I get there to watch it."

Most scouts seldom get to see their own teams play because they're on the road all season. Last season, the only time King saw the Phillies in person was during spring training when he attended meetings with the staff. "You see other scouts, and they tell you what's going on with your team," King said. "But this is a job in which you end up watching the scoreboard a lot to see how your team's doing. The only trouble is, when

Filling out reports and working long hours are two of the requisites of Hank King's job as a major league advance scout.

the other team scores, you think, damn, maybe there was something I left out of my report."

Actually, scouts like King don't follow the course of the game they're watching, either. "Sometimes," he said, "I'll get back to the hotel room and I honestly don't know who won the game. You watch every pitch and every ball that's hit, you're writing it all down, and you're so thoroughly into the game that you're not focusing on the score. In fact, you're so into the game that you can't just get up and get a soda or walk out to the bathroom. You have to sit there and tell yourself that you're going to grind it out for three or three and one-half hours."

When it comes to accommodations, major league clubs make a special effort to help scouts from other teams do their jobs. They reserve special seating areas behind home plate where anywhere from 12 to 15 scouts can sit at one time. The lower the seat, the better a scout can see. Atlanta's Turner Field is regarded as having the best seats for scouts because they are directly behind the catcher and umpire, and a scout can pick up the ball right as it comes out of the pitcher's hand. Dodger Stadium in Los Angeles provides the worst seats because they're too far from the playing field. Some ballparks also have seats from which the corners of the outfield can't be seen.

"The one trouble at some ballparks," King noted, "is if the seats aren't all taken by the scouts, the teams sell them to fans. Invariably, you'll be sitting there working away, and somebody will start asking you questions. I just try to be very nice and politely say, 'I work the second shift. You work the nine-to-five shift. I have a job to do, just like you do. This is my job.' I don't try to be smart or obnoxious. I just can't sit there and carry on a conversation. I need to concentrate totally on the game."

During the season, King is on the road an average of 28 days a month. He flies an estimated 60,000 to 65,000 miles per year, although that figure would be higher if he didn't drive from his home to games in New York and Baltimore. One year alone, he drove to New York for either Mets or Yankees games 27 times.

"The biggest headache is traveling," King said. "The airports are unbelievable. And airlines are offering fewer flights. In my case, I have to take 5:30 or 6:30 flights when I'm at home just so I can get to the airport before rush hour comes and all the roads are jammed. Then I get to my destination at 9:30 or 10 in the morning, and I can't get into the hotel room. I make my own travel arrangements, which I do a couple months ahead. And I've gotten to know a lot of the hotel managers. If I know I'm getting in town early, I can call them a month or so before I leave and ask them to have a room ready. But overall, travel is definitely the hardest part of the job."

King has missed only two assignments since he's been on the job. The first time, Charlie Manuel filled in shortly after he'd joined the Phillies. The second time, John Vukovich substituted for King. Both Manuel and Vukovich said they would never do it again.

"I think Jim Fregosi said it best when he said every manager and every coach should do this job for one month, and then you would get the respect you deserve," King recalled. "Both Pat [Gillick] and Ruben [Amaro] have said this is the hardest job in baseball. And you known what? They're right."

chapter 25

FROM ERA TO CIA

I t is safe to say that the life of Pete Sivess was not an ordinary one.

A pitcher with the Phillies in the 1930s, Sivess jumped directly from Dickinson College to the big leagues, and spent parts of three seasons toiling in the service of the National League club at decrepit, old Baker Bowl. It was a colorful time in baseball, and Sivess was very much a part of it. But viewed from the perspective of a lifetime, Pete's career in baseball was merely a diversion, a brief stop along the path to a higher calling.

While some former players dwell on their baseball careers, placing them as the central parts of their lives, Sivess did no such thing. That is not to suggest that he belittled his six-year career in professional baseball. It was simply far less significant than his later pursuits.

Sivess, you see, was an important member of the Central Intelligence Agency for 25 years. Before that, he had a significant role in World War II as well as immediately following the war in the reconstruction of Europe.

Pete's professional baseball career may have been short, but it had its special moments.

A native of South River, New Jersey, the six-foot-four, 200-pound Sivess had been an outstanding athlete in a town that became noted for breeding football players such as Joe Theismann, Drew Pearson, and old Philadelphia Eagles Hall of Fame center Alex Wojciechowicz.

"As a kid, I played a lot of sandlot baseball," Sivess recalled. "Every little town had teams. I spent all my time pitching. I pitched a lot of no-hitters."

In high school, Sivess earned letters not only in baseball, but also in football, basketball, and track. In baseball, he pitched and played the outfield. One year, he hit .511.

Sivess was hailed as one of North Jersey's finest schoolboy athletes, and was a member of the All-State baseball team. His reputation stretched to Pennsylvania where he attracted the attention of Dickinson College coaches. Soon, he was headed for Carlisle, Pennsylvania where he would spend four years as a four-sport star.

"When I went to Dickinson, I had one object," Sivess said. "That was to play professional baseball. If I didn't play baseball, I was going to teach and coach."

Sivess became one of the top college pitchers in the East. During three years of varsity ball, he won 20 of 27 games. In his senior year, he struck out 104 batters in 72 innings. Professional scouts flocked to the campus to watch him play.

"In my senior year in 1936, I was playing basketball in Philadelphia in a game against Temple," Sivess recalled. "Jimmie Wilson, the manager of the Phillies, called me and asked me if I was interested in playing with the Phillies. I actually signed after the game. The Cardinals had also offered me a job. They wanted to pay me $65 a month. The Phillies offered $400 a month, and I took it.

"I went back and completed my senior year at Dickinson. After graduation, I joined the Phillies in Chicago. Wilson invited me to breakfast. Now, I'm not one to spend other people's money. I ate very cautiously. He said, 'What's wrong with you?' I said, 'I thought you were paying for it.' I would never take advantage of anybody."

Sivess saw just one professional baseball game before he pitched in the big leagues. "But I didn't give a hoot for anybody," he said. "I was in charge. I never gave the hitters or the crowds any thought. I was never scared. I just went out there and threw. I never gave a damn if there were 500 or 50,000 people in the stands."

Sivess could throw hard, and he had a big, roundhouse curve. "I wasn't a smart pitcher, though," he said. "I just went out there and overpowered people. Nothing bothered me. In fact, I used to whistle when I was on the mound. It kept my mind relaxed."

After joining the Phillies during the summer of 1936, Sivess pitched in 17 games, starting six of them, and compilng a 3-4 record and a 4.57 ERA in 65 innings. "One game I started against the Brooklyn Dodgers lasted just one hour and 38 minutes," he said. "Another game, I lost, 5-4, to Carl Hubbell and the New York Giants. It was his 16th straight win." (Hubbell went on to win 24 games in a row, which also included a one-hit shutout against Sivess and the Phillies.)

Sivess also remembered a game in which he was paired against Dizzy Dean and the St. Louis Cardinals. The Gashouse Gang rode Pete from the start. "They were yelling stuff like, 'Who's that farmer out there?' At one point, I went over to their bench, dropped my glove and hollered, 'Which one of you SOBs wants to know?' Nobody said a word.

"Dean was so fast his pitches looked like a pea. After the game, he came over to the clubhouse. I said, 'I thought you had something. Hell, I saw better stuff in college.' The whole clubhouse roared. [Chuck] Klein and [Pinky] Whitney invited me out to have a drink with them. From that point on, I was one of the boys."

For Sivess, the fun of being a brash rookie was soon over. Wanting to give their young hurler some minor league experience, the Phillies sent him to the Milwaukee Brewers of the Class AA American Association at the start of the 1937 season. Shortly after his arrival, however, Pete's elbow swelled so much that he couldn't straighten his arm. The Phillies then dispatched him to the Baltimore Orioles where he overcame his arm problems and became one of the Class AA International League's top pitchers with a 15-5 record and 2.43 ERA in 34 games.

After spending three months in Baltimore, Sivess was recalled by the Phillies at the end of the season. He appeared in six games, winning one and losing one.

The following spring, the Phillies held training camp at Biloxi, Mississippi. Sivess reported with the expectation of having a banner season. Instead, he pitched mostly in relief, starting just eight of the 39 games in which he appeared while compiling a 3-6 record with a 5.51 ERA for a team that lost 105 games.

"I did strike out Tony Lazzeri three times in a game with the Chicago Cubs," Sivess remembered. "Early in the season, I beat the Cardinals, 2-1, at Baker Bowl. They got a run in the top of the ninth, and we got two in the bottom of the inning." Legendary sportswriter Red Smith, who was covering the Phillies at the time for the Philadelphia *Record*, was so impressed with Sivess that he wrote the following prose:

"Long, scrawny Sivess, making his first appearances as a major league starter this season, made that little white pill duck and weave and bob and soar like a kite in a hurricane. Babes in arms were the mighty Medwick, the mammoth Mize, the slashing Slaughter...Pete mixed 'em up, serving a fastball now, a curve, now a hipper-dipper low over the outside corner, now a scorcher just under the batter's chin. And down went the Cards like shooting gallery ducks."

Sivess didn't have any more games like that. And the following spring, he was sent to the Newark Bears of the International League in exchange for first baseman Ed Levy. Sivess ended his Phillies career with a 7-11 record. He pitched in 62 games, starting 16, and working 201 innings, allowing 257 hits, striking out 58, and walking 116. Toiling in the claustrophobic confines of Baker Bowl with its right field wall only 280 feet from home plate, he concluded with a 5.46 ERA.

"I never thought about that wall," Sivess said many years later. "Against lefthanded batters, the trick was to keep the ball away from them so they couldn't pull it."

Early in the 1939 season at Newark, Sivess was spiked on a play at the plate by Danny Murtaugh, a future Phillies second baseman then playing with the Rochester Red Wings. Sivess never really recovered. Cut by the Bears, he tried to hook on with Baltimore, managed by Rogers Hornsby—called by Pete "a strange duck"—but was released again. He finally finished the season with the Jersey City Giants. In 23 games with three International League teams, Pete posted a 3-2 record.

In 1940, at the invitation of Wilson, then a player and coach with the Cincinnati Reds, Sivess went to spring training with the Ohio club, but wound up spending the season with its American Association farm team at Indianapolis. He registered a 7-12 record in 26 games. The following year with Springfield (Ohio) in the Class A Eastern League, he went 4-8 while playing for manager Rabbit Maranville, who Sivess described as "a prince of a man."

Several months after the season ended, the Japanese attacked Pearl Harbor, and the United States went to war. Sivess was about to begin a new life.

Sivess' new career began in 1942 as his baseball career was winding down. "I had some arm trouble," he said, "and I was not one to pursue a dead horse. I could have tried again in the minor leagues, but an athlete has to face reality. I sensed that I had had my day. I saw no useful purpose in trying to make a comeback. The war had come on, and in due course, I enlisted in the Navy."

Baseball no longer was important. "The war was on, and wearing a baseball uniform was the last thing I wanted," he told John Steadman in a 1984 article in the Baltimore *News-Journal*. "I went in to get the job done."

Sivess attended officers' training school at Quonset Point, Rhode Island, and then was commissioned as an ensign. Along the way, naval authorities learned that he could speak Russian fluently and had a thorough knowledge of that country's politics and culture.

"My parents were from Russia," he said. "They didn't know any English, so Russian was all we ever spoke at home. I grew up being able to speak both languages."

With that skill, Sivess was assigned to the Chief of Naval Operations. His specific duty was to help train the Russian Navy. Pete spent most of the war years working with the Russians while stationed in Miami, Florida and the Aleutian Islands. When the war ended, he was on duty in Cold Bay, Alaska, helping to prepare for an amphibious assault on mainland Japan.

After the war, Sivess remained in the Navy, and was sent to Europe where he had the title of Assistant to the U.S. Naval Member of the Allied Control Commission for Romania. The war had stripped Romania of its government, and Sivess and his colleagues were charged with the responsibility of running the country for two years while a new government was established.

The world was being reshaped, and it was a critical time for anyone involved with that responsibility. Sivess excelled in

After pitching with the Phillies, Pete Sivess eventually
wound up holding an important job with the CIA.

his job and was awarded a special citation for his work by the
State Department. When that job was finished, Sivess joined
the newly formed CIA. And another career far from the clamor
and crowds of baseball was launched.

A member of the CIA from 1948 until his retirement in 1972,
Sivess was in charge of a clandestine operation on a 62-acre
plot at the confluence of the Chesapeake Bay and the Chop-
tank River on Maryland's Eastern Shore. Called Ashford Farm,
the secret facility gave diplomatic asylum to and processed de-
fectors and other political refugees, most of them from Com-
munist countries in Eastern Europe. It was the job of Sivess
and his staff to debrief all such people who came to the United
States, and to indoctrinate them in U.S. culture and beliefs, train
and help them get jobs and places to live, and in some cases
relocate them with new identities. Thousands of people passed
through the Chesapeake Bay installation, and went on to spend
productive lives in this country.

One of the "guests" was the notorious double-agent,
Nicholas Shadrin, a Russian naval officer who worked for the

FBI and who later disappeared while on a mission in Vienna. Although Sivess avoids comment about Shadrin and his espionage activities, just as he does about most of his other military and CIA adventures, the two did become good friends and fishing buddies while they were in Maryland together.

While most of the visitors at Ashford Farm were foreign-born, a few of them were Americans. One of Sivess' most prominent residents was U-2 pilot Gary Powers, who came under Pete's domain in 1962 after getting released from a Soviet prison. Powers had been incarcerated after his airplane was shot down while flying on a spying mission over the Soviet Union. He was eventually traded back to the United States in exchange for Soviet spy Rudolph Abel.

As an international celebrity, Powers was soon discovered to be a temporary resident of the Chesapeake Bay base. Naturally, the media flocked to nearby St. Michael's, Maryland in pursuit of stories. The media attention exposed the presence of the facility run by Sivess, and with that discovery came protests from the previously unsuspecting local residents. They opposed the presence of such a place so close to where they lived.

With the existence of the covert operation thus uncovered, it became necessary for the CIA to shut it down. When it did, Sivess was reassigned to a job in Washington, D.C. He worked there until his retirement.

Some years later, in his attractive home in St. Michael's, not far from the place where he directed the CIA operation, Sivess proudly displayed the government commendations and tributes he'd received over the years. The ex-pitcher looked back on his 30 years of government service with a justifiable sense of satisfaction.

"It was an interesting career," he said. "I wouldn't trade it for anything."

It was a career that proved to be full of intrigue and excitement, the kind only a few ex-players, much less anybody else, ever experience. In the long run, it would overshadow Pete's baseball career. But more significantly, it gave Sivess the best of two worlds.

Pete was a major league baseball player. And he played in the major leagues of government service.

chapter 26

THE 1950 PHILADELPHIA DODGERS

For many years, while they were still in Brooklyn, the Dodgers had a heated rivalry with the Phillies. Geographically, the teams were not too far apart, their fans were similarly intense, ownership was just above the poverty line, and when they met, the two clubs often demonstrated their mutual dislike with varying kinds of ill-mannered behavior.

The clubs shared a somewhat similar history, too. Through much of the 1920s and 1930s, the Dodgers and Phillies usually ranked as two of the worst teams in the National League. There was even the time in the '20s when the Phillies had lost 11 games in a row just before arriving in Brooklyn for a series. But all their trunks had been lost, including the ones carrying the team's uniforms. The Phillies were forced to wear the Dodgers' away uniforms. The Phils won the game. By the next day, their trunks had arrived, and back in their own shirts and pants the Phillies proceeded to lose the next 12 straight games.

While the Phillies dominated last place, much of the time the Dodgers were not far above them. It took until the 1940s for both clubs finally to unburden themselves from the dismal failures that had plagued them for years.

The Dodgers were the first ones to rise above calamity, winning a pennant in 1941 and thereafter becoming one of the National League's top teams with more first-place finishes in 1947 and 1949. The Phillies, meanwhile, took until the late 1940s to shed the cloak of dreariness before finally winning the NL flag in 1950.

No Phillies season was more memorable or more exciting than 1950. That was the year of the Whiz Kids, one of Philadelphia's most revered sports teams.

The Whiz Kids had been given that name because the nucleus of the team consisted mostly of young players. Outfielders Del Ennis and Richie Ashburn, infielders Willie Jones, Granny Hamner, and Mike Goliat, and pitchers Robin Roberts, Curt Simmons, Bubba Church, and Bob Miller were all part of that youthful group, whose average age was 23.

Veterans Andy Seminick, Dick Sisler, Eddie Waitkus, and Jim Konstanty, among others, also manned key spots on the team, managed by off-season college professor Eddie Sawyer. But it was the youngsters who commanded the most attention during the 1950 season, and they all played key roles in driving the team toward only its third first-division finish since 1917.

Starting in late July, the Phillies had spent every day of the previous three months in first place. The team had a seven-game lead with 11 games left to play, and appeared a virtual certainty to lock up the club's first National League pennant since 1915.

But suddenly, the Phillies began to crumble. The Whiz Kids turned into Fizz Kids. They lost seven of nine games, while the Brooklyn Dodgers won 12 of 15. Entering a two-game series in Brooklyn on the final weekend of the season, the team that earlier in the season had been dubbed "The Fightin' Phils" had a mere two-game lead over the Dodgers. Two losses would drop the Phillies into a first-place tie, necessitating a best-of-three playoff.

The Dodgers would be favored in such a battle, not only because they were a team made up mostly of seasoned veterans who were accustomed to pennant races, but because the Phillies were a team playing on fumes. The club was exhausted, injuries to Seminick, Church, and Miller had put them on the sidelines, and in a final stroke of misfortune, the Korean War had started and Simmons had been tapped for military duty. A member of the Army National Guard, Curt had finally blossomed during the season into a standout pitcher, and by September when he was drafted, he had won 17 games, highest on the staff.

Brooklyn was at the time the class of the National League. The Dodgers had won pennants in 1947 and 1949, and would win again four times in the next seven years (plus tying for the flag before losing in the legendary 1951 playoffs). Although the team won just one World Series during that span (in 1955), there was no club in the league as powerful as the Dodgers.

Jackie Robinson, Duke Snider, Pee Wee Reese, Roy Campanella, Gil Hodges, and Carl Furillo gave the club a devastating offense, and Don Newcombe, Preacher Roe, and Erv Palica led a formidable pitching staff. Brooklyn also had the best defensive team in the league.

The Dodgers team was also loaded with Philadelphia connections, not the least of which was that manager Burt Shotton had been the skipper of the Phillies many years earlier. Shotton, a big league outfielder for 14 seasons, all but one spent either with the St. Louis Browns or Cardinals, was a protégé of Branch Rickey.

After managing Syracuse in the International League for two years, Shotton became the Phillies manager in 1928. That season, the Phils lost 109 games, at the time a club record, while winning just 43. The next season, with Lefty O'Doul hitting a league-leading .398 and setting a major league record with 254 hits, and Chuck Klein bashing a league-record 43 homers to go along with his .356 batting average and 145 RBI, the pitching-poor Phils surged to a 71-82 record. After plummeting to 102 losses in 1930 and posting a 66-88 mark the following year, the Phils staged their first first-division finish since 1917 when they landed in fourth place with a 78-76 record. The Phillies would not finish in the first division again until 1949.

That elevated finish was short-lived. In 1933, despite an MVP season by Klein, the Phils rejoined the dregs of the league, losing 92 of 152 games. At the end of the season, Shotton was dismissed. In six years with the Phillies, he posted a 370-549-4 record. Burt spent the next 12 years as a coach and minor league manager. Then in 1946, he was hired by Rickey as a scout with the Dodgers.

When Dodgers manager Leo Durocher was suspended for "conduct detrimental to baseball" in 1947, Rickey summoned Shotton to manage the club. It was Jackie Robinson's first year

in the big leagues, and Shotton thus became the first manager
of an African American major league player in the 20th century. Brooklyn captured the National League pennant, but then
lost to the New York Yankees in the World Series.

Durocher returned in 1948, but in the midst of the season
quit the Dodgers and took a job with the New York Giants.
Again Shotton became the Brooklyn manager. This time, Brooklyn finished third as the Boston Braves, who that season had
acquired Philadelphia native Eddie Stanky from the Dodgers,
won the pennant. But Shotton's club returned to the World Series against the Yankees the following season before losing once
again in the Fall Classic.

Then in 1950, the Phillies entered the picture and threat-
ened to disrupt the Dodgers' dominance. The Phils had previously won just one pennant since the team was formed in 1883.

But on the next-to-last day of the season, the Dodgers ripped
the Phils, 7-3, at Ebbets Field with the help of another Philadelphian. Roy Campanella, a native of the city's Nicetown section
who in the early 1940s had sought but been denied a tryout
with the Phillies, blasted a three-run homer to cement the win.
And the Whiz Kids' lead was down to one game.

The final game—on Sunday, October 1—pitted Robin
Roberts and Don Newcombe. Both pitchers were going for their
20th victories of the season. For Roberts, it was his third start
in the last five days.

A standing-room-only crowd of 35,073 packed Ebbets Field.
An estimated 30,000 more were turned away. A sizeable crowd
from Philadelphia was in attendance, while back at home virtually every fan sat by a radio to hear Gene Kelly call the game.

Willie Jones' single scored Dick Sisler for the first run of the
game in the top of the sixth inning. Then in the bottom half of
the frame, Pee Wee Reese hit a ball that lodged in the screen
in right-center that was ruled a home run.

The score was tied at 1-1 as the game reached the bottom
of the ninth. Leading off for the Dodgers, Cal Abrams drew a
walk. Reese singled him to second. Then Duke Snider lashed a
single to center. And the irony of ironies intensified.

As Richie Ashburn fielded the ball on one hope in shallow
center, Dodgers' third-base coach Milt Stock waved Abrams
around third. A speedy runner, Abrams streaked toward the

Two of the Brooklyn Dodgers who played key roles in the final game of the 1950 season were Cal Abrams, getting tagged out at the plate in the bottom of the ninth inning by the Phillies' Stan Lopata (top left), and third-base coach Milt Stock, who injudiciously sent Abrams home.

plate, but he was no match for Ashburn. Although not noted for a strong arm, the Phils' center fielder rifled a throw to the plate that catcher Stan Lopata caught and tagged Abrams some 15 feet up the line. Ashburn's throw not only saved the Phillies from a loss, but became known as the greatest defensive play in club history.

Robinson, who had been treated more viciously by the Phillies and then-manager Ben Chapman than by any other NL team when he broke baseball's color barrier in 1947, was intentionally walked. Then Roberts escaped a bases-loaded jam by retiring Carl Furillo, a native of Reading, Pennsylvania, on a pop-up and Gil Hodges on a fly to right. That sent the game into extra innings. In the top of the 10th, Sisler, adding his name to Phillies lore, slammed a three-run homer to left that gave the Phillies a 4-1 victory and the pennant. Sisler's blast has since been regarded as the greatest home run in Phillies history.

Greatest throw, greatest home run, and a thrilling victory to win the pennant, all in one game. It was a game that no Phillies fan who was alive at the time could ever forget.

The Dodgers' Philadelphia connection loomed large in the victory. Not only was Shotton a former Phillies manager; not only was Campanella a native of Philadelphia; not only had Robinson born the brunt of the Phillies' brutal verbal abuse and also forced the trade of Eddie Stanky when he was moved to the Kensington-raised player's position at second base—there were even more Philadelphia footprints in the battle.

Milt Stock, who had made the unwise decision to send Cal Abrams home when he could have given the hold sign, thereby creating a bases-loaded situation with no outs, was the Phillies' third baseman when the team won its first pennant. A credible guardian of the hot corner, Stock had hit .260 for the 1915 Phillies after he was inserted into the regular lineup during the season. Nicknamed "Handle Hit" because many of his hits came off the handle of the bat, Stock was a regular with the Phillies through the 1918 season during a major league career that lasted 14 years. He was also the father-in-law of Stanky.

Both Shotton and Stock were fired after the season.

Of all the ironies, though, none was odder than the one involving Abrams. The runner who was thrown out at the plate in a play that had he been safe would have given the Dodgers a 2-1 victory and forced a playoff, was of all things born in Philadelphia. He was a resident of the city until moving to Brooklyn at the age of five. Much maligned in Brooklyn after his ill-advised romp to the plate, Abrams was otherwise a respectable player who spent eight years in the big leagues.

Among other Dodgers players, reserve infielder Eddie Miksis was also a native of the Philadelphia area, having been born and raised in nearby Burlington, New Jersey. Although he did not get into the game, Miksis, a key utilityman, spent parts of seven years with the Dodgers during a 14-year career in the majors.

Few paid much attention to it at the time. But from ex-Phillies Shotton and Stock, from Philadelphia natives Campanella and Abrams, and from Robinson, Stanky, and Miksis, the Dodgers had some prominent ties to the city in 1950. The Whiz Kids, of course, won the pennant. But Brooklyn's Philly guys played a noticeable role in that effort.

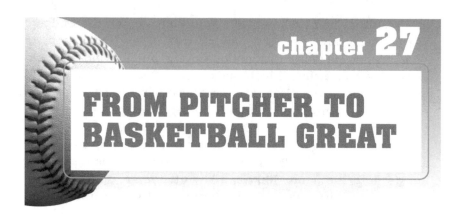

chapter 27

FROM PITCHER TO BASKETBALL GREAT

O ne of the most prominent professional basketball players ever to perform for a Philadelphia team was
a squared-jawed, bony native of Ohio named Neil
Johnston.

Johnston spent his entire pro basketball career with the
Philadelphia Warriors, playing for eight seasons from 1951
through 1959. During that time he led the National Basketball
Association in scoring three straight times and was a member
of six NBA All-Star teams. In 1955-56, he reached the pinnacle
of success as one of the main cogs on the Warriors' NBA championship team.

With a deadly hook shot and a precision one-hander, Johnston could shoot with uncanny accuracy from inside or outside.
Accordingly, he led the league in field goal percentage three
times. And when he wasn't scoring, he was a superb rebounder,
leading the league in that category once, even though at six
feet, eight inches he was far from being among the league's
tallest centers.

Although a reserve in his first year and injured much of his
final season, Johnston finished his NBA career with 10,023
points, an average of 19.4 points per game.

By the time he retired after the 1959 season, Neil—whose
nickname was Gabby, a reverse tribute to his quiet and reserved personality—was regarded as one of the top pivotmen
of all time.

Johnston's brilliant career was rewarded in 1989 when he was inducted into the Basketball Hall of Fame.

As successful as he was on the hardwood, however, basketball was not Johnston's first sport of choice. He was more interested in baseball. And, as hardly anybody on the planet knows, he once played in the Phillies' farm system, and was determined to become a major league pitcher.

Johnston had come out of Chillicothe, Ohio, where he was a high school basketball and baseball star before entering Ohio State University. He played freshman basketball and baseball with the Buckeyes, then made the varsity in both sports in his sophomore year.

"He was very, very good in both sports," recalled Tippy Dye, OSU's head basketball coach and an assistant coach in baseball when Johnston played. A peppy 93-year-old when he was interviewed, Dye said he watched Johnston play both sports in high school, and knew if he could recruit the skinny young kid for the Buckeyes, they would have a standout player in both basketball and baseball. "In baseball," Dye said, "he was a pitcher who could throw very hard, and was also a good hitter. When he got to Ohio State, we used him in the outfield when he wasn't pitching."

Although he wasn't particularly tall in high school, Johnston grew nearly one foot after he got to Ohio State. He made the varsity basketball team as a sophomore, but Dye took him out of the pivot and moved him to forward, while inserting Dick Schmittker at center. On what Dye described as a "not very good team," Johnston averaged nine points per game. Then that spring, he made the baseball team, by which time he was attracting the attention of professional baseball teams.

One of those teams was the Phillies. At the time, the Phils were nearing the end of a disastrous era in which they had only one winning season between 1918 and 1948. But when the Carpenter family took over the team in 1944, the Phillies began a long, uphill climb that would eventually lead them to the National League pennant in 1950.

Team president Bob Carpenter was determined to sign as many young players as possible, and by 1946, he had nine minor league teams in the system with rosters waiting to be filled.

Carpenter was especially partial to big, strong pitchers, and Johnston was a perfect fit.

"My father's first love was baseball," recalled Nancy Banks, one of five Johnston children, "and his aspirations were to become a professional baseball player. He was a very gifted, natural athlete—he was a good football player and later became a scratch golfer and an outstanding pitcher in local fast-pitch softball leagues—and had perfect hand-eye coordination. But his favorite sport was baseball, and he really wanted a career in it."

Johnston got a start in that direction when he learned about a Phillies tryout camp. Neil was on his honeymoon at the time, but that didn't prevent him from attending the session.

Although Johnston's height was a matter of some concern—the era of hurlers who towered above hitters had not yet been launched—Phillies scouts Heinie Groh and Eddie Kranick liked what they saw, and soon afterward signed him to a contract.

Over the years, the Phillies occasionally showed more than a passing interest in basketball players. Outfielder Frank Baumholtz (1956-57), first baseman Howie Schultz (1947-48), pitcher Gene Conley (1959-60), shortstop Dick Groat (1966-67), and pitcher Ron Reed (1976-83) all played in the NBA or one of its predecessors.

In the spring of 1949, Johnston—called Don (his first name was Donald) by some local newspapers—reported to the Phillies' training camp at Clearwater, Florida. To some, including Maje McDonnell, then a coach and batting practice pitcher with the Phils, Johnston made a quick impression.

"The first time I saw him throw, I couldn't believe it," remembered McDonnell, still an employee of the Phillies. "That's how good he was. He had a really good arm, and could throw very hard. I was very impressed."

Johnston had a buggy-whip delivery, which at the time was a term used to describe a pitcher who threw sidearm. Phillies scouts thought that Johnston could become another Ewell Blackwell, a hard-throwing sidearmer who was the ace of the staff on the Cincinnati Reds.

In the spring of 1949, the Phillies sent their 20-year-old pitcher to Terre Haute, Indiana, where they had a Class B team in the Three-I League. Johnston compiled an 11-7 record under manager Lee Riley (ironically, the father of another future NBA great, Pat Riley) as Terre Haute finished third. Future Phillies pitchers Bob Miller and Paul Stuffel were also members of that team.

The following year, Johnston was moved up to a slightly higher Class B level at Wilmington, Delaware, in the Interstate League. There, under playing-manager Skeeter Newsome, the Blue Rocks edged the Hagerstown Braves for the league championship with Johnston posting an 11-12 mark with a gaudy 2.08 ERA. He was definitely in the sights of the Phillies, who now had Robin Roberts and Curt Simmons in the fold, but were looking for additional help on the mound.

As he had done before, Johnston spent the early part of spring training in 1951 in Clearwater with the parent Phillies. Then, after camp broke, he was sent back to Wilmington.

While Johnston played for the Blue Rocks, he was followed closely by Al Cartwright, a budding young sportswriter who would become a legendary columnist and sports editor for the Wilmington *News-Journal*. Cartwright clearly remembers those days.

"He was very intimidating as a pitcher because of his size," Cartwright recalled. "But by the time I got to know him, he talked more about basketball than baseball. He told me he wanted to try out for the NBA. He was a big, gawky guy, and I thought he was really reaching to think he could play pro basketball."

Johnston's renewed interest in basketball was not just a passing fancy. The 1951 season for Neil, who in the off-season played semipro basketball and attended classes at Ohio State— getting a degree in education a few years later—was not a good one. Neil could do no better than a 3-9 record for the third-place Blue Rocks, and along the way he developed arm trouble. Or, as Nancy Banks said, "He threw his arm out."

With none of the current medical treatments available to pitchers at that time, Johnston's aspirations to become a major league baseball player suddenly appeared shattered. Even with a bad arm, though, Neil could still play basketball. The NBA appeared to be a suitable solution.

"I decided I was going nowhere in baseball," Johnston told Hugh Brown of the *Evening Bulletin* in 1957. "So, from then on, I put all my athletic apples in the peach basket."

Before becoming a three-time NBA scoring champion,
Neil Johnston (left), shown at spring training with
pitchers Blix Donnelly (center) and Schoolboy Rowe,
was a pitcher in the Phillies' farm system.

At the time, the Blue Rocks' business manager was a man named Jim Ward, and he had a connection with Warriors coach and soon-to-be owner Eddie Gottlieb. Ward called Gottlieb and asked if he'd give the youngster a tryout. Never one to turn his back on a guy who stood six feet, eight inches, Gottlieb invited Johnston to Philadelphia.

"I was just another guy trying to make the team," said Johnston, who when asked by Gottlieb how tall he was, replied that he was six feet, three or four inches. Not believing that, Gotty measured the youngster and found that he stood six feet, eight inches. When asked to explain the difference, Johnston told Gotty he hadn't been measured since college.

But Gotty liked what he saw, offered Johnston a contract, and soon the 23-year-old from Ohio had gone from minor league pitcher to major league basketball player.

The switch was certainly fortuitous. Although in his first season in 1951-52, Johnston played mostly behind George Mikan's younger brother Eddie, he moved into a starting role the following year and quickly became a star.

In his second season, Johnston, who by then resided in Sharon Hill in a house next door to longtime Warriors ticket manager, Mike Iannarella, led the NBA in scoring, pumping in 1,564 points for a 22.3 average. He led again in 1953-54 (1,759, 24.4) and in 1954-55 (1,631, 22.7), a year he also led the league in rebounds. He set a career high with 50 points in a game at Madison Square Garden against the Syracuse Nationals.

But even though he had become a nationally prominent basketball player, Johnston never gave up his love for baseball. After getting established with the Warriors, he resumed pitching, joining a team called Norway Cleaners, which played in the Delaware County (Delco) Baseball League, a fast-paced semi-pro circuit. The league, which in 2007 celebrated its 100th anniversary, has over the years been a temporary base for many past, present, or future professional players, ranging all the way back to Frank (Home Run) Baker and including such other more recent luminaries as Mike Scioscia, Lew Krausse Jr., and Jamie Moyer.

Pitching in the early to mid-1950s, Johnston was one of the league's top hurlers. In one game, he struck out 16 batters, a Delco League record that still stands.

"Standing out there on the mound, he was very imposing," recalled Angelo Tiburzi, one of the league's all-time greats and a player in the league for five decades. "He was certainly the biggest guy I ever batted against. Because of his size, when he took a step off the mound, he looked like he was halfway to home plate. He was scary. But he could throw, too. He had a terrific fastball and a very good curve. The way things are today, he'd be in the big leagues if he was playing now."

After he stopped pitching but while he was still playing in the NBA, Johnston coached a basketball team, also sponsored by Norway Cleaners, that played in a strong outdoor summer league in Narberth, Pennsylvania. The league, one of the more prominent amateur circuits in the Philadelphia area, was made up of high school and college players.

In 1955-56, Johnston, joined by hometown All-Americans Paul Arizin from Villanova and Tom Gola from La Salle, formed an awesome trio that led the Warriors to the NBA championship, eventually beating the Fort Wayne Pistons four games to one in the final. Arizin and Johnston placed second and third in the scoring race behind Bob Pettit of the St. Louis Hawks.

Arizin, who had won the scoring title in 1951-52, repeated in 1956-57 while Johnston, then living in Broomall, finished fourth. All the while, Johnston was working for a master's degree in physical education at Temple University. He was awarded the degree in 1957.

On the basketball court, Neil was suffering from knee problems. After the 1958-59 season, he retired from the Warriors. He was just 30 years old.

The following year, Johnston became the coach of the Warriors, piloting the team during Wilt Chamberlain's first two years in the NBA. After resigning from that job, he became the coach of the Pittsburgh Rens of the short-lived American Basketball League.

Eventually, Johnston moved to Bedford, Texas, where he became the athletic director and basketball coach at North Lake College. He died in 1978 at the age of 49 while playing basketball.

Today, Neil Johnston is saluted as one of Philadelphia's greatest professional basketball players. Who'd have thought, though, that he almost pitched with the Phillies?

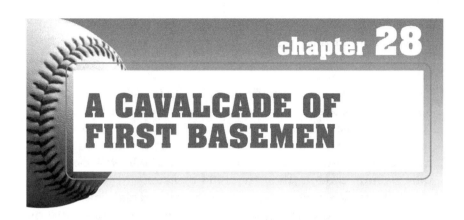

A CAVALCADE OF
FIRST BASEMEN

No Phillies season ever produced more pain and suffering than the 1964 campaign when the team had the National League pennant in its back pocket and blew it. It was a season that drove a whole city into a mammoth depression, the scars from which have never quite disappeared.

The gory season has been documented to the point of nausea, but to recap once more, the Phillies had a six and one-half game lead with 12 games left in the season. Then suddenly and without warning they imploded, losing 10 straight games and plunging out of first place in the most devastating collapse ever seen in baseball until challenged in 2007 by the New York Mets.

Even today, the Phillies' disastrous plunge is regarded as the darkest moment in the club's history, and still produces attacks of angst among those who were around to see it happen. It was not a pretty sight for the team, its players, or its fans.

The 1964 season—the Phils wound up tied for second after winning their last two games of the season—was the poster child for what was a highly dysfunctional decade. Eddie Sawyer saw it coming when at the start of his third year of managing the Phillies for the second time, he quit the job after just one game of the 1960 season. When asked why he left so abruptly, Sawyer replied, "I'm 49 and I want to live to be 50."

Give Sawyer credit for exceptional foresight. The 1960 Phillies lost 95 games and finished last. Then the 1961 Phillies lost a major league record 23 straight games and 107 games altogether, and finished last. Improvement was noted in 1962 when the team reduced its losses to 80 and climbed all the way up to seventh place.

The 1962 season actually launched the team on an upward spiral that reached its summit in 1964 before it tumbled back to another dismal stretch that this time would hang around until 1974 when the Phillies passed through the entrance to their most glorious era. Nothing during that stretch was more brutally painful, though, than the 1964 disaster.

With rookie Dick Allen—then called Richie—and Johnny Callison sparking a strong offense, and Jim Bunning and Chris Short leading a competent stable of pitchers, the Phillies had what could be regarded as their best squad since the early 1950s. And that showed as Bunning pitched a perfect game in June, Callison won the All-Star Game with a ninth-inning home run in July, Allen (the 1964 Rookie of the Year) hit balls over the roof at Connie Mack Stadium, and the Phillies roosted in first place through most of the second half of the season.

As conspicuous as the exploits of its key players were, though, something much more subtle was happening. Maybe it didn't seem terribly significant at the time, but in the overall picture, it would play a major role in the Phillies' ultimate demise.

As the season progressed, the Phillies were changing first basemen about as often as the hot dog vendors changed aisles. By the time the season ended, no less than nine different players had spent time at first base. That is a lot of players for one position.

True, the Phillies have used more players at some other positions. In 1884, they set an all-time record by using 13 players at catcher. In 2000, they set a club mark by using 27 pitchers. And the all-time major league record for most first basemen in one season is 13, held jointly by the 1895 Louisville Colonels and the 2000 St. Louis Cardinals.

But in 1964, wearing the red and white uniform of the Phillies, Roy Sievers, Ruben Amaro, John Herrnstein, Danny Cater, Costen Shockley, Johnny Briggs, Gus Triandos, Frank Thomas, and Vic Power all performed at the initial sack. Never in Phillies history have so many players played first base in the same season.

The Phillies' first basemen had little in common. Only one—Shockley—was a full-fledged first baseman. Some, such as Sievers, Thomas, and Power, had originally been outfielders. Cater and Briggs were also outfielders. Amaro was essentially a shortstop. Triandos was a catcher. Herrnstein, Cater, Shockley, and Briggs were all rookies. And the nine first basemen played in varying amounts of time, ranging from one game each for Briggs and Triandos to 68 games for Herrnstein.

Phils manager Gene Mauch, of course, was right in the middle of the game of musical first basemen. As he always did throughout his 26-year managerial career, the Little General switched lineups almost as regularly as he changed socks. Rare was the week when Mauch played the same lineup two days in a row.

In the case of the first basemen, there were sometimes extenuating circumstances. Injuries, slumps, and shifting defensive alignments all played parts in the seemingly constant changes.

The season had started with Roy Sievers at first. Acquired in a trade with the Chicago White Sox, the 1949 American League Rookie of the Year (with the St. Louis Browns) had been a steady although unspectacular first sacker for the Phils since 1962. Expected to lend power to the lineup again in 1964, the aging veteran was a big disappointment. Although Sievers had hit a three-run homer early in the season to defeat the Mets, 5-3, he was hitting just .183 after 49 games.when he was sold to the Washington Senators.

The weak-fielding Sievers had often been removed late in games and been replaced by Ruben Amaro. His regular position was shortstop, and he alternated there through much of the season with Bobby Wine, but he was often used as a defensive replacement, not only for Sievers, but for some who followed. In 1964, Amaro wound up appearing in 58 games at first, and hit .264 for the season.

After Sievers' departure, the regular spot in the lineup was taken by John Herrnstein, a part-time outfielder/first baseman and onetime University of Michigan football captain. In his first full season with the Phillies in 1964, Herrnstein had been a good hitter with significant power in the minor leagues, but showed no such traits once he got to the majors. He appeared in 68 games at first in 1964 (and in 69 games in the outfield), and his .234 average for the season showed why he was never more than a part-timer.

The Phillies' first base job got another visitor in late May when Danny Cater appeared at the position. Also in his first year with the Phillies, Cater was normally an outfielder, but also played in seven games at first during his only year with the Phils.

Costen Shockley was yet another rookie in 1964 and also played in just one season with the Phillies. The former Penn State star had been called up from Little Rock to the Phillies during the season. Once he got to the big club, he played in 11 games, nine of them at first base. He hit .229. Shockley wound up getting sent back to Little Rock were he hit .281 for the season while leading the Pacific Coast League in home runs (36) and RBI (112).

Along the way, the Phillies used Johnny Briggs, another rookie and normally an outfielder, as a defensive replacement in one game at first, even though he had not previously played the position in his one prior year in the pros. Gus Triandos, the veteran catcher who had come to the team from the Detroit Tigers in the same trade that brought Jim Bunning to the Phils, had played some first base in his early years, but in his first year in Philadelphia, he appeared in one game at that position.

After all the changes, the Phillies seemed to have a solution to the parade at first base when they acquired Frank Thomas in a trade on August 7 with the Mets. Originally an outfielder, Thomas had played both third and first bases during a lengthy career that began in 1951, but when he got to the Phillies, his sole destination was first base.

Thomas had an immediate impact. In his first 34 games with the Phillies, he drove in 26 runs and was hitting just under .300. But on September 8, he suffered a broken thumb while sliding into third base, and was lost for the season. It was a devastating blow to the Phillies.

Desperate for help, the club picked up the veteran Vic Power in a trade on September 11 with the Los Angeles Angels. Ironically, the deal made Power possibly the only player ever to have been traded for himself. The Phillies gave pitcher Marcelino Lopez and a player to be named later to the Angels. After the season, Power went back to the Angels as that player.

The Phillies used nine first basemen in 1964. It has sometimes been said that if one of them, Frank Thomas, hadn't gotten hurt, the team would have won the pennant.

Before that, though, the Phillies seemed to have bailed themselves out of trouble. Power, a hard-hitting, fancy-fielding, seven-time Gold Glove winner who had begun his big league career in 1954 with the Philadelphia Athletics, seemed to be a perfect choice to fill the hole. But it wasn't to be. Power hit just .208 in 18 games, and as the Phils went into their late-September dive, he contributed little more than a name in the lineup.

It has often been said that the Phillies' swoon was largely caused by the way Gene Mauch handled the team's starting pitching during that fateful 10-game losing streak. Jim Bunning and Chris Short each started three times in those 10 games. Bunning, a 19-game winner that year, and Short, who won 17, each pitched with two days rest between each start. In the other four games, however, Art Mahaffey and Dennis Bennett, both 12-game winners and both pitching with ample rest, each started twice.

Certainly, the way the rotation was handled played a major role in the collapse. But there were other reasons. The situation at first base was surely one of them.

Thomas' injury was devastating. But there are those who insist that it was compounded by Mauch's failure to use Cater as his replacement. The energetic Cater was having a splendid year and would hit .296 for the season. Wouldn't he have been more useful than the over-the-hill Power?

There are those, including some members of that infamous 1964 team, who think that he would have been and that playing Power instead of Cater was a major mistake. A look at the numbers says they are probably right.

THE BASEBALL EVANGELIST

chapter 29

I t might have been in a massive tent. It might have been in a gigantic tabernacle. Whatever the case, the picture is not hard to imagine, especially for those who've seen the movie, *Elmer Gantry*.

Thousands of people are jammed inside, filling every available space. Women are dressed in their fanciest clothes—long, flowing dresses and big, floppy hats. Men, also in their finest attire, wear long, straight suits, stiff-collared shirts, ties, and top hats.

Dignitaries and other special guests are seated in a roped-off area in front of the crowd. A choir made up of the best singers in town and that might number as many as 1,500, sits behind the stage. The stage is covered with ornate vases filled with flowers of all colors.

The air is thick with anticipation. Finally, the reason for this extraordinary setting is announced. And suddenly, out of a wing on one side of the stage comes a man immaculately dressed, hair perfectly coifed, excitement and enthusiasm exploding from his body.

He sprints across the stage. And then—feet out front—slides perfectly into the pulpit.

William A. Sunday—Billy to most people—did not make such a grand entrance every time he spoke. But when he did slide into a specially braced pulpit, he not only immediately captured the attention of the audience, he also revealed the reason he was called "The Baseball Evangelist."

Billy Sunday, you see, was a former major league baseball player. He spent eight years in the big leagues, including the last part of his career with the Phillies. In fact, it was during the appropriately named Sunday's days with the Phillies that his life as a world-renowned evangelist began.

The man who would become known as the Father of Evangelism in the United States was born in 1862 in a two-room log cabin in Ames, Iowa. His father, a private in the Union Army, was killed during the Civil War, and soon afterward, his mother, considering herself unable to raise her children in a suitable manner, placed Billy and his brother in an orphanage for the children of deceased soldiers.

While there, young Billy developed a passion for track, and in time built a reputation as one of the fastest sprinters in the nation, a speedster who was one of the few in the country who could run the 100-yard dash in 10 seconds.

Sunday resided in the orphanage until graduating from high school, by which time he had developed a consuming interest in baseball. Ultimately, as the star player for a town team in Marshalltown, Iowa, where he worked for $3 a week for an undertaker, Sunday was discovered by the legendary Adrian (Cap) Anson, also a resident of Marshalltown and the playing-manager of the National League's Chicago White Stockings.

Anson signed the local baseball hero to a contract, and the 21-year-old outfielder reported immediately to the White Stockings. Without benefit of minor league experience, Sunday struck out in his first 13 times at bat.

Despite such a feeble start, Sunday soon became known as the fastest player in the league. It was said that he could circle the bases in 14 seconds, a dazzling time even by today's standards. One writer claimed that Sunday "probably caused more wide throws than any other player in the game because of his specialty of going down to first like a streak of greased electricity."

But Sunday couldn't hit. In 1883, his first season with the White Stockings—and also the season in which the Phillies joined the National League—he hit just .241 in 14 games. His playing time increased to 43 games the following year, but his average dropped to .222, although the young outfielder was attracting attention with his vitality and enthusiasm. Although Chicago won the National League pennant in each of the next two seasons, Sunday hit just .256 and .243 in reserve roles.

When Sunday's playing time increased to 50 games in 1887, he responded by hitting .291. But that winter he was sold to the Pittsburgh Pirates. It turned out to be a good move for Sunday. Billy became a regular, playing in 120 games, but hitting only .236. He did, however, steal 71 bases.

Baseball, though, was becoming a secondary interest for Sunday. In Chicago, he had become deeply involved in religion, and that would become his focus for the rest of his life. Eventually, Sunday would be known throughout the world, ultimately reaching his peak during World War I before his popularity faded in the 1920s.

Although he had been a practicing Christian since his early childhood, Sunday's first decisive encounter with religion occurred one Sunday afternoon in Chicago. After leaving a bar, Sunday and some of his teammates from the White Stockings, as well as a few players from the visiting New York Giants, were strolling along a downtown street.

As the group, a few of whom were drunk, approached what was normally an empty lot, they saw a gathering of men and women holding an outdoor religious meeting. Sunday and his friends stopped to listen. Soon, the meeting had captured their attention, and the players sat down on a curb to hear the entire service.

Afterward, a man, noticing Sunday's interest in the service, approached him, inviting him to a meeting at a nearby mission. Sunday accepted. Shortly after attending that first meeting, Sunday became a regular at the mission services. Ultimately, he accepted the call to devote his life to God, stopped drinking, taught a Sunday school class, and married a young lady he'd met at the mission named Nell Thompson.

According to *The Real Billy Sunday*, a book written in 1914 by Elijah P. Brown, the ballplayer from the plains of Iowa initially feared that in the rough and heavy-drinking world of professional baseball, he would be ridiculed by his teammates because of his newfound religious fervor. That feeling, however, was put to rest when one day after reporting to the clubhouse,

Sunday was approached by the team's star, future Hall of Famer Mike (King) Kelly. "Bill, I'm proud of you," Kelly said. "Religion ain't my long suit, but I'll help you all I can."

Within a few years after his religious awakening, Sunday, who now refused to play on Sunday, was sold to the Pirates. He spent two years in Pittsburgh, and while reduced to a reserve role in his second season, he hit .240 in 81 games.

In 1890, after playing in 86 games with the Pirates, Sunday was sold to the Phillies. It was in Philadelphia that Sunday's career as an ordained Presbyterian minister and an evangelist, who eventually was said to have preached to more people of Christian faith than anyone else in history, began to take shape.

Although he had preached to smaller audiences, Sunday appeared before his largest crowd to date when he took the pulpit in front of some 1,500 people at the First Presbyterian Church of Manayunk.

Sunday was a smashing success. Directing his sermon mostly to the many young people in the audience, he urged them to resist temptation, and to live "a moral and upright life."

Many in the audience were "visibly affected by the clearness and earnestness with which the layman addressed them, in a voice of tender pleading," reported one newspaper covering the event. Another newspaper that covered the service noted that "It is something of a novelty to see a professional ballplayer get up in the pulpit." But, the article continued, Sunday's "eloquence astonished the assembly." "It is evident that his baseball energy has been transferred to his new calling...his vitality shows in every sentence," wrote still another publication.

Sunday continued to preach in the Philadelphia area and elsewhere. As he did, his reputation as a staunch fighter of "Satan" and his popularity increased tremendously. Soon, Sunday's treatment of the gospel had driven him to such heights that he had little time to be a ballplayer.

For the rest of the 1890 season, Sunday played in 31 games with the Phillies, hit .261, and earned $400 a month. Then, before the 1891 season, according to *"Billy" Sunday, The Man and His Message*, authored by William T. Ellis, also in 1914, Sunday was offered a three-year contract by the Phillies. "I said to God," Sunday was quoted as saying, "'Now, if you want me to quit playing ball and go into evangelistic work, then you get

Just before launching a career that would lead to
his becoming a world-famous evangelist, Billy
Sunday was an outfielder with the Phillies.

me my release.' I left it with God to get my release before the
25th day of March, and would take that as evidence that he
wanted me to quit ball.

"On the 17th day of March, St. Patrick's Day—I shall never
forget it—I was leading a meeting and received a letter from
Colonel Rogers, president of the Philadelphia club, stating that
I could have my release."

As the meeting ended, Jim Hart from the Cincinnati Redlegs
raced to the platform with a contract that offered to pay Sunday
a salary of $3,500. "He threw a check down for $500, the first

month's salary in advance," said Sunday. But the fledgling preacher declined the offer. Afterward, he consulted friends and family, who gave him mixed responses. Some said, take the money; others said, stick to your promise. Finally, after praying until five o'clock in the morning, Sunday decided to leave baseball. He did so with a .248 career batting average compiled in 499 games. He had stolen 236 bases, including 84 in his final season.

Soon afterward, Sunday's preaching career skyrocketed, and by the late 1890s, he was in demand throughout the nation. His energy, his enthusiasm, and his showmanship were limitless. And the message he brought captivated his audiences, which dug deep into their pockets when it came time to collect the offering. Often, thousands were turned away at his appearances because there was no more room in the auditorium.

Sunday became more popular still in the 1900s, while developing strong friendships with leaders such as Theodore Roosevelt, William Jennings Bryan, and John D. Rockefeller. He even unsuccessfully sought the nomination for president in 1920 as a Republican. Often, he returned to Philadelphia where it was not uncommon for him to preach two or three times in one day. He preached in factories, in prisons, in schools and colleges, in shops, even in sanitariums. He preached to the rich and the poor, to business leaders and laborers, to socialites and lowlifes. Of course, he also preached in churches and tabernacles where his audiences often numbered in the thousands. One such tabernacle was located on the site now occupied by the Free Library.

In 1913, more than 800 churches in the Philadelphia area put out a joint call for Parson Sunday to conduct a campaign in the City of Brotherly Love. Sunday accepted, and according to Tom Granahan, writing in the *Today* magazine of the *Philadelphia Inquirer*, he preached some 280 sermons in 11 weeks. In one session, he spoke to an audience of 60,000. On another day, some 3,000 city employees and a police band led a parade to the tabernacle located on the Benjamin Franklin Parkway. And at yet another service at the University of Pennsylvania, Sunday preached to 3,000 students, some sitting on windowsills or on rafters, with several thousand turned away at the gate.

Sunday rode to his engagements in a Chalmers limousine owned by retail mogul John Wanamaker. He cavorted with the city's most notable—and wealthy—citizens. And on Mondays, when he took the day off, he played golf at the club now known as Whitemarsh Valley Country Club or walked the boardwalk at Atlantic City.

Speaking with a rapid delivery that was estimated to be 300 words per minute and spoken with perfect grammar, Sunday, who died in 1935, railed against smoking, swearing, drinking, dancing, and people he considered to be unscrupulous politicians. With oratorical delivery second to none, he loudly condemned those who sinned, praised those who led righteous lives, and urged those in his spellbound audience to commit their lives to God, all the while stressing conservative values while shadowboxing with the devil.

"Bull-necked, infamous, black-hearted, white-livered, hog-jowled, God-forsaken, Hell-bound gang," Sunday called sinners in his electrifying sermons. Often, converts numbering in the thousands would step to the front of the auditorium to be saved.

But the theatrical preacher, whose mission was to save souls, was never too far from the game he once played professionally. Constantly, he referred to baseball in his sermons. Using his athletic skills, he leaped, whirled, and ran around the stage. Sometimes, he deliberately fell to the floor in prayer. He jumped on chairs and sometimes off the stage to make a point. Once, according to Granahan, he smashed 10 glass jugs with a baseball bat to illustrate a point about breaking the Ten Commandments.

"No posture is too extreme for this restless gymnast," Ellis wrote. Sunday retained his athletic prowess so well that even after shaking the hands of thousands of converts at a single service, his hands remained strong and his grip firm.

"No doubt, the ex-ballplayer's experience on the diamond has had much to do with making him always have a clear and definite purpose," Brown wrote. "As a ballplayer, he soon learned that no ball was ever to be thrown just to keep it in motion, but it should go with a true aim whenever it left the hand.

"As a ballplayer, it had been his habit to try to send the ball right where it ought to go to hurt the other side and help his own—and do it quick. And so it may be that his athletic training was due to some of the earnestness and precision with which he [now] preaches."

And to think, it all began in Philadelphia when Sunday played with the Phillies.

chapter 30

INSIDE THE CLUBHOUSE

I t is three hours before gametime, and in the Phillies' clubhouse deep beneath the stands at Citizens Bank Park, players are occupying themselves in a variety of ways.

One player sits in front of his locker, a boom box blaring the latest tunes. Another reads his mail. Several are talking on their ubiquitous cell phones, while a few others play a video game. A couple of players are engaged in conversation, several are watching television, and another is being interviewed by a local writer.

Many of the players are not in sight. They are in other rooms of the clubhouse, working out, eating, getting medical treatment, watching videos of their past performances, swinging away in the batting cage, or conferring with a coach. But regardless of the activity, the Phillies clubhouse, far from the clatter that will soon engulf the ballpark, is a busy place.

Like all major league clubhouses in new stadiums, the Phillies' clubhouse is a sumptuous tribute to the evolution of the players' off-the-field workplace. And it is a far cry from the old locker rooms, a term which meant exactly what they were—rooms with lockers.

For the Phillies, the metamorphosis of the locker room has been stunning. It has gone from no locker room at all at Recreation Park (the teams dressed in a nearby hotel) to the dank, austere quarters at Baker Bowl where a swimming pool adjoined the second-floor clubhouse and where pitcher Claude

Passeau once cheerfully confided to the author that each year players received new nails on which to hang their clothes.

That was followed by the snug and frill-free clubhouse at Shibe Park/Connie Mack Stadium with its metal lockers, small manager's office off on one end, and trainer's room in a small loft above the main floor of the clubhouse. Then came vastly expanded digs at Veterans Stadium where there were wide lockers—wide enough for Darren Daulton to put a lounge chair in his—with a broad space down the center of the room and separate side rooms that included a manager's office, coaches' dressing room, eating area, trainer's room, storage, clubhouse manager's office, video room, and a large workout area.

When the Phillies moved to Citizens Bank Park in 2004, the era of the super clubhouse was officially launched in Philadelphia. Far exceeding the combined attributes of all of its predecessors, the new Phillies clubhouse is both luxurious and efficient, spacious and comfortable, a place where no player should be reluctant to prepare for battle.

"It is a top of the line facility," said Frank Coppenbarger, the team's clubhouse director. "It doesn't take a back seat to any clubhouse in baseball. In fact, I think ours is the best because the Phillies didn't cut anything out when they built the ballpark. We have everything right here.

"It's a real showplace," added Coppenbarger, who has managed the clubhouse and the equipment with the Phillies for 19 years, before which he worked for seven and one-half years as an assistant in the clubhouse of the St. Louis Cardinals. "And because it is, it's a very good recruiting tool. We bring free agents down here, and they see how nice it is. It gives them a little extra incentive to play with the Phillies."

The clubhouse sits along a wide corridor that runs below the stands. Groundskeepers equipment, storage rooms, the Phillie Phanatic's quarters, a media room for press conferences, Dan Stephenson's video production room, the umpires' dressing room, and the visitors' clubhouse—a smaller but equally functional version of the Phillies' clubhouse—are among the many other facilities that line the corridor.

"Having a nice visitors' clubhouse is critical," Coppenbarger said. "Most of the time, the only things a visiting player sees are the airport, the hotel, and the ballpark. If a clubhouse doesn't have top of the line amenities, he assumes we're a second-rate organization. We want him to think we're a first-class ballclub in a first-class city."

To enter the Phillies' clubhouse, one must pass through a door along the corridor. Immediately inside sits Coopenbarger's office on the right. A few steps farther are the manager's office and coaches' quarters on the left. Running past those rooms is a walkway lined with pictures and brief biographies on Phillies Hall of Famers that leads down a slope to a large room with three batting cages, beyond which is the entrance to the home dugout.

The Phillies' clubhouse is back up the walkway across from the coaches' room. When entering, the first things that are noticeable are a large sign with the day's starting lineup and the players' mail boxes. Then the main clubhouse comes into view.

The facility is huge, deluxe, and impressive.

Forty-four lockers, all made of oak and 40 inches wide, line both sides of the massive, slightly curved dressing room. Each locker has ample room to hold the large quantity of equipment, uniforms, street clothes, and sundry other paraphernalia players carry during the season. A thick rug, at least equal to the rugs in most people's living rooms, covers the floor.

Behind one side of lockers is the shower room, which includes 16 showers, a sauna room, and a steam room. Then, beyond the main locker room, a place that is off-limits to all but members of the team, is the business end of the clubhouse.

There is a large room featuring an oversized hot tub and a treadmill at the bottom of a four and one-half foot deep pool that not only offers the necessary resistance to the user, but is equipped with a camera and can record underwater movement on a computer. In addition, there is a doctor's office and a medical examination and treatment room that serves injured players from both the Phillies and visiting teams. (A back door allows visiting players to enter the room without having to come through the home team's locker room.) Equipped with an x-ray machine and assorted other medical devices, a computerized system allows doctors and trainers, even when they're on the road, to review a player's injury.

Also located in the spacious area behind the locker room is a dining area with tables, chairs, and up-to-date kitchen equipment. When day games are scheduled, players often arrive early to eat breakfast. For night games, most players come to the park between 1 and 2:30 p.m. Many have a snack—usually a sandwich containing cold cuts, a cheesesteak, a slice of chicken, or a veggie tray—after batting practice. Following the game, players are served a hot meal. The meals are all organized by nutritionist Synthia Sass, a Tampa resident widely known in her field, who was hired by the team in 2007. Sass makes sure players eat only foods that among other things are nutritious, that nourish muscles, and that help players maintain high energy levels. Naturally, trans fats are not on the menu.

Along a wall outside the dining area is a bulletin board with special notices to players, most of them from Major League Baseball, explaining rules and regulations. Most of the notices are written in both English and Spanish. One even instructs pitchers about preserving the pace of the game. Another advises players on the appropriate conduct toward official scorers.

The showpiece of the back end of the clubhouse is the training room. It contains virtually every piece of workout equipment imaginable. Some 25 machines, ones made for any kind of exercise, form the centerpiece of the room. There are also nonmechanical devices and suitable space for floor workouts. Players spend countless hours in this spacious room, and it is more than amply furnished for their special needs and demands.

The rear flank of the clubhouse also contains a small locker room for batboys and others; an office for clubhouse personnel Phil Sheridan and Dan O'Rourke; a large storage area for uniforms, bats, balls, and other equipment; a room with washing machines, and a few sundry nooks and crannies. Overall, every need seems to be met in the elegant clubhouse that players call their second home.

"It's a lot different than it used to be," said Coppenbarger, who typically arrives at the ballpark for a night game at 11 a.m. and leaves one hour or so afterward. "Guys today want to have ultra-modern facilities. And that's what we have here."

Providing facilities that rival those of an exclusive country club is not, however, the only clubhouse activity conducted by Coppenbarger and his associates. Dealing with the players' uniforms and equipment is also a primary task.

The Phillies' clubhouse at Citizens Bank Park has all the amenities. Frank Coppenbarger directs the elaborate operation.

During the season, the Phillies use eight to nine dozen balls in each game. Some are hit into the stands, some are thrown into the stands by players, and some are thrown out of games by pitchers and umpires. Including spring training and the regular season, the Phillies buy 300 cases of baseballs each year. There are 12 boxes, each containing one dozen balls, in a case. If you do the math, that comes to more than 43,000 balls a year.

Bats, which like balls are ordered by the Phillies, also enter the clubhouse by the truckload. In any given year, a position player uses about eight dozen bats. They break, they chip, they don't feel right; a player might even detect a minuscule difference in weight or length—even though all his bats are ostensibly the same. Pitchers use six to 12 bats per season. All add up to an ongoing order that by year's end may number upwards of 2,500 bats.

The Phillies, like all major league teams, are not permitted by MLB to purchase chewing tobacco anymore, but they do buy chewing gum, sunflower seeds, soap, shampoo, towels, pine tar, and numerous other products. Chewing gum, for instance, comes with six boxes in one case. The Phillies purchase between 300 and 500 cases each season.

Spiked shoes are another heavily used product. Because they get stretched or torn or the spikes wear out, position players use four or five pairs a year. Many players also wear up to eight different caps each season, although some players keep the same, grungy headpiece the entire year.

Most position players keep three gloves in their lockers. One is used in the game, one is kept in reserve, and one is in the process of getting broken in. Like their shoes but unlike their bats, gloves are owned by the player.

One of the biggest jobs of Coppenbarger and his crew involves uniforms. At the start of the season, each position player is issued two home and two road uniforms (shirts and pants). Pitchers get one of each. But a player such as Jimmy Rollins or Chase Utley goes through six to eight pairs of pants every season. Some get too worn or torn to use again. Some have tears small enough that Coppenbarger or someone else on the crew can mend the pants on a sewing machine kept in the clubhouse. Sometimes, a player gets a nice, new pair of pants, but his older shirt is too faded to match. So, the player must be outfitted in a new shirt, too.

What happens to the old uniforms that don't get thrown out? At the end of the year, most players keep one or two jerseys. Others are given to charity or wind up in the hands of memorabilia dealers and collectors. If the uniform was worn during a noteworthy performance, it (or just the shirt) might be put on display, stored for a future special event, or sent to the Hall of Fame at Cooperstown.

A major issue with uniforms concerns their numbers. While young players just arriving are assigned numbers by Coppenbarger, most veteran players want a say in what numbers they use. They can't, of course, wear retired numbers such as Richie Ashburn's 1, Jim Bunning's 14, Mike Schmidt's 20, Steve Carlton's 32, or Robin Roberts' 36. Nor can they wear Jackie Robinson's 42 unless they wore it before MLB retired the number in 1997, in which case they're grandfathered in. The Phillies are also reluctant to issue high numbers or the number 13, unless a player really insists on one of them. Number 69 is never given out.

Sometimes, a problem arises when a veteran player joins the Phillies and asks for a number that had previously been his, but an existing member of the team already has that number. In such cases, a round of negotiations usually takes place. If the holdover player relents and gives up the number to the new guy, he is usually rewarded with a suit, a watch, a case of beer, or some other token of appreciation. Shane Victorino has done well, having given away his number twice (to Alex Gonzales and Wes Helms) in the previous two years.

Although John Kruk changed his number four times while he played with the Phillies, when a member of the team requests a new number, that can create a problem, too. Such a change requires uniforms bearing the player's former number to be recalled from retail stores, displays, and other public places. That happened one year when Chase Utley wanted a new number. He changed his mind after it was pointed out that thousands of his old jerseys would have to be returned.

For a number of years, Coppenbarger demurred from issuing Tug McGraw's old number 45. But when Mitch Williams requested number 99, he got it. And when Tim Worrell joined the Phillies, he was given number 38, his brother Tom's old number.

"I'm constantly thinking about numbers," Coppenbarger said. "As soon as we get a new player, I start thinking about what number to give him."

Also the team's traveling secretary, Coppenbarger, who devotes time to that job at home in the mornings before leaving for the ballpark, has not only flight and hotel reservations to think about when the team is on the road, he must also devote a considerable amount of time to loading and sending the team's baggage. On each trip, the Phillies take three giant trunks and 10 large duffle bags. They're filled with uniforms, including extra ones for possible new players or to replace damaged ones, along with bats, balls, food, trainer's equipment, medical supplies, and many other items.

Packing the gear is no ordinary job, but it's one that is made easier by the convenient facilities in the Phillies extraordinary clubhouse. It is a clubhouse with many special features, all of them designed to accommodate the modern era and the modern player.

chapter 31

AN EARLY WOMAN EXECUTIVE

ntil a couple of decades ago, few women occupied high-level executive positions in professional baseball. Except in rare instances, the top posts on teams were dominated by men. Men owned the teams, men ran the teams, and men performed all the necessary tasks required to keep their teams afloat.

A woman's place was certainly not on a baseball team unless she was somebody's secretary. And those few times when a woman did pierce the men's front-office monopoly were often not due to normal circumstances.

Such was the case with Helene Robison Britton, the first woman known to have reached the upper echelon of a baseball team. In 1911, Britton inherited the St. Louis Cardinals from her father and uncle, owners of the team since 1899. An advocate of women's rights, Britton played an active role in the operation of the team until she sold it in 1916.

Among other women in baseball, Florence Dreyfuss became owner of the Pittsburgh Pirates after her husband, Barney, died in 1932, and retained ownership until 1946. Edith Dunn owned the Cleveland Indians for five years after her husband, James, died in 1922. Margaret Donohue worked as a secretary/treasurer for the Chicago Cubs in the 1930s. Marge Schott owned and operated the Cincinnati Reds from 1985 to 1999. But otherwise, no woman was visible on a baseball team.

And then there was Mae Mallon Nugent. Her place in baseball was unlike that of any other woman. Nugent was a true pioneer who worked for the Phillies from 1916 to 1943, serving the club much of that time as vice president, treasurer, and secretary, and with her husband, Gerry, as part owner. Until then, no other woman had been a full-time baseball executive for that length of time.

Nugent was an active participant in the daily operation of the Phillies. She was known for her encyclopedic knowledge of baseball and its history, and for her intimate knowledge of the way the game was played. She knew every player's batting average, and she was as familiar with the business end of the game as any man.

"[Nugent] knows baseball as well [as] or better than any man connected with the organization with the possible exception of her husband," baseball writer (and former Phillies pitcher) Stan Baumgartner once wrote in a piece for the *Inquirer.*

No one disputed that claim. Although Nugent was involved with the Phillies during the most dismal era in club history—the team had one winning season between 1918 and 1949—her diligence and devotion to the National League nine was never in doubt. The Phillies represented Mae Nugent's entire professional life.

A native of Conshohocken, Nugent had been a baseball fanatic since she was a child. As Mae Mallon, she wore knee pants, tied her hair in pigtails, and rooted relentlessly for the Phillies. So strong was her allegiance to the team that she even persuaded her mother to buy a few shares of stock in the Phillies.

In 1916, having just graduated from business school, Mae applied for a job with the Phillies. She was hired as a secretary to Phils president and majority stockholder William A. Baker, and a career in baseball was launched.

Mae was still working at that job in 1919 when she met a young man who was a corporal in the 108th Field Artillery and had just returned from service overseas in World War I with two medals for bravery. His name was Gerald P. Nugent, a former football and baseball star at Northeast High School in Philadelphia.

Like Mae, Gerry Nugent, soon to be a purchasing agent for a leather company, was an avid Phillies fan. He regularly attended games at Baker Bowl, sitting in the stands behind third base. Gerry also had a broad knowledge of baseball, and, having gotten to know Baker through his fiancée, frequently presented ideas and gave suggestions to the Phillies owner. Mae often tried to persuade Baker to give Gerry a job with the Phillies. Eventually, Baker, a former New York City police commissioner, saw the merits in having such a fertile mind on the payroll, and in 1925 he gave Gerry a job as his assistant. Soon afterward, Mae and Gerry were married.

The team's office, located in the Packard Building in Center City, was a bare bones operation with never more than a handful of people working there. The Phillies were always on the verge of bankruptcy, a condition largely created by a lack of attendance and a team that in the 1920s finished in eighth place six times, and in seventh twice.

But the Nugents plugged away, and in 1926, Gerry was named the team's business manager, replacing longtime Phillies employee Billy Shettsline. There wasn't much Gerry could do with such a financially challenged baseball team, but he did hit the lottery at one point when he bought the contract of a promising, young minor league outfielder named Chuck Klein for $7,500. In the next six years, Klein would win a Triple Crown, four home run titles, and two Most Valuable Player awards on the way to a berth in the Hall of Fame.

Baker died in 1930, and when his will was probated, it was learned that he had left the controlling interest in the Phillies to his wife, Laura, Lewis Ruch, and Mae Nugent. Mae received 500 shares valued at $25,000, which, Baker had written in his will, was done "in appreciation of the faithful services she and her husband rendered me during the time I controlled the club." Laura and Mae were also named co-executrixes of Baker's estate.

Overall, Baker had owned 1,257 shares valued at $62,850. Ruch, who succeeded Baker as president, owned the same number of shares, while the remainder of the club's 5,000 shares were owned by a group of minority stockholders.

Ruch, a local businessman, had been a Phillies stockholder since 1913 when Baker took control of the team. Although he had not taken an active part in the team's operation, he was listed as the Phillies' vice president. Elevated to Baker's former position, he took to the job with enthusiasm and energy. But Ruch had health problems, and in 1932, less than two years after becoming president, he had to resign. Gerry, then just 40 years old, was selected as his successor.

Under Ruch, Mae had been the club's treasurer and assistant secretary. After Ruch's departure, she was also named vice president and elected to the board of directors. With her new jobs, Mae joined Gerry as the first wife-husband team to operate a baseball club.

Mae was an integral part of the operation. While Gerry looked after the baseball end of the Phillies' activities, including serving as the team's general manager, Mae took care of all the business matters. Yet, she stayed in the background, rarely garnering any public attention.

"I don't think women are news," she once said. "All I do is sign the checks. Gerry does all the talking for this family."

Despite that statement, Mae was determined to increase women's interest in baseball. She explained that opinion in a lengthy interview with sportswriter Bill Duncan.

Few women have held high-ranking executive posts in big league baseball, but the Phillies' Mae Nugent (with her husband Gerry [left] and pitcher Si Johnson) was one of the first.

"Women flock to big football games more for the color than for the game itself," she said. "Here in Philadelphia, we see this illustrated every year by the great interest in the Army-Navy game. They [women] almost battle for a chance to witness that classic.

"In the stands will be thousands of women who do not know a forward pass from a placement kick. They are there to see the cadets and midshipmen march and to see the brilliant displays between halves. Also, they want to see what milady is wearing because there is a certain social angle to the game.

"I am not going to be ridiculous and say there can be a social angle to a game between the Phillies and Brooklyn. But I do think efforts can be made to provide something unusual for the women. Maybe a band, brass or string, or a stunt of some kind. Old-type magnates may still think people come only to see a man make a base hit and run to first, but when you are going after the patronage of women, a little touch here and there will help.

"By this suggestion," she added, "I do not want to create the false impression that I favor making a burlesque out of baseball. But I have been around baseball a long time, and I know that attendance means more money in the treasury, and that is what interests club owners."

One of the ways the Nugents attracted more women to Phillies games was to introduce what they called "ladies' days" in which women were admitted to games at discount prices. These events were extremely popular and in many cases served as a foundation for building an interest in baseball for numerous women.

Mae's interest in the Philles increased again in 1936 when Laura Baker died. The wife of the team's late president, who had lived with the Mallon family when she first arrived in Philadelphia after her husband had taken over the club, willed to Mae $10,000 and the 757 shares she still held in the Phillies. That made Mae the team's biggest shareholder. And with shares Gerry had purchased over the years, the couple now had 52 percent of the stock, giving them controlling interest in the Phils.

Yet, the Phillies' financial woes continued. Three times during the 1930s, Phillies attendance was under 200,000 for the season and it never reached as high as 300,000. Gerry had to unload star players such as Chuck Klein, Ethan Allen, Johnny Moore, Pinky Whitney, Jimmie Wilson, Dick Bartell, Dolph Camilli, Bucky Walters, Spud Davis, Morrie Arnovich, Kirby Higbe, and Claude Passeau just to get the funds to stay in business. Had they all remained with the Phillies, the club could've been a National League power.

The Phillies' annual payroll was usually around $200,000. Overall, it cost about $350,000 to operate the team each year. Visiting teams didn't even make enough money at Baker Bowl to cover their expenses. At least once, Gerry used his own salary to pay a debt. Often, he had to borrow money. Once, the Phils even had to sell their office furniture to finance spring training. Another time, Nugent used his own stock as collateral to obtain funds to pay some bills. On top of all their financial problems, a plot to kidnap the Nugents' son, Gerry Jr., was uncovered, although the crime was thwarted before it happened.

The Nugents were not immune to public attack. One newspaper went so far as to say, "The present ownership of the Phillies had made this city the laughingstock of the sports world." Yet, the Nugents did what they could. They began a Knot Hole Gang, which allowed boys from the ages of 10 to 16 to be admitted to games without charge. In 1936, they began broadcasting Phillies games on radio. They broke their 99-year lease at decrepit, rundown Baker Bowl and moved the team into the much more suitable confines of Shibe Park. And they developed a working relationship with several minor league teams in an attempt to build a small farm system, hiring the astute former pitcher Johnny Ogden to run it.

There was always hope. Mae said her burning ambition was to make the team solvent. "We'll get going one of these years," she said. "Then watch our smoke."

The smoke, though, never came. In 1940, a group of minority stockholders tried to oust the Nugents, saying they wanted to bring in new investors and players, and make the team a contender. Among several charges, they said that Gerry's annual salary of $15,000 and Mae's earnings of $5,000 were far too much.

"Every time [the team] gets a good player, it sells him to get money for the Nugents' salaries and other operating expenses," fumed stockholder William Harman, the vice president of Baldwin Locomotive Works and owner of 60 shares of Phillies stock. "Stockholders haven't received a dime on their investment for as long as I can remember," he added. "And I never saw an operating statement. All I know is that it [the team] continually operates at a loss. A wholesale shakeup is urgently needed."

The rebellion was squelched, but the handwriting was on the so-called wall. The Nugent regime had serious problems that would not easily go away. Mae knew it. Gerry knew it. And the National League hierarchy knew it.

Some National League owners urged dismantling the franchise and moving it to another city. They found a willing listener in National League president Ford Frick.

Ultimately, Frick and the four owners who comprised the league's board of governors made their move.

In 1942, with huge debts that reportedly totaled about $330,000, including $132,000 owed to the league and another $35,000 in back rent for Shibe Park, the Nugents were forced to sell their stock to the league. Including their 2,600 shares and stock that belonged to minority shareholders, the league wound up purchasing 4,685 shares for $75,000.

When the Nugents closed the office door in the Packard Building for the last time, there was hardly a dry eye to be seen. It was, said Ed Pollock in the *Evening Bulletin*, "what you would expect at a funeral. Club employees looked like red-eyed mourners."

"It was a real shame," recalled Danny Litwhiler, the Phillies' left fielder at the time. "The Nugents were very nice people. Mae didn't have any contact with the ballplayers, but you would see her around the office. I know she and Gerry tried very hard to keep the team afloat. It was just too bad things didn't work out better for them."

Frick appointed a group from the league office to run the team until a new owner was found. That owner turned out to be a friend of Frick's, William D. Cox, owner of a lumber company in New York. In March 1943, Cox, heading a 30-man syndicate, bought 4,950 of the team's 5,000 shares, paying $190,000 in cash, plus a $50,000 note. (By November, Cox would be banned for life from baseball for betting on the Phillies.)

The Nugents, meanwhile, returned to their home in Conshohocken to lament their fate. Finally, in 1946, Gerry took a job as president of the Class B Interstate League. Mae was named the league's secretary. They held those posts until the league disbanded in 1953 after which Gerry became a stockbroker.

In 1966, Mae died at the age of 73 at Eugenia Hospital in Whitemarsh Township. At the time, she and Gerry lived in the Cambridge Apartments in the Germantown section of Philadelphia.

Mae's passing was duly noted in the obituary sections of the Philadelphia newspapers. What none of them said, however, was that she was a woman who had made not only an indelible mark on baseball, but had struck a major blow for women's rights.

In her own way, Mae Nugent played a substantial role in baseball by leading women to the upper levels of management in a business in which men had nearly exclusive control. She was unquestionably a pioneer of the highest degree.

chapter 32

TRADING AWAY THE FUTURE

Few areas of baseball produce livelier discussions or are more thoroughly dissected than trades. Especially when they involve major players, trades attract a high level of attention when they're made, and, in many cases, are still being scrutinized years later.

It used to be that players were mostly traded without their knowledge or consent. Teams simply agreed to swaps that seemed to make sense to both sides. That process has, of course, changed drastically in recent decades. Trades have become enormously complex with factors that go far beyond the mere act of exchanging players dictating the mechanics of every deal.

Some of these factors, such as the resolution of contracts, influence the assessment of swaps. Now, it's not just who you got and who you gave up, but what other concessions you had to make.

Naturally, every team makes good trades. And every team makes bad trades. The key is to make more good ones than bad ones. Which is not exactly a description that fits the Phillies.

Over the years, the Phillies have made brilliant trades that have landed players such as Steve Carlton, Cy Williams, Jim Bunning, Dick Sisler, Garry Maddox, Johnny Callison, Tony Taylor, Tug McGraw, Curt Schilling, and Bobby Abreu. In every case, these players were obtained without surrendering equal value, and all went on to become major Phillies players.

Then there were the clunkers: Grover Cleveland Alexander, Chuck Klein, Billy Hamilton, Bucky Walters, Jack Sanford, Dolph Camilli, Gary Matthews, Claude Passeau, Dave Bancroft, Eppa Rixey, Ferguson Jenkins, Richie Ashburn, Dick Bartell, Dick Allen, Scott Rolen, Schilling, and Abreu. All—seven of whom were future Hall of Famers—departed in trades in which the Phillies got far less in return. In most cases, you could say that the Phillies were fleeced.

In no trade, however, were the Phillies more taken to the cleaners than the deal of the three shortstops in which they gave up not only Larry Bowa, but also Ryne Sandberg to the Chicago Cubs for Ivan DeJesus. It was a swap that was ill-conceived then and has given the Phils grief ever since. And to think, the deal was made by Paul Owens, the best general manager the Phillies ever had and normally a master at pulling off lopsided trades that favored his team.

The swap was made on January 27, 1982, soon after Sandberg had completed his fourth banner season in the Phillies' farm system. Just 22 years old at the time, the Spokane, Washington native would go on to have a sparkling career and a seat in the Hall of Fame.

The key figure in the deal was Bowa. The Phillies' regular shortstop since 1970, he was locked in a contract dispute with the club and had lost favor with some members of the team's top management. It was virtually certain that the fiery shortstop would be playing in a different uniform in 1982.

Bowa was one of the premier shortstops in baseball, a five-time All-Star who was—and still is—holder of the National League career record for highest fielding percentage (.980 in 2,222 games) by a shortstop. DeJesus, on the other hand, was a journeyman shortstop who played for seven different teams during a 15-year career in which he posted a lifetime .254 batting average.

Just a few months before the trade, a group led by Bill Giles had taken over ownership of the team, and trade winds were blowing heavily. That winter, the new owners would sanction three other major swaps, dealing Lonnie Smith, Keith Moreland, and Bake McBride, all key members of the 1980 championship team, in separate exchanges, none of which benefited the Phillies.

While Owens was the Phillies' point man in the deals, the instigator of the trade with Chicago was Dallas Green. The man who had been the director of the Phillies' farm system and manager of the 1980 Phillies, Green had become vice president and general manager of the Cubs just a few months earlier. He knew that the lowly Cubs needed to make changes, and he knew the whereabouts of some of the talent he needed to make those changes.

"We were struggling," Green remembered. "We didn't have anybody. I knew Bowa could bring something to my table, and I wanted to bring guys to the Cubs who knew about winning and what it took to win a championship. Bowa was that kind of guy. But to get him I knew that I needed to give them a shortstop to take his place, and it so happened that one of the few people I had available that the Phillies could use was De-Jesus."

The Phillies were willing to make that swap. Along with Bowa, they offered the Cubs a choice of one of five players. One of them was minor league pitcher Kevin Gross, who was wanted by the Cubs' new manager, Lee Elia. "I said. 'Get me Gross,' because we needed pitching and I knew he was going to be a pretty good pitcher," Elia recalled.

But Green wanted the pot sweetened another way. Initially, he had talked the Phillies into adding another player to the deal, instead of settling for a one-for-one swap. The extra player he wanted was Ryne Sandberg.

A few years earlier, Sandberg had been expected to be a high draft pick out of high school, but he was a *Parade* magazine All-American quarterback and had signed a letter of intent with Washington State University. Figuring he was going to opt for football, he was ignored in the June 1978 baseball draft until the Phillies chose him in the 20th round. Soon afterward, Sandberg had what he called "a total change of heart," and when the Phillies offered to sign him for $39,000—a figure that third-round picks usually got in those days—he decided to become a baseball player. And Green became one of his early supporters.

"I drafted him. I signed him, I watched him grow up in our minor league system when I was with the Phillies," Green said. "So I knew the kid inside and out. At the winter meetings, I saw Pope [Owens] and Hughie [Phillies superscout Hugh Alexander], and I said that 'I'm not making any trade unless I get inventory. And the inventory I want is Sandberg.'"

The one problem with Sandberg at the time was that he was a man without a clear-cut position. He had originally been a shortstop, and had played that position exclusively in high school and at Helena, Montana and Spartanburg, South Carolina in his first two years in the minors. He played mostly shortstop at Reading in 1980 and at Oklahoma City the following year. While at Oklahoma City, Sandberg had hit .293 and combined with outfielder Bob Dernier to steal 103 bases. But it was clear that Sandberg wasn't cut out to be a shortstop. "I managed him in Puerto Rico one winter," said former Phillies shortstop and coach Bobby Wine, "and he couldn't play shortstop."

Along the way, though, Sandberg had started to play some at second and third bases. One of his early tutors at second was the Phillies' stellar keystone sacker, Manny Trillo, who worked with Sandberg in winter ball in Venezuela. "He really helped me out a lot when I was trying to learn to play second base," Sandberg recalled some 26 years later.

The Phillies, however, were still not sure where Sandberg fit in. And when they called him up at the end of the 1981 season, he played five games at shortstop and one at second base. But with Julio Franco being a highly regarded prospect in the organization and also a shortstop, there was even talk that the Phillies would try Ryne in center field.

"There had been some discussion about him when I was with the Phillies," Green recalled. "A lot of people in the organization weren't real sure he was going to be a shortstop. And a lot of people didn't think he was going to have enough power, either. But that didn't matter to me. I knew he was a great athlete, and I knew he could help the Cubs.

"I said to Pope, 'You can't use him. You have Schmitty [Mike Schmidt] at third base, you have Trillo at second, and if I give you a shortstop, Sandberg's not going to play there. You have [Garry] Maddox in center field. There's no place for him to play. So you'll have to send him back to Triple-A, and if you do, you're going to kill that kid.' I said, 'I don't know where he's going to play, either, but I will play him somewhere.'

"I felt I had the upper hand in the discussion because I had the only viable shortstop that was available, and the Phillies were going to need a shortstop. I was determined to make the trade if I could get Sandberg, too."

Ultimately, the deal was made. Bowa and Sandberg became Cubs. To the young Sandberg, it was a stunning shift in his career. "For me, it came out of a clear blue sky," he said. "I had always dreamed I would someday step in at short for Bowa, and I had tried very hard to improve my game every season. Then when I came up at the end of the '81 season, I was so happy that I was even ready to become a utility outfielder. But I never expected at that point to be traded. I was just trying to put the uniform on one day at a time and play ball every day."

While Bowa would play three and one-half years with the Cubs before his career ended in 1985 with the New York Mets, and DeJesus would spend three mediocre years with the Phillies before moving on, Sandberg played the rest of his career with the Cubs, retiring in 1997.

When the Phillies traded infielder Ryne Sandberg to the Chicago Cubs, little did they realize that he would one day become a Hall of Fame second baseman.

In Sandberg's first season with the Cubs in 1982, he reported to spring training as a man without a position. He was tried at most of them. "I think I had every glove in my locker but a catcher's mitt," Sandberg told Barry Rozner, writing in the Hall of Fame's 2005 Yearbook. "Some days in spring training, I played either center, left, short, second, or third."

Sandberg wound up his first season playing 133 games at third base and 24 at second. The following year, he performed in all but one game at second. From then on, Sandberg was a full-time second baseman.

Again, it was a man with a Phillies connection who masterminded that decision. Elia, a former infielder who had been a manager in the Phils' farm system and a coach with the parent club before Green called him to Chicago, saw Sandberg's potential at second base and decided that's where he should play. "Don't worry," he told the youngster. "Focus on your defense and the offense will come."

Bowa also played a major role in getting Sandberg established at second. "We worked very hard together," Sandberg said. "He was always helping me, giving me advice. One year, he even came to spring training a month early to work with me."

Over the years, it became obvious that second base had been the right choice. With a strong, accurate arm and exceptional range, Sandberg won nine straight Gold Gloves at the position. He is tied for the major league record for best career fielding average (.989) by a second baseman. He led major league second basemen in fielding four times. And he set a major league record for most consecutive errorless games (123) by a second baseman.

Sandberg could also hit. When he retired, he carried a .285 lifetime batting average with 282 home runs, the fourth-highest total in Cubs history. He had made 10 consecutive appearances in the All-Star Game, and in 1984 won the National League's Most Valuable Player Award while leading the Cubs to their first postseason appearance since 1945.

Equally important, Sandberg had a relentless work ethic. "Ryne Sandberg worked harder than any player I've ever seen," said Pete Rose. "A lot of guys with his athletic ability get by on that and have nice careers. Sandberg worked his butt off because he knew it was wrong not to."

Much of the foundation for that attitude was initiated when Sandberg was a kid in the Phillies farm system. "The Phillies organization had a lot of pride, and it preached on a daily basis how to play the game properly," Sandberg recalled. "The Phillies farm system laid the groundwork for me for what occurred later. When I was coming up the ladder, I was very fortunate because I had great people helping me. No one helped me more than Larry Rojas, my manager in Montana and then a Phillies minor league instructor for many years. He had a huge influence on me."

Currently a manager in the Cubs' farm system, Sandberg tries to apply the lessons he learned with the Phillies. "I try to reflect back on those days, and instill what I learned," he said. "The lessons I learned as a young player are well worth passing along to the players I manage."

In 2005, Sandberg was inducted into the Hall of Fame, capping what had been a brilliant, 16-year career in the major leagues.

During that career, the Phillies used five second basemen. Manny Trillo, Joe Morgan, Juan Samuel, Tommy Herr, and Mickey Morandini were all excellent second basemen. But none was on a level with Sandberg, a star who was nurtured by the Phillies but was allowed to get away in one of the worst trades the club ever made.

chapter 33

THEY WON SOME, TOO

During the summer of 2007, when the Phillies became the first major league sports team ever to lose 10,000 games, the newspapers and airwaves were filled with stories and commentary about how poorly the team had played through much of its 125 years.

This is a team, the pundits proclaimed, that once lost 100 or more games five years in a row and 14 times overall. It's a team that has finished in last place 31 times. Once, it lost 23 straight games. Another time, it blew a six and one-half game lead with 12 games left in the season. And during one 31-year stretch, it finished in the first division just once. The Phillies, it was said with some truth, have over the years rendered a lot more bad news than good.

It seemed only fitting. The Phillies play in a city that has a reputation for harboring one of the largest crowds of malcontents. They're the loudest of boobirds. They threw seat cushions onto the field at Baker Bowl. They've caused games to be forfeited. And, of course, they've booed with considerable lust some top Phillies players such as Del Ennis, Dick Allen, Mike Schmidt, and Pat Burrell.

Losing 10,000 games is certainly an extremely inglorious feat that drags an uncommonly high collection of distressing moments along behind it. There is big-time baggage tied to this dismal achievement, and it is quite obviously not something that would send the home fans dancing into the streets.

Looking back on that dubious milestone, surpassed only by the Washington Generals, the patsy of the Harlem Globetrotters, and reached by the Phillies on July 15 when they lost, 10-2, to the St. Louis Cardinals, it's safe to say that the subject was amply covered, both locally and nationally. By the same token, the other side of that record wasn't covered at all. But there have been a number of success stories. This seems like a good place to mention some of them.

Phillies wins. They fall well short of Phillies losses. But they—and other notable feats—are, nonetheless, worth discussing.

At the end of the 2007 season, the Phillies had won 8,853 games. That figure is the eighth highest in the National League and trails all teams (each of which has won more than 9,000 games) that began in the circuit in the 1800s. Of those eight teams, the Chicago Cubs, Cincinnati Reds, and then-Boston Braves all began seven years (1876) before the Phillies, and the New York Giants started the same season (1883). Only the Pittsburgh Pirates (1887), Brooklyn Dodgers (1890), and St. Louis (1892) began after the Phillies got under way.

The Phillies have winning records in five of the 11 decades in which they've played (1890-99, 1910-19, 1970-79, 1980-89, and 2000-07). And, of the five main ballparks that they've called home, they have winning records (not counting postseason games) in Baker Bowl (1,957-1,778-29), Veterans Stadium (1,415-1,198-3), and Citizens Bank Park (348-300).

In their first 86 years, or before the National League was divided into divisions, the Phillies finished in the first division 34 times, including second or above eight times. Since the league was recast in 1969 into divisions, the Phils have finished in the top two 15 times in 39 years. In their last 34 years, starting in 1974, the Phillies have finished below third place 12 times. Overall, the Phils have nine first-place finishes, 14 seconds, 16 thirds, and 22 fourths.

The Phillies have posted 52 winning seasons. They have won more than 100 games twice, winning 101 in both 1976 and 1977. The team has won 90 or more games 11 times, starting in 1899 when it won 94. The last time was in 1993 when it won 97.

In the period from 1974 through 1983, generally regarded as the finest decade in Phillies history, the team posted a club-record 10 straight winning seasons, won five division championships, two NL pennants, and two trips to the World Series. (The team also appeared in the postseason playoffs in the strike-shortened 1981 season.)

Overall, the Phils have won seven division titles, five pennants, and have appeared in five World Series (1915, 1950, 1980, 1983, 1993), winning one fall classic. That isn't all that bad considering that the Cubs haven't won a World Series since 1908.

As few as there are, the Phillies' pennant winners have all been noteworthy. There were the Whiz Kids (1950), the Wheeze Kids (1983), the first pennant winner (1915), the only Series winner (1980), and the last pennant winner (1993).

The 1915 team won the flag by seven games, and the 1950 club, one of the most popular teams ever to play in Philadelphia, won in the 10th inning of the last game of the season. The star-studded 1980 Phillies came from a 5-2, seventh-inning deficit in the last game of the National League playoffs to beat Nolan Ryan and the Houston Astros in 10 innings, then went to the Series where they erased the Kansas City Royals in six games in a scintillating fall classic. The 1983 squad, with a lineup heavy with older players, won the division title by six games and squashed the Los Angeles Dodgers in four games in the playoffs. And the hugely popular 1993 Phils won 97 games, the third-highest total in club history, before whipping the Atlanta Braves four games to two in the National League Championship Series.

Although only one of these teams won the World Series—the Phillies lost in five games to the Boston Red Sox (1915), in four games to the New York Yankees (1950), in five games to the Baltimore Orioles (1983), and in six games to the Toronto Blue Jays (1993)—they have provided some of the most memorable moments in Phillies history.

There have been others. The Phillies have won 16 games in a row three times (1887, 1890, 1892) and 13 straight twice (1977, 1991). They have scored as many as 29 runs in one game (1985 versus the Mets), and three times (1906, 1922, 1979) have scored 23 runs in a single game. They have beaten opponents

Among Phillies winners, who can forget the 1980 World Series victory parade down Broad Street, led by Paul Owens (left) and Dallas Green, or the 1950 pennant-winning celebration when the whole team joined the fun?

three times by 18-0 scores (1910, 1930, 1934). And the Phils have slugged 36 hits in one game (1894), 27 hits in one game twice (1930, 1985), 26 once (1922), and 25 once (1901).

Of the current National League teams, the Phillies have a winning record against seven of the 15, including the Milwaukee Brewers, Colorado Rockies, Florida Marlins, New York Mets, San Diego Padres, Houston Astros, and Washington Nationals/Montreal Expos. Although there are far fewer games involved, the Phils also have .500 or better records against the American League's Baltimore Orioles, Chicago White Sox, Cleveland Indians, Detroit Tigers, Kansas City Royals, Minnesota Twins, Oakland A's, Texas Rangers, and Toronto Blue Jays. (The record is exactly .500 against the Orioles, Indians, Tigers, Twins, A's, and Blue Jays.)

Among team statistics, the Phillies have led or tied for the league lead in batting average 12 times, in home runs 16 times, and in runs scored seven times. The Phils have led or tied for the league lead in earned run average six times, and in fielding percentage 12 times.

Phillies players have led the league in batting average nine times (Richie Ashburn twice; Billy Hamilton, Sam Thompson, Ed Delahanty, Sherry Magee, Lefty O'Doul, Chuck Klein, and Harry Walker each once). Twenty-six times, the Phillies—led by Mike Schmidt with eight, then Gavvy Cravath with six, Chuck Klein with four, Cy Williams with three, Sam Thompson with two, and Ed Delahanty, Jim Thome and Ryan Howard each with one—have won or tied for home run titles. Phils have won the RBI crown 22 times with Schmidt leading the way with four, followed by Delahanty and Magee with three each, Cravath and Klein each two, and Thompson, Nap Lajoie, Elmer Flick, Don Hurst, Del Ennis, Greg Luzinski, Darren Daulton, and Howard with one apiece. And the league has been led in runs scored 14 times by Phillies: three each by Klein and Hamilton, including his all-time record 196, and once each by Roy Thomas, Sherry Magee, Gavvy Cravath, Dick Allen, Von Hayes, Lenny Dykstra, Chase Utley, and Jimmy Rollins.

Among pitchers, Phillies have won or tied for the league lead in wins 16 times (Grover Cleveland Alexander five times, Robin Roberts and Steve Carlton each four, and Tom Seaton, Jumbo Elliott, and John Denny one apiece). Phils have led in complete games 15 times, five each by Alexander and Roberts, three by Carlton, and one apiece by Terry Mulholland and Curt Schilling. The league has been led 19 times in strikeouts by Phillies pitchers—five times by Carlton and Alexander, two by Roberts and Schilling, and one each by Seaton, Earl Moore, Kirby Higbe, Jack Sanford, and Jim Bunning. And the ERA crown has gone eight times to Phils hurlers with Alexander winning three of them, and Charlie Ferguson, Dan Casey, Al Orth, George Mc-Quillan, and Carlton with one apiece.

Thirty-six men who represented the Phillies on the field (including managers and coaches) are members of the Baseball Hall of Fame. Some—such as Alexander, Ashburn, Bunning, Carlton, Delahanty, Hamilton, Klein, Roberts, Schmidt, and Thompson—spent the best parts of their careers with the Phillies.

Phillies players have earned Most Valuable Player Awards eight times (Schmidt three times, Klein twice, and Jim Konstanty, Howard, and Rollins each once). Six Cy Young Awards—four to Carlton and one each to Denny and Steve Bedrosian—have gone to Phils pitchers. Although presented by different

Eight-time Gold Glove winner Garry Maddox is interviewed by Richie Ashburn after the Phillies won the 1983 League Championship Series.

organizations, the Phils have had nine Rookies of the Year—Ennis, Ashburn, Sanford, Ed Bochee, Allen, Lonnie Smith, Juan Samuel, Scott Rolen, and Howard. Silver Slugger Awards have gone to Phillies players 16 times, including six times to Schmidt, twice to Manny Trillo, and one each to Pete Rose, Samuel, Daulton, Dykstra, Bobby Abreu, Howard, Utley, and Rollins. Six Manager of the Year honors have been awarded to Phils skippers, including Gene Mauch twice, and Eddie Sawyer, Danny Ozark, Jim Fregosi, and Larry Bowa once each. Roberts and Howard have been named Major League Players of the Year.

Since the All-Star Game began in 1933, Phillies players have been selected 163 times to wear the uniform of the National League. Roberts made seven of those teams and was the starting pitcher in five of the games. Schmidt was chosen 12 times, Carlton seven times, Bowa five, and Ashburn, Greg Luzinski, Pete Rose, and Jimmy Rollins have each made it four times. All five Phillies managers (Sawyer, Mauch, Dallas Green, Ozark, and Fregosi) who piloted All-Star teams have emerged winners.

The Phillies have won 39 Gold Gloves since the award was first presented in 1963, including 10 by Schmidt, eight by Garry Maddox, and three each by Trillo and Rolen.

So, as it turns out, Phillies history may not be as bleak as it's made out to be. The team has had some significant achievements, too. The Phils and their players have won some games, captured some titles, and collected some awards. There's something to be said for all that.

Sources

The Baseball Encyclopedia. Macmillan, 1997.

Brown, Elijah. *The Real Billy Sunday*. Fleming H. Revell, 1914.

Hanneman, David. *Diamond in the Rough — The Legend and Legacy of Tony Lucadello, One of Baseball's Greatest Scouts.* Diamond Books, 1989.

Harrison, David. *Jimmie Foxx — Baseball Hall of Famer.* McFarland, 1996.

Johnson, Lloyd, and Miles Wolff. *The Encyclopedia of Minor League Baseball.* Baseball America, 1997.

Nemec, David. *The Great Encyclopedia of 19th Century Major League Baseball.* Donald I. Fine Books, 1997.

Nineteenth Century Stars. Society for American Baseball Research, 1989.

Orem, Preston. *Baseball, 1845-1881*, Preston Orem, 1961.

Shiffert, John. *Base Ball in Philadelphia — A History of the Early Games, 1831-1900.* McFarland, 2006.

Westcott, Rich. *Native Sons — Philadelphia-Area Baseball Players Who Made the Major Leagues.* Temple University Press, 2003.

Westcott, Rich, and Frank Bilovsky. *The Phillies Encyclopedia*, 3rd Ed. Temple University Press, 2004.

Yastrzemski, Carl, and Gerald Eskenazi. *Yaz — Baseball and Me.* Doubleday, 1990.

Other Sources

The Complete Baseball Record Book, *The Sporting News*

Dittmar, Joe — *Alexander the Great*

Granahan, Tom — *Philadelphia Inquirer Magazine*

Johns Hopkins University Magazine

Lauber, Scott — Wilmington *News-Journal*

New York Times

Official Baseball Guide, *The Sporting News*

Official Baseball Register, *The Sporting News*

Philadelphia Daily News

Philadelphia *Evening Bulletin*

Philadelphia Inquirer

Philadelphia *Public Ledger*

Philadelphia *Record*

Phillies Media Guides

Phillies record books

Phillies Report

Phillies Yearbooks

Wikipedia

Photo Credits

Philadephia Phillies, pp. 53, 85, 135, 209, 238, 244, 247

Photos by Miles Kennedy, courtesy of the Philadelphia Phillies, pp. 5, 95, 151, 222

Urban Archives, Temple University, Philadelphia, p. 189

Photos courtesy of Edith Houghton, pp. 12, 14, 16

National Baseball Hall of Fame and Museum, p. 173

Photos by Alan Kravetz, pp. 41, 69

Photo courtesy of Chuck Randall, p. 118

Photo courtesy of Hank King, p. 181

All other photos provided by Rich Westcott.